RECLAIMING SCIENCE FROM DARWINISM

Kenneth POPPE

HARVEST HOUSE PUBLISHERS

EUGENE, OREGON

Cover by Terry Dugan Design, Minneapolis, Minnesota

Back cover author photo © Phyllis Dwyer; Cover photo © Lawrence Lawry / Photodisc Green / Getty Images

RECLAIMING SCIENCE FROM DARWINISM
Copyright © 2006 by Kenneth Poppe
Published by Harvest House Publishers
Eugene, Oregon 97402
www.harvesthousepublishers.com

Library of Congress Cataloging-in-Publication Data
Poppe, Kenneth, 1948-
Reclaiming science from Darwinism / Kenneth Poppe.
   p. cm.
ISBN-13: 978-0-7369-1833-6
ISBN-10: 0-7369-1833-7
1. Evolution (Biology) 2. Creationism. 3. Natural selection. 4. Intelligent design (Teleology) I. Title.
QH366.2.P663 2006
576.8—dc22
                          2006015510

Printed in the United States of America

RECLAIMING
SCIENCE
FROM
DARWINISM

To the One Supreme Designer,
whose true Spirit has been sought by people
throughout the ages under many different names,
and who made a Way to reclaim me from my former self.
May He fit my little story into His big Story.

Acknowledgments

I would like to thank my wife, Sidney, for her unwavering love and intuitive support, and for being an excellent lightning rod when I was generating too much static. I would also like to thank my children—Andrea, Kenny, Morgan, Caleb, Ethan, and Emma—and my mother, Retha, and sister, Lois, for patiently listening when I would launch into yet another discourse.

I would like to acknowledge my math and science students from 30-plus years of teaching, who have taught me so much—especially the sixth-grade class of 2005/2006 and their parents at Lyons, Colorado, who were unique beyond belief ("Who loves ya?!").

I would also like to acknowledge the majority of competent public-school science teachers—who are not strict Darwinists—and encourage them to stand up for objectivity in the origins issue and teach the balance that the topic deserves.

Furthermore, I would like to thank Dr. John Terry Rickard, Dr. William Dembski, and Dr. John Walker for their excellent information and advice—scientific and otherwise. And my thanks to others who have contributed greatly such as Gordon Hampton, Sally Helms, Dr. Dale Johnson, Jerry Lancer, Mark and Pat McDowell, George Putnam, Dave Sonnesyn, and Dan Williams.

Finally, my deep appreciation goes to my main editor at Harvest House Publishers, Paul Gossard, for his straightforward and tireless assistance, and to the entire warm staff at Harvest House, who have been the consummate friendly professionals each step of the way.

Contents

PART FOUR
Physics and the Laws of Thermodynamics

PART FIVE
Paleontology and Genetic Change

No Rational Connection

Foreword by William Dembski

Dad: Josh, Mom tells me you've been having some trouble at school. What's going on?

Josh: Uh…she's right, Dad. Yeah, I've been late to class a few times and I punched a teacher and then the other week I tripped a guy in the hall—but that was really an accident.

Dad: Well, I can understand an accident happening. But what was that second thing you said?

Josh: I…uh…punched a teacher.

Dad: What on earth! We need to talk more about this.

Darwinism is like Josh's confession. A number of its claims are innocuous, such as that organisms have changed over time, that organisms can adapt to changing environmental conditions, or that gene frequencies may vary in a population. But, as with Josh's confession, tucked in among these innocuous claims is a whopper. The whopper, in the case of Darwinism, is this: All organisms, including ourselves, are the result of a blind, purposeless evolutionary process (namely, the Darwinian mechanism of natural selection and random variation).

Moreover, at no place did this process require the services of God or any guiding intelligence.

Like Josh, Darwinists try to conceal this whopper, only they do it not to befuddle a parent but to beguile the public. For instance, when parents press school boards and biology teachers about what they are teaching their children concerning biological origins, they typically get the innocuous version of evolution: *Of course you believe that organisms have changed over time...Surely you've heard of bugs developing antibiotic resistance...This is evolution in action.*

Indeed, this is evolution in action. But it is small-scale microevolution, which no one disputes and which is irrelevant to the really big claim of evolutionary theory, namely:

1. The bug that developed antibiotic resistance and you, the poor human whose immune system cannot resist the bug, are both offspring of some common ancestor in the distant past; and

2. The process that brought you and the bug into existence is Darwinian, operating by chance and necessity and without plan or purpose.

In particular, you, your aspirations, and the entire human family to which you belong are simply an accident of natural history, here for a brief moment and destined for extinction. This is Darwinism in its full glory.

Can We Get from A to B?

Suffocating as Darwinism is to the human spirit, we cannot reject it simply because we don't like it. If the truth hurts, deal with it. But is it true? Is it the case that we evolved through a blind Darwinian process? What evidence supports this grand view of evolution, and what evidence disconfirms it? In this book, Kenneth Poppe answers these questions brilliantly and decisively. In particular, he shows that Darwinism needs to be defeated not as a ploy to promote Christian theism—but because it is demonstrably false.

At this point, valiant defenders of evolution, of which there are many, usually play the "overwhelming evidence card." Accordingly, they tell us there are "mountains and mountains of evidence for evolution." (Richard Dawkins used precisely those words in his recent attack on religion in the BBC series *The Root of All Evil?*) When I hear Darwinists use the phrase "overwhelming evidence" to tout their theory, I think of a story my colleague Del Ratzsch of Calvin College tells. According to a certain tabloid, the wife of an entertainer is descended from aliens. The key piece of evidence cited to support this hypothesis was that the woman had slightly lower-than-average blood pressure. Obviously, the problem with such an argument is that there is *no rational connection* between blood pressure and alien descent.

Likewise, there is no rational connection between the mountains of evidence cited by Darwinists and the grand claim they make that all organisms are descended from a universal common ancestor via a purposeless material process (which they understand as the interplay of natural selection and random variation). Because no such rational connection exists, evolutionary theory, in its grand macroevolutionary Darwinian form, *flies in the face of the scientific method. It should not be taught except as a discredited speculative hypothesis that properly belongs to nature religions and mystery cults—not to science.*

It's a fact: The grand claim of Darwinian evolution has never been tested. All the evidence and experiments cited to support that claim have no rational connection with it. At best, the evidence and experiments support that there was a gradual progression of living forms. But they do not support that such a progression occurred without the need for intelligent input.

As *Reclaiming Science from Darwinism* makes clear, *intelligent design* is the real science here. Intelligent design studies patterns in nature that are best explained as the result of intelligence. As such, it merges the natural sciences (such as physics, chemistry, and geology) with the engineering sciences (such as information theory, communication theory, and computational intelligence). Intelligent design makes testable predictions about the forms of complexity we should find in biological systems—and the inherent limitations we should observe in evolutionary processes not controlled by intelligence. As this book demonstrates, these predictions are now being consistently borne out.

———•••——

Kenneth Poppe is not an armchair general. He has been an active participant in the fray about which he writes. He is competent in the relevant science, and he is a card-carrying member of the educational establishment in which this controversy over evolution and intelligent design is being played out. You will be hard-pressed to find a better guide through this minefield. And once you are through it, you will realize why the famous words of Malcolm Muggeridge are finally coming true:

> I myself am convinced that the theory of evolution [read "Darwinism"], especially to the extent to which it has been applied, will be one of the greatest jokes in the history books of the future. Posterity will marvel that so very flimsy and dubious an hypothesis could be accepted with the incredible credulity it has.

This Book Is for You If...

If you've picked this book off a shelf or a table, you're likely in one of the groups of readers I had in mind when I wrote it:

- parents with school-age children who need effective answers to pro-evolutionary content taught in public schools
- officials in school boardrooms, legislatures, and courtrooms whose positions require them to weigh the merits of Darwinism and Design
- people who were raised in religious households but rejected faith as young adults before all the evidence was heard
- people who are convinced that strict Darwinism will always be the answer and need to become well-educated about Design in order to try to refute it
- private-school science teachers or homeschoolers who need proven non-evolutionary content
- public-school biology teachers who desire to balance Darwinism with reasonable objections
- faith-based individuals who need answers for atheistic or agnostic acquaintances
- people who desire stronger personal faith in the face of evolutionary science, which on the surface can seem so convincing
- individuals who, in general, want to assist in breaking the monopoly Darwinism exerts on science, and who want to require natural evolution to prove itself in the face of reasonable objections

GETTING SCIENCE OUT OF JAIL

An expanded title to this book might read, *Today's powerful scientific and mathematical challenges to Darwinism show it to be a failed theory, and it is time that science no longer be captive to its control.* This is my answer to the past 100-plus years of science history—history that has told the public that the entire universe, especially life here on Earth, was "self-made." And the body of this book will present resounding scientific and mathematical proof to show that natural processes can in no wise account for our existence.

If you have never done so before, pause and reflect on the tremendous implications of believing that all we see was able to make itself, by itself, without any outside intelligence. For starters, it means all the physics, biology, and chemistry producing us had no direction or preset goal whatsoever. There was no awareness that something as monumental as creation was underway. In short, everything was one huge accident.

Next it follows that celestial objects, life-forms, and molecules can have a *function,* but—without a "purposer"—never a *purpose.* Then ultimately it means that our personal existence, and the existence of the ones we think we love, has no meaning in an altogether random and indifferent universe—and in the end, all life is compost. I would say that is a very somber viewpoint—one that is as dismaying as it is totally incorrect.

The Random Alternative

Prior to the 1850s, most people did not have to contemplate such a grave outlook. It was generally standard for a person to believe that some type of god had a hand in creation, whether Jehovah, Allah, Manitou, and so on.

Not long after that time, however, a small band of scientists and philosophers, influenced by the work of Charles Darwin, set out to expunge from science all theological aspects. Their alternative was firmly in place by the 1900s, and over time these people became our true atheists—that is, those who believe "god" is a psychologically generated illusion and an adult form of Santa Claus one should outgrow. You can also add to these the agnostics—people who believe the truth about "god" is unknowable and therefore a waste of time. And although agnostics may not have the strength of conviction that atheists do—and may even occasionally engage in a benign form of religion for reasons only they know—their aggressive defense of Darwinism is surprisingly often the same.

The growing late-1800s entourage of outspoken people believed science, not "god," could answer *every* question on the origin of the cosmos and life, and they eventually were able to convince mainstream science of the total efficacy of natural processes. From there, the theory of evolution reigned supreme throughout most of the last century.

Let's look at the theory of evolution in its pure form. The famous "Darwin Fish"—the fish with a legged body—is a well-known symbol of the theory. It implies that over time totally natural processes can change any life-form into something more advanced, like the fish that spontaneously grew limbs and climbed out on dry land to eventually become a walking reptile.

The essence of natural evolution could be summed up this way:

KEY CONCEPT In the beginning, our universe, our galaxy, our solar system, and our planet were produced over immense periods of time by random forces. Following that, cellular life on Earth arose spontaneously by another series of accidental biochemical events, and then was slowly driven forward to become today's complex multicellular life by yet another unintended process called *natural selection*. All this was possible by the science existing within the system, and no intelligent involvement was required.

That is my view of the mind-set of people who profess no faith, and this view is in the minority in our population. Interestingly, they are in contrast to that equally small number of people who will always practice a faith actively regardless of what they think science says.

An Unwarranted Arrangement

However, we are still left with the large majority of people. Though perhaps not practicing an active faith, they inherently believe that in the origin of the universe, "god"…in some form…had a role…in some way. They show this belief on some highly charged issues, such as rejecting that a monkey turned into a human all by itself. Yet at the same time they generally accept the tenets of evolution—some to a lesser degree but others almost entirely—and have little or no objection to the fact that evolution dominates the scientific scene.

For this large majority, it is crucial to know that the many defenses for "self-made" that Darwinists have used for decades can be easily debunked by even the nonscientific mind—and that strict evolutionists are not telling you the full truth. You may well agree as you read further.

In keeping with the title of my book, I say we must break this unwarranted arrangement in which so few decide what science is taught to so many. I can guarantee you that aggressive or subtle evolutionists still dominate university science and philosophy faculty, school-board policymakers and district science supervisors, teacher licensing and hiring officials, grant funders and research underwriters, textbook authors and adoption committees, media programmers and news reporters—even spiritual leaders and clergy of those aforementioned benign religions.

And let's not forget that Darwinism dominates even the science and philosophy teachers teaching in public elementary and secondary schools. This situation is now unacceptable because the evidence has gone completely against self-made. Yet Darwinists still insist that only strict evolution be taught in public-school classrooms, and any concept that even remotely suggests divine involvement be confined to religious programs outside of school time.

The ground is far from equal in public education. Though some non-believers may dismiss faith diplomatically, others say straight out what the rest believe—"Take your religious fables and your other superstitions and go join the rest of the Flat Earth Society." But their turf is slipping away. Debates in boardrooms, legislatures, and courtrooms are being less and less favorable to evolution, and even people in coffeehouses, teacher lounges, and business gatherings are less inclined to hold their tongues when Darwinists pontificate.

The Rise of a New Alternative

In large measure this change is coming about because of a revolution that began to get the general public's attention toward the end of the twentieth century. A group of scientists and mathematicians arose to challenge natural evolution in a new way. They were not invoking the names of deities, and they were using few or no quotations from religious or holy writings. Furthermore, these were not spiritual leaders who had learned to incorporate a touch of science into their rhetoric. They were professors and researchers with impeccable academic credentials and impressive scientific achievements who worked with formulas, specimens, charts, and glassware.

These thought-provoking individuals did not seek to dismantle sub-theories pertaining to origins, such as the big bang, primordial soup, or survival of the fittest. Instead, they were challenging the scientific community with new concepts such as *irreducible complexity, universal probability bound,* and *complex specified information*—"unreligious-sounding" concepts that forcefully explained how the blind luck so indispensable in Darwinism could never do the impossible. Though they were working outside the monopoly of mainstream science and were frequently ostracized by it, from PhDs to people on the street, they were still turning heads. The reason? To borrow a political phrase, their logic "resonated" with the general population in a way Darwinism never had.

These new spokespersons eventually coalesced under the banner of the word *design,* and going into the twenty-first century, the phrase *intelligent design* became the most recognized and repeated identifier. Regardless of their backgrounds, the arguments by these dissenters to Darwinism were, and still are, basically the same. In contrast to the above summary of evolution, the key concepts of Design could be stated thus:*

KEY CONCEPT

The processes and phenomena currently operating within the universe and on Earth are insufficient to produce themselves. No amount of natural evolutionary theory can account for the complexity and compatibility that are continually observed by science. Therefore, there must be a guiding intelligence repeatedly involved in creating the complexity, but not subjected to it. Such complexity must always be the result of intended information because there is a mathematical limit to what blind luck can accomplish.

The strength of these words becomes more evident when we see how Design has helped level the playing field. Now people in state and national legislatures, governor's mansions, courts of law, and school boardrooms are calling for the academic honesty to at least allow theories challenging natural evolution to be taught as well.†

Design's superior appeal is not evident just from the many high-profile governmental initiatives promoting it, but also from the surging grassroots approval of people who study it. By comparison, Darwinism's influence is waning as further probes beneath the attractive artificial turf

---

* Throughout this book, I use *Design* (capital D) to refer to theories of origins that propose the involvement of a guiding intelligence.

† See chapter 14 for some comments on key legal cases.

of blind luck continue to hit only infertile soil. Additional evidence of the failure of Darwinism is that in debates or response papers over Design, strict evolutionists increasingly look like people backed into a corner, resorting more and more to name-calling, irrational statements, and temper flashes rather than scientific rebuttal.

Where We're Headed

From the table of contents and this introduction, it should be evident I intend to demonstrate the need to reclaim science from Darwinism with a wealth of challenges to natural evolution. Part one will further discuss the two basic choices to explain our existence—luck or intent. Part two will then look at mathematical impossibilities, part three will expose weaknesses in supposed chemical evolution, part four will examine challenges from physics and the laws of thermodynamics, and part five will show the difficulties with the fossil record and supposed genetic changes. Finally, part six will look at some concluding thoughts about individual issues a person should resolve. I also add for your further reading an appendix on the true substance of Darwin's famous book *The Origin of Species.*

Many excellent writers have covered the above subjects in other books, and I heartily recommend them for their depth. But between the covers of this volume you will find an overview of just about *all* of the key objections to self-made. Furthermore, you will find the challenges explained in clear and concise language, and reinforced with diagrams and graphics to make them understandable.

After more than three decades of personal laboratory research and teaching in the biological sciences, I am thoroughly convinced that the

Choice, Not Chance

If you haven't already noticed, I have been adding the word *natural* to the term *evolution*—thus, "natural evolution." I consistently do so because when scrutinized, Design generally says there is no reason to abandon the view that life has changed over long periods of time (the basic meaning of "evolve" without the recent anti-theological connotation). Neither does the more specific Intelligent Design object that some of the change mechanisms espoused by science might have happened as described (the big bang, for instance).

These processes were not the result of chance, though, but of choice ("Let there be light!"). Therefore, science, math, and logic dictate that "natural" can no longer be the only force necessary to drive all of creation. In a paraphrase of biochemist Michael Behe, *"Natural science may be able to explain mountains, but not Mt. Rushmore."*

However, I do not hold to the view that the power of science is to be revered in the same measure as the power of a Creator. Have you ever heard something akin to, "Well, maybe God started it, but then science took over and did all the rest"? Even if this is true, all scientifically observed processes are the creation of their Creator, and this is where *sole* credit belongs. If the science we study exists only because of intelligence outside the system, then "natural" still operates only where and when intended. It has no power to redirect or reinvent itself by itself.

And further, if a Designer has been operating, the information in this book will show that He has to have been *actively* orchestrating scientific processes throughout geologic history, even in the most recent of times. But we do need the flexibility to break free from the confining human interpretation of time. After all, cannot the unfettered Creator choose to work first in a microsecond and then in a millennium?

very scientific fields once liberally employed by Darwinism through sleight of hand, so to speak, have thoroughly betrayed it in the end.

Today the arguments against natural evolution come from physics, chemistry, astronomy, molecular biology, zoology, botany, genetics, human biology, and paleontology—to name just the headliners among the branches of science.

If you doubt this, look at the present flow of scientific discussion on origins. No longer is it people of faith searching for a bit of scientific leverage, but the faithless frantically trying to explain...

- the perfect universe, solar system, and planet
- the near-total lack of fossil intermediates
- the complexity in molecular machines
- the idea of "good" mutations, which is unsupported by observation
- the math that never ceases to confound "self-made"

Make no mistake. Strict Darwinism—the "self-made" portion—is destined to become a footnote in scientific history. The jury of academic inquiry has already made its ruling, and the public currently reviewing the decision concurs: Natural evolution must release its stranglehold on science.

This does not mean, as some accuse, that the acceptance of Design will halt or even curtail scientific research in any field, especially in the origin of life, because all is now "magic." On the contrary, Design merely says the processes whose secrets we try to unlock were not the result of chance. That's it.

The only real caveat is that further investigations cannot be done under the untenable assumption that science alone has done the impossible. Rather, reclaiming science from Darwinism will lead to more exacting conclusions, fewer dead ends, and greater harmony between what is proposed and what is observed.

PART ONE

A SURVEY OF THE LANDSCAPE

Chapter 1

CAN LIFE REALLY
MAKE ITSELF?

*How the "self-made" approach
plays out in the real world*

I have never seen a biology textbook that did not examine a few of the old-time scientific myths and superstitions that have since been debunked. If you check a text, you may read how Mendeleev's periodic table with its eventual hundred-plus elements put to rest Aristotle's faulty view that all matter was made up of just four elements—fire, water, air, and earth. You might also find how Copernicus finally proved the Earth revolved around the sun, and not vice versa, or how Pasteur's vaccinations replaced bloodletting and leech treatments as a cure for infections.

Furthermore, you are almost certain to find such a textbook critical of the notion of *spontaneous generation*. This medieval concept was that cellular life could just arise out of nonliving material. To explain the erroneous concept, my high-school biology book included a crude drawing of critters crawling out from under a rotting log. Other depictions might show swamp life climbing out of the oozing mud, maggots emerging from a piece of raw meat, or a sack of grain generating the rodents that invariably show up for the food. The author's comments on such drawings usually point to the folly of people thinking life just "happened."

These blind alleys dismissed, the book usually gives the correct view for the origin of cellular life, using Pasteur's famous "soup in a flask" experiment. Pictures show how boiled broth left in an open container developed the contamination of bacterial life, while boiled broth in a flask sealed from microbes in the air did not—thereby proving that only life gives rise to life. And to be sure that the impressionable young reader understands that superstitious theories cannot account for life, the author is likely to close with the cell theory. This theory has three tenets:

1. The cell is the basic unit of life.
2. All organisms are made of cells.
3. All cells come from other cells.

The heart of the cell theory is the third statement, which says a new cell can only come from a preexisting cell.

Life from Nonlife?

This poses a dilemma for the theory of natural evolution: to first say spontaneously generated cells are a medieval myth, but then to say inorganic (nonliving material) went to organic (living material) at least once in Earth's history. To escape the dilemma, Darwinists need a powerful explanation for unintended life, and a really good one, or they are back on "maggots just appear on dead meat" footing.

Of course they have one to offer. It bears careful examination because if it is believable, Design must take a giant step backward, so to speak. If it is unbelievable, then Design wins, even if only by default.

The following will give you a taste of the complex processes said to be necessary if life is to evolve from nonlife. (To fully comprehend the various theories would take a lifetime of study.) In brief you are about to read of a string of random events that begin with our Earth as a raging and inhospitable planet full of intense heat, toxic gases, and violent storms.

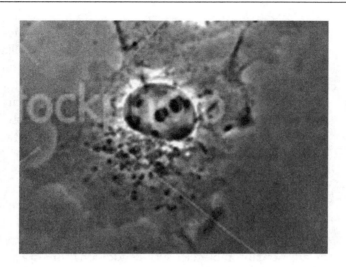

KEY CONCEPT

Following the big bang, the first cell evolved on Earth when—after about 1.1 billion years—conditions on our violent and inhospitable planet finally settled sufficiently for chemical complexity to move forward.

By about 3.5 billion years ago, a powerful *reconfiguring force*, probably the sun's ultraviolet rays, had eventually fractured enough simple inorganic molecules like carbon dioxide and methane to release their atomic carbon contents. These then reassembled into the carbon-chain configurations that are the backbones of organic molecules in our carbon-based life-forms.

As water, hydrogen gas, ammonia, and nitrogen gas were also fractured by UV rays, all four atoms that make up 99 percent of organic tissue—hydrogen, oxygen, nitrogen, and additional carbon—were able to begin attachment to the existing carbon chains. Though this may have taken many millions of years, the simplest organic carbohydrates finally appeared in the *primordial soup*.

Now the oceans—or perhaps freshwater ponds which were not subject to harsh salinity—contained organic molecules like simple alcohols (ethanol), weak organic acids (acetic acid), and monosaccharides (glucose, and later deoxyribose and ribose). At this point, perhaps it was lightning, another powerful reconfiguring force, that fractured sulfuric and phosphoric acids to free necessary sulfate and phosphate radicals. These ionized groups, perhaps further catalyzed by superheated iron and nickel sulfides, then interacted with the present carbohydrates to produce at least some of the "alphabet" of 20 amino acids. And now that these amino-acid building blocks were appearing, they polymerized into the all-essential proteins necessary for any type of future cell structure.

Besides UV rays and lightning, there were other reconfiguring forces present on ancient Earth to aid in molecular advancement. X-rays, volcanoes, earthquakes, tornadoes, and meteor strikes may have also played a role in the assembly of larger organic molecules such as additional amino acids, vitamins, ATPs, and simple enzymes. The appearance of enzymes would be particularly important in that they would accelerate molecular development.

At this juncture, critical components made their appearance. Certain amino acids were somewhat altered to produce the nitrogenous bases of cytosine, adenine, guanine, and uracil, which combined with sugars and phosphates to produce nucleotides that served as the building blocks for the first nucleic acid, RNA. (The template for assembling such a *macromolecule* could have been the intricate lattice arrangement of inorganic crystals.)

With RNA now present, acting as both a coder of additional nitrogenous base sequences and a ligase-type catalyst, it began to self-replicate. Portions of the RNA molecule were now able to construct longer proteins, such as those needed for protective cell membranes, and were also able to code for a unique molecule called chlorophyll. The chlorophyll in developing chloroplasts would then take over carbon-chain construction through the extremely reliable process of photosynthesis.

With RNA and photosynthesis both producing further organic molecular complexity and abundance, these large particles began adhering to each other, eventually forming well-known prebiotic *coacervates*—subcellular particles bringing us to the verge of a living cell.

Other portions of mutating RNA molecules could now begin to code for proteins necessary for the eventual appearance of organelles such as mitochondria, ribosomes, and plastids. Meanwhile, another nitrogenous base, thymine, had already been added to the soup. It was now only a short step to transform RNA into the double-helix marvel of DNA, the ultimate holder of all future genetic codes. This freed RNA to adopt its present role of messenger in the production of subsequent proteins and allowed DNA to assume full "blueprint duties" for all other cell structures. Then in short order, the first asexual prokaryotic cell appeared in the form of a single bacterium, and life was born.

As proliferating prokaryotic cells continued nucleic acid production, individual strands of DNA eventually traveled in twos, leading to the homologous chromosome pairs that are basic to all of today's organisms.

Then, as these evolving cells engulfed other less complex bacteria through *endosymbiosis*, they were transformed into organelles for added capabilities rather than being digested. This produced the first true eukaryotic cell, and the world now had an organism capable of going beyond simple asexual reproduction to utilize a sexual mating process allowing for great variations among offspring. It did not take long for these advanced cells to clump together in multicellularity for protection and division of labor, producing perhaps worms and primitive fish. Though this entire process may have taken 3.5 billion years to complete, the forces of natural selection were now coming into play through survival of the fittest, which would drive organisms to improve or die. For this reason, one might say that in the next billion years or so, the appearance of the complex plant and animal species of the twenty-first century was a foregone conclusion.

Obviously, research for more specifics on the actual mechanisms above continues. On other fronts, the search on Earth for structurally related but unusable molecules has been inconclusive, as have attempts to generate molecular complexity in substantive quantities under laboratory conditions. But nature continues to divulge her secrets, albeit reluctantly, and the work goes on.

This highly detailed explanation stops at the appearance of the ancient chordates—fish—which Darwinists believe went on to eventually become species like the North American wood duck (which I use as an example in the next chapter). And if that could happen, then I guess mammals could appear and become monkeys, and so on.

Get Out the Magic Wand

On the surface, the entire package appears to constitute a powerful argument. Darwinists I know fully believe in this and think nothing more needs to be said. At first glance, how could anyone argue with this explanation? How could you challenge the details unless you were as highly trained as the researchers? The rapid bombardment of high-powered vocabulary, and the dizzying mosaic the terms paint, surely cannot be the product of a vivid imagination, can it?

And what about the explanation's obvious lack of need for an Unseen Hand? How can "In the beginning, God..." compete with this? Is natural evolution the truth and Design the fraud? Does Darwinism still have every right to monopolize science, rendering the title of this book meaningless?

We can see why, to Darwinists, theological explanations for the origin of life must seem like magic-wand waving and smoke and mirrors. I'm sure this is the reason evolutionists have told me to my face that I've forsaken cognitive facts and the left-brained reasoning of science, and instead am now drawing on the emotionalism of the right-brained superstitions of religion—not too far from voodoo and witchcraft. (Flattering, isn't it?)

Another Accidental Marvel

However, before we pursue the issue further, I would like to present an explanation that parallels the one above: an explanation of the unintended processes that produced another first—the first television.

KEY CONCEPT

The television came into use when conditions in the civilized world finally made electronic communications a possibility. It began long ago on a deserted tropical island. Violent volcanic activity due to tectonic plate movement crystallized sand into glass in the shape of a cathode-ray tube. This tube fell into a phosphorescent "soup" composed of the remains of millions of ancient fireflies, and the oozing liquid coated the glass. Though natural erosion eventually wore away the outside phosphor coating, the inside coating dried and remained.

Later, a random lightning strike placed two lumps of iron at each end of the tube. These lumps became magnetized, one positively and one negatively, by the heat dissipation of the ancient cooling Earth, and simultaneously began to function as an anode and a cathode, collecting and repelling electrons. Random oxidation-reduction reactions driven by intense heat from a thermal vent separated and refined sufficient copper from available ore to shape several strands of wire, which were belched ashore by an underwater earthquake and subsequent tidal wave. Hurricane-force winds attached these wires to the magnets in the glass tube in the exact required position. Suction from these same winds produced a vacuum in the tube, which was sealed in by cork insulators blown into place from destroyed trees.

Finally, a burst of ultraviolet radiation from an uncommonly intense solar flare energized the two electrodes, and they began to fire electrons at the phosphor coating at the precise angle that would cause it to glow. The very first operational cathode-ray tube was now a reality.

As all this was taking place, over the same lengthy time period the same reconfiguring forces had shaped the less complex components of tubes, circuit boards, dials, and wood cabinetry. These lay scattered all over the island where the cathode ray tube lay glowing. The light and the other strange-looking objects attracted the curious monkeys on the island, and they began to randomly manipulate the pieces.

As luck would have it, the primates somehow managed to assemble the components, and before they could disassemble them, a man walking the deserted island found the device and named it the "tele-vision." This man was an entrepreneurial sort who realized its potential to display specified electronic signals, perhaps for profit. He brought the "TV" back to civilization, where he applied for and was granted a patent.

Now it has been many years since that first simple glowing cathode-ray tube was discovered, and through serendipitous results of the random actions of bungling repairmen, it has evolved into such sophisticated devices as plasma screens and HDTV. However, much of the original accidental technology is still being duplicated, and even the name "television" is still used today.

Electronic engineers around the world still marvel at the luck of the original patent owner. This is because no similar "pre-television" components have ever been found anywhere else on Earth, either nonfunctional or near-functional, which could corroborate the bizarre tale told by the man who once walked that tropical island. Also, attempts to piece together the natural processes thought to have taken place, and then recreate them under tightly controlled simulated conditions, have met with unsatisfactory results. And yet faith in the truth of the process causes the work to go on.

Well—there you have it. The product has changed from cell to television, but the reliance on potentially lucky processes is basically the same. Perhaps the only other difference is that the vocabulary in the TV scenario isn't as intimidating and doesn't produce the hoodwinking element of mystery due to the unfamiliar.

Choose Your Smoke and Mirrors

Is it perhaps possible that evolutionary science also employs its fair share of magic-wand waving and smoke and mirrors? When you understand what natural evolution is really trying to sell, do you get the feeling someone should tell the king sporting his new clothes that he is really naked?

The story is told of a consortium of scientists who bet God they too could make a living cell from scratch. The challenge was accepted, and the group proceeded to gather the most renowned molecular biologists, cytologists, and geneticists from around the world. As word spread, funds began pouring in from all over. The team built an impressive research facility and equipped it with powerful supercomputers, high-tech microscopes, state-of-the-art electronic machinery, and all the best tools and glassware. When all was in place, the team prepared to go out and collect the necessary chemical compounds to begin their experiments. At this point, God stepped in and said, *"Hey, not so fast—get your own raw materials."*

> Constructing a vital organelle within a cell, such as a mitochondrion, is unthinkable due to complexity of an unimaginable magnitude.

Even if organic components—in this case, prelife molecules already assembled by living cells—were available, I wonder if lab experiments have shown that we are anywhere near making a living cell.

Consider the following:

- Cutting-edge laboratory work can barely identify and safely alter organic molecules from those already present in nature.
- Even constructing a vital organelle within a cell, such as a mitochondrion, is unthinkable due to complexity of an unimaginable magnitude.

Therefore, the correct answer as to whether we can make a living cell in a test tube is not "inevitable," "likely," "probably," or "maybe"—or even "remote"—but most definitely "impossible." However, the incongruity is, many of those same reputable scientists believe that without our story's state-of-the-art research facility with supercomputers, microscopes, electronic machinery, tools, and glassware, a living cell could still accidentally happen in nature.

Now here's where the cheese binds. Why will Darwinists say the random processes making the first cell are within the realm of believability...and then slam the door, as we all must, on my goofy scenario about the first TV? Why the double standard? In both processes we have all the necessary raw materials. In both we also have identical reconfiguring forces with the tremendous yet unguided power to bring about change. Both even have a selection mechanism to drive development forward after the central unit is in operation. All we need in both is a "little" luck.

Can it be intellectually honest to reject the second set of processes while accepting the first? Think about it as we move on to the "either... or" challenge in the next chapter.

Chapter 2

EITHER...OR

A description of the two basic origins choices

Believers in the tenets of Darwinism often state that accepting natural explanations frees one from the necessity of believing in any kind of deity. Conversely, however, religious or spiritual people often incorporate many evolutionary theories in their explanations for how God made the world.

Religious or spiritual people might wonder if God's power directly intervened in human evolution—or if nature had enough power to accomplish this advance on its own. Meanwhile, the opposing crowd firmly believes nature has the power to make these and all other changes, and God is irrelevant.

I encourage the people who believe in a God to be like the Darwinist believers in one respect—dispense with the fence-sitting. The introduction to this book pointed out that recent mainstream science has endorsed only one view, with no blend of the other: Science is *all*, and no deity is required.

So if you suspect Divine intervention but are not quite sure, I urge you to get off the wall of indecision or indifference. Go with one of the two choices because when both views are stated in pure form, they *cannot* be blended.

- *Either* there is a natural explanation for everything, and no type of theology is needed—

- *Or* a supernatural designing entity of some type gets full credit for bringing into existence that which otherwise would have remained a void.

These two views are based on two mutually exclusive presuppositions:

- *Either* we are here through a mindless, random set of events that made an entire universe and then produced life through time and chance—

- *Or* any form of life is too complicated and organized to arise spontaneously, and the science we study reveals that this complexity is born out of information that exists by Design.

If you decide now on which side you fall, you will see much more plainly whether the information in this book supports or refutes your position.

Proposing a Test

As a preface to further considerations, and to emphasize the stark difference between the two choices, here's a review of the two contrasting summaries I gave at the book's beginning:

KEY
CONCEPT

Natural evolution: In the beginning, our universe, our galaxy, our solar system, and our planet were produced over immense periods of time by random forces. Following that, cellular life on Earth arose spontaneously by another series of accidental biochemical events, and then was slowly driven forward to become today's complex multicellular life by yet another unintended process called *natural selection.* All this was possible by the science existing within the system, and no intelligent involvement was required.

Design: The processes and phenomena currently operating within the universe and on Earth are insufficient to
produce themselves. No amount of natural evolutionary
theory can account for the complexity and compatibility
that are continually observed by science. Therefore, there
must be a guiding intelligence repeatedly involved in
creating the complexity, but not subjected to it. Such complexity must always be the result of intended information
because there is a mathematical limit to what blind luck
can accomplish.

To assess the two stances, I would like to test each through an application in nature. (I'll pick up the story where we left off in the previous
chapter—at the appearance of the chordates.) Specifically, how would
natural evolution and Design explain the existence of a unique living
organism?

Out of life's myriad of examples, the male North American wood
duck *(Aix sponsa)* is an appropriate choice because by anyone's standards,
he is one of the most strikingly beautiful birds ever to grace a wetland
or an artist's canvas. Since his extreme beauty seems to go far beyond
necessity, does this point to the artistic talent of a Designer? Or can
science give a thorough explanation for the beauty of the wood duck
through entirely natural means?

Choice #1

If you want to be conversant with Darwinism you need to understand its most highly regarded mechanism: *natural selection.* It was
natural selection, so it is said, that caused that duck to develop. This
is how life advanced of its own accord. Though the following explanation is a bit technical, in a nutshell, natural selection involves a good
mutation that is favored by environmental factors, which then carries
a species forward.

To explain natural selection, Charles Darwin frequently
used the phrase *descent by modification* for how certain

species gave rise to advanced relatives. In this method, you assess ancestry and relatedness is through the scientific classification system of *taxonomy*, and then the simpler relatives give rise to more complex ones. For sufficient detail, the system assigns seven names to all living organisms— according to seven different taxa based on morphology, physiology, and genetic comparisons.* Obviously, the closer the seven names match for two species, the more closely they are related.

The seven steps, from broadest to most specific, are *kingdom, phylum, class, order, family, genus,* and *species,* with the last two steps being the exact name of the organism in a binomial (two-name) naming system. Using this system, the natural differentiation of the wood duck from related species can be outlined by the numbers below.

In the very early stages of life on Earth, organisms split into two main kingdoms. The first was the kingdom Plantae, which are autotrophs that could make photo-synthetic food using solar power. The other was the ① kingdom Animalia, which are heterotrophs that must capture food. (Ducks would obviously arise from the latter, but not until vast numbers of years passed.)

Simple fish in the ancient Paleozoic seas were probably the first animals in the ② phylum Chordata, those animals with spinal cords from fish to ducks to humans. These fish later transitioned through amphibians to establish themselves on land as reptiles in the Age of Dinosaurs. Then certain ancient reptiles began adapting feathers for limited flight, and these eventually mutated into all birds in the ③ class Aves, which obviously includes all ducks.

With ancient birds beginning to dominate the land after the extinction of dinosaurs, a separate group of birds developed the necessary adaptations to live on water. In a few million years, these water birds expanded into the

---

* According to Webster, *taxonomy* is "classification; especially orderly classification of plants and animals according to their presumed natural relationships." A *taxon* (plural, *taxa*) is "a taxonomic group or entity."

④ order Anseriformes, which includes just the duck water-fowl, as well as geese and swans.

Many thousands of years ago, one branch of these ducks acquired an adaptation allowing them to build their nests in the security of trees rather than on the ground, and close relatives of the wood duck could now be grouped into the duck ⑤ family Anatidae, just those ducks that nest in trees. Now, all that is left in the last few thousands of years is to produce today's wood duck, ⑥ genus and ⑦ species *Aix sponsa*, and the final process is easy to explain.

Just as the dictates of survival of the fittest carried life forward from the simplest of animal life to tree-nesting ducks, so can the "nuts and bolts" of natural evolution explain the male *Aix sponsa*'s dazzling colors—quite a contrast to those of the drab, brown female. As to sexual reproduction, ducks are *polygynous*, which means one male will mate with as many fertile females as are available. (If you have ten female wood ducks and one male, you can have ten broods of ducklings, but if you have ten males and one female, you still have eleven adult ducks but one brood of ducklings for the next generation.)

Obviously, once the males have done their reproductive duties, they are most certainly expendable. So if a predator like a coyote should happen by, a more easily visible male will likely fall prey, while the camouflaged female hides quietly with her young. The advantage is this. If a duck must die—and predators need to eat as well—the male's death better serves any duck population, removing the male's drain on available resources while allowing the female to pass on not only her but his genes to the next generation.

So where did the wood duck get such extraordinary colors beyond most male birds? Somewhere in the past, a random and unexpected mutation, or a series of natural variations during breeding, accidentally caused a new gene combination to produce at least one beautiful male. And his bright colors actually enhanced that new gene's

survivability due to the improved way it attracted predators. Now, suddenly, compared to other ducks, the wood
duck species suffers more losses in expendable males and
fewer losses in essential females, and that gives the breed
a better chance to outcompete other ducks by survival
of the fittest. (Some biologists say it is actually the DNA
molecules that are in the fight for survival, and they conveniently wrap themselves with the most advantageous
organisms in an attempt to outcompete each other.)

With time available (4.6 billion years), a mechanism
(random mutations), and a driving force (natural selection), then chance has been able to give us all the diversity
of life—from diatoms to daffodils, from dinoflagellates
to dinosaurs to ducks, even amazingly gorgeous wood
ducks—and all without the aid of an "unseen hand."

Choice #2

Now the Design point of view would be quite different. It goes
something like this:

KEY CONCEPT

First of all, that a ground-nesting duck was lucky enough to
adapt into a tree-nesting duck hardly proves the entirety
of natural evolution. Assuming ducks arose from other
waterfowl that sprouted from other birds that diverged
from other chordates that developed from other animals
that originated from protozoans, can you just assume an
estimated 30 million other life forms also received new
and radically different DNA codes from their progenitors
through the blindness of chance in the time allotted? Also,
is it fair to assume unintended processes could accidentally
piece together the complex biochemistry necessary for the
initial cell? Finally, is evolution automatically allowed to
spot itself a suitable planet in a stable solar system, both of
which were random products of a violent explosion?

Even if evolution is allowed to answer yes to all the above questions, there still must be some proof for how ducks suddenly took to trees. It must have been rather instantaneous because there are no intermediates. In other words, past or present biology cannot provide evidence of a duck that could nest in both locations and finally chose the safety of trees.

And while we are at it, where did the duck suddenly get its webbed feet, strainer bill, and oily feathers? Surely not from the penguin. However, the penguin is genetically closer to a chicken than a duck. Besides, evolutionists say, as a flightless bird, the penguin is a much later arrival than the duck—the penguin's increasing swimming ability eventually rendered its wings unusable for flight and turned it into a fish-eating carnivore.

So it must be that the chicken—which is at least a duck's barnyard cousin and is said to have been a flyer farther back in time—has to be the progenitor of both the duck and the penguin. However, since there is no fossil evidence of a prehistoric chicken that could "almost" swim, we must ask if primitive chickens spent too much time close to water and began to gradually pick up swimming adaptations while hiding them from the fossil record. If not, then did chickens just fall in the water suddenly and quickly get the necessary adaptations before they drowned, with one group swimming to North America and the other to the Antarctic?

Sorry. The unique existence of the male wood duck, or any life-form for that matter, can never be fully explained by the natural forces now governing the world. To try to reduce such complexity to a series of random events leads to scientific and mathematical futility. Rather, the explanation for the duck's existence ultimately requires an intelligent designing entity responsible for, and undefined and unfettered by, these natural forces.

Humans have intuitively acknowledged such an entity in every culture ever known, calling Him by many names. But by whatever name, this "God" is the creative power behind all the science that now operates. Certainly He employed several of the scientifically observed change mechanisms and operational principles studied today (for example, colorful male birds help draw attention away from nesting females), yet it all depends on the science He alone created and fully understands.

Therefore, the rhythm of life is not a cacophony of random and banging noises that somehow fell together, but a symphony by a Master Composer in which all players are unfamiliar with the composition and their as-signed instruments...and yet never miss a note. So in the final summation, if the Designer is responsible for the ex-istence of the universe, fashioning a beautiful duck by the method and in the time frame of His choosing is a small task.

———————

The foregoing explanations offered by natural evolution and Design pose an interesting choice. The first explanation appears organized, documented, researched, quantified, and so...well..."scientific." In con-trast, the second explanation could be viewed as a lot of magic-wand waving and smoke and mirrors—rather like the "God of the gaps" notion. (Instead of searching for the real scientific cause, just say, "God did it.") On the other hand, it's obvious the Darwinian explanation is full of gaps as well. It has always been easy to make evolution attractive at first glance, but it only takes a bit of digging to show how much is based on broad speculations.

So in the end, no matter how you look at it, the choice is still one of only two. *Either* all science is filtered through natural theories, with God being irrelevant or nonexistent. *Or* science is only properly interpreted in light of the Creator who made it.

Again, I suggest both approaches are not of equal value. Only one leads to more truth and resolution of the origins issue, while the other leads to more misconceptions, blind alleys, and questions without answers. The next chapter will examine preconceptions leading to mind-sets that rob a person of needed objectivity on such crucial issues.

Chapter 3

MIND-SETS THAT
ALTER OBJECTIVITY

Preconceptions in religion and science

If my life is typical, I imagine it is difficult for most of us to see the origins issue with a clear set of eyes. As with other hot-button topics (capital punishment, abortion, and so on), we tend to come out of adolescence with our minds already made up on evolution versus creation, based largely on the legacies of our home lives.*

These legacies create mind-sets in people that can become very solidified and recognizable by early adulthood. For example, if the following terms are well-known to you and carry positive connotations, consider yourself a confirmed Darwinist: *big bang theory, natural selection, mutation, survival of the fittest, microevolution, macroevolution, stratification, geologic timeline, fossil record, intermediate species, evolutionary tree, molecular evolution, vestigial structures and behaviors, homologous and analogous structures, punctuated equilibrium, coacervates, radiometric dating, panspermia, endosymbiosis, primordial soup, archaeopteryx, Lucy.* These weighty-sounding terms are not related just to the great debate on origins, but are those that tend to define the evolutionary concept. If you consider these a checklist, your level of familiarity with them indicates your depth of basic understanding in the theory of self-made life.

---

* I was raised in a small fundamental church in a small town in central Wisconsin. So I sometimes contemplate the different views I would have if I had been raised in Tokyo, Paris, Baghdad, Salt Lake City, or somewhere else.

If you buy into the theological angle, your checklist of terms is a bit more exclusive. People professing faith view the hand of God in creation from so many different angles that perhaps only one of the following terms has personal significance to you: *Genesis literalism, creation science, theistic evolution, evolutionary creation, fully gifted evolution, scientific creationism, empirical creation, pantheistic evolution, reincarnation science, deistic evolution, spontaneous creation, teleological evolution, guided gradualism.* Though you probably don't recognize all of them, the above represent someone's attempt to explain the extent of God's role in creation. For convenience, I have organized them from maximum divine involvement (*Genesis literalism*—the Christian Scriptures explain divine control and rapid appearance of every creative and historical detail) to minimum tinkering (*guided gradualism*—just one little holy shove in the right direction). I'll wager if one of these strikes the right chord, I could recite to you several of your personal beliefs.

Locked into a Mind-set

At any rate, whether you are represented by the evolutionary laundry list or identified by a choice from the religious smorgasbord, you could easily be living your life locked into a scientific or a religious preconception.

If your thinking is confined within a preconception, this means you have accepted a basic premise beforehand, and supporting ideas considered for acceptance must conform to the premise or they are automatically rejected. Therefore, the body of information under the premise may grow, but the premise itself has no chance to change or mature into a more substantive belief. In simple words, the mind is closed.

As an example, I had a colleague who believed that the answer for how the simplest of single cells (called *prokaryotes*) became more advanced cells (called *eukaryotes*) was endosymbiosis (larger cells engulfed smaller cells, but used them internally rather than digesting them). However, when it came to *punctuated equilibrium* (the idea that life moved forward in stair-step fashion—no change followed by sudden change), this same fellow felt there were no reasonable mechanisms that would allow a species to lunge forward in complexity. Therefore, in the course of my friend's research, you could tell he quickly adopted any piece of information that could be squeezed or bent into his preconception of endosymbiosis. And any idea that smelled of punctuated equilibrium—or "punk eek" as he called it—was immediately rejected out of hand.

Preconceptions can be equally powerful in religion. For example, that loose confederation of people who support a belief system called *creation science* interpret the six days in Genesis chapter 1 to be literal 24-hour periods, leaving the Earth less than 10,000 years old. The result is that all information on the origin of the universe, fossils, geology, and so on, must be interpreted in light of a "young-earth" generalization. On the other end of the continuum, for those who believe in it, *guided gradualism* seems to mean that some vaguely defined supernatural being could have had a hand in the science governing the world, but that force is now gone. Therefore, all evolutionary mechanisms thought to have operated over the last 4.6 billion years are potentially valid, and any inclusion of Genesis, the Bible, or any religious thought at all is unneeded speculation. Once again, as such people study and do research, information is scrubbed through their own personal filters.

Stagnation

One of the pitfalls inherent in being locked into a preconception is stagnation of thought. Potentially enhancing points of view fail to get a true hearing. If you are in such a trap, the signs are rigidity and ridicule. And the more closed off you become, the more others see you as being rather far out on the limb you are sawing off. Here are two of my favorite examples: 1) An atheistic group demands that crosses be removed from highway locations where people's loved ones have died because they can't stand the sight of religious symbols on taxpayer-maintained highways. 2) A highly segregated religious group loudly accuses atheists of being singlehandedly responsible for destroying the American family. (I would say that neither of these groups is filled with open-minded and nonjudgmental folks.)

There are ramifications to a mind

> Those who get the thumbs-up in history's assessment, I would say, are those who have the ability to use both the "parachute" and "garbage can" approaches with equal effectiveness.

under lock and key. Consider if Galileo had been determined to keep his mind closed to the ramifications of the observations he was making by telescope. Thus any evidence that seemed to contradict the idea that the Earth was at the center of the cosmos would have been planted by the devil to undermine the teaching of the Church.

You escape preconceptions by weighing evidence based on merit and not bias. For those who do, history seems to have a way of vindicating their records. For example, science books remain derisive of Jean-Baptiste Lamarck's early nineteenth-century speculation that giraffes got their long necks by stretching them to reach tree leaves. However, Lamarck's contemporary, Gregor Mendel, is extolled because his extensive testing showed such traits were passed on from parents to their offspring through dominant and recessive genes. Similarly, theologians of nearly every type tend to view faith healers with extreme skepticism, while lauding the efforts of Mother Teresa.

Those who get the thumbs-up in history's assessment, I would say, are those who have the ability to use both the "parachute" and "garbage can" approaches with equal effectiveness. ("The mind is like a parachute. It only works when open"; and, "The mind is like a garbage can. Leave the lid off, and people will throw any kind of trash inside.") The way I would put it is, you must have the readiness to be open to new ideas that have merit, as well as the discernment to not accept intellectual refuse. So with respect to Darwinism and religion, an effective use of both parachutes and garbage cans can help a person keep from getting locked into preconceptions.

———— • ————

Without a doubt, history is full of instances where religious preconceptions have been responsible for unconscionable activities. Yet crucial problems have likewise arisen in science because of preconceptions. Mainstream science can be so passionate about the cause of Darwinism that all other points of view are excluded. The next chapter shows that objectivity-altering mind-sets can operate at the highest levels.

Chapter 4

WHAT THE OLD GUARD
FIRMLY BELIEVES

*An encounter with the National
Association of Biology Teachers*

If there is any doubt over the unity of science teachers in good professional standing, consider the following definitive document by the National Association of Biology Teachers (NABT). On the NABT Web site you can find a link to a document titled "Statement on Teaching Evolution." After some background information and general positioning, the heart of the document presents 22 different bulleted points that state very clearly how the experts believe evolution is to be taught to public school students.

Before I look at some key excerpts from this document, let me say it certainly reveals the extent to which old-guard public-school biology teachers and university biology professors agree that a "natural evolution only" curriculum is the single proper classroom approach. In other words, this document shows how much confidence the NABT places in the explanations for a naturally existing universe, the random processes that supposedly produced complex molecules and cellular components, and the natural selection theory for how life became increasingly complex. It also obviously rests on a "case closed" mind-set, because you will see the NABT does not consider Darwinism open to examination from legitimate sources.

If there is any doubt a preconception is in place, bullet #1 of 22 immediately dispels that doubt. It says,

> The diversity of life on earth is the outcome of evolution: an unpredictable and natural process of temporal descent with genetic modification that is affected by natural selection, chance, historical contingencies and changing environments.

Not much gray area here, is there?

Testability

The remaining 21 bullets are an interesting combination of accuracy and supposition, so let me select those with the most noteworthy points. For example, bullet #3 says that evolution enjoys "clear empirical testability of its integral models." This reads as if something like the following has happened—a researcher in a lab began with a population of ground-nesting ducks and watched them mutate into tree-nesting wood ducks. Unfortunately, today's most intensive and carefully managed breeding programs only produce variations of the same species—or as an old principal of mine once said, "When I breed pigs, I get pigs."

In actuality, the "testability" notion is based on what was *thought* to have happened by observing the very sketchy fossil record. Speaking as if I was an evolutionist, I would tell you all life-forms came from some prehistoric progenitors whose fossils we sometimes find to give us our proof. *True,* we have not found an ancient ancestral bird that was developing into a duck. *True,* since the chicken is a better genetic match to a penguin than a duck, we must say chickens, not ducks, turned into penguins. And yet, *true,* we have complete assurance our position is not flawed.

The Fossil Record

Bullet #4 follows with one of the most inaccurate observations in the entire document. It says,

> The fossil record [includes] abundant transitional forms in diverse taxonomic groups [that establish] extensive and comprehensive evidence for organic evolution.

Nothing could be farther from true, and many evolutionists familiar with the fossil record agree. Back in 1859 when Darwin had the all-impacting *Origin of Species* published, he also knew the fossil record was woefully inadequate, and he also knew the danger this posed to his favorite concept, "descent by modification." Consider his words:

> The number of intermediate varieties, which have formerly existed on earth, [must] be truly enormous. Why then is not every geological formation and every stratum full of such intermediate links? Geology assuredly does not reveal any such finely graduated organic chain: and this, perhaps, is the most obvious and gravest objection which can be urged against my theory.

Of course, in Darwin's day paleontology was in its infancy, and he knew time would have to provide subsequent fossil finds to underwrite his hypothesis. Also, like almost all the educators who contributed to the writing of the NABT document, Darwin was not an experienced paleontologist. Then let's consider the words of an authentic paleontologist, David Raup, Curator of Geology at the Field Museum of Natural History in Chicago. Raup, who had every likelihood to write anything but the following, gave us this quote from his own professional reflections in 1979:

> Well, we are about 120 years after Darwin, and the knowledge of the fossil record has been greatly expanded.... Ironically we have even fewer examples of evolutionary transitions than we had in Darwin's time.

As to bullet #4, who is more credible—Raup, or the NABT?

Directionlessness

After further related points on the mechanisms of natural selection, bullet #7 does make a very true statement. It says,

> Genetic variants within a population under an existing environmental state [have] no specific direction or goal.

Of course, mutations have no preset destination. "Random" cannot possibly know where it is headed. Eminent paleontologist Stephen Jay Gould remarked that if life were to happen on Earth all over again, the outcome would have to be very different, and who knows what new looks life would have then assumed. We all have to say a resounding "amen" to that. But then how do you explain "wingedness"? Birds have feathery wings. Mammals (bats) have leathery wings. Insects display a dizzying array of different wings. Even some of today's fish have wings, as well as some extinct reptiles like the pteranodon!

It does not take an ornithologist or an aviation engineer to appreciate the complexity of flight. Who can fathom the incredible numbers of body structures and adaptations that must be absolutely perfect? Who also can argue that with flight, "nothing works until everything works"? Yet how would weird mutational parts and processes not yet functional just hang around on a body waiting until luck put all the rest in place? And not once, but five different times! No direction, you say? If you flew an airplane blindfolded for a long period of time, as Gould says evolution has to have done, would you arrive at the same most unlikely of destinations five separate times?

Order from Disorder

Bullet #9 says,

> Evolution does not violate the Second Law of Thermo-dynamics: producing order from disorder is possible with the addition of energy, such as the sun.

I was impressed that the document did not ignore the implications of the second law because to so many, it is the single most damaging piece of evidence to strict Darwinism. The second law, also called the law of universal decay, says, among many other postulates, that systems never become more dynamic of their own accord, only more chaotic. Or in simpler words, nothing improves without outside assistance, such as monkeys becoming men.

You cannot just sweep the implications of the second law under the carpet, because many respected scientists believe that this "immovable rock" of physics dooms evolution before it gets out of the gate. (I will provide more details on the laws of thermodynamics in chapter 11.)

But for now, if you want to negate the second law's far-reaching effects, then first complete the following simple three-step experiment:

1. Construct a closed-in room divided by a wall with a door in it.

2. Use solar energy to heat the left side of the room to 65 degrees and the right side to 75 degrees.

3. Open the door in the partition and find some unassisted way for 5 degrees to move right instead of left, and have a 60-degree/80-degree set-up instead of a 70-degree/70-degree one.

In other words, find a way to stop the calm of equilibrium in any unguided dynamic state from happening. Then you will have set aside one of the inviolate second law corollaries, "Heat always flows to cold." Accomplish this first, and then we'll talk.

Time Scale

Bullet #10 is rather short.

> Although comprehending deep time is difficult, the Earth is about 4.5 billion years old. *Homo sapiens* has occupied only a minuscule moment of that immense duration of time.

If the Earth is indeed on the order of billions of years old, the *Homo sapiens* comment still creates a huge problem: how to transition through as many as a dozen species of prehistoric humans, with extensive overlapping and regression, in the blink of an evolutionary eye. (More details ahead on this highly misunderstood and falsely represented topic.)

Molecular Biology

After #4 and #9, bullet #13 is the next major position built on a foundation of shifting sand. The statement has an aggressive counterattack quality, as if intended to strike down a serious challenge. The wording in its entirety is,

> Recent findings from the advancing field of molecular genetics, combined with the large body of evidence from other disciplines, collectively provide indisputable demonstration of the theory of evolution.

Unfortunately, the statement is in direct contradiction to the latest research being done by molecular biologists themselves, who are becoming the leading dissenters from Darwinism. What's more, some of these dissenters were once considered leaders in evolutionary thinking, such as Dean Kenyon. Kenyon's landmark textbook—with the revealing title *Biochemical Predestination*—was the molecular-evolutionary bible of the 1970s. One overriding premise in the book was that due to their functional groups that allowed a multiple of side chains, amino acids *had* to eventually organize themselves into present-day proteins without the help of DNA.

However, by the 1990s Kenyon finally realized the fantastic impossibilities of randomly generating proteins without a macromolecule like DNA. Nor could DNA precede smaller proteins. In Kenyon's own words, his belief in self-made reached the "intellectual breaking point." Now his expert opinion is that organizing the first living cell through random processes (which science says seemed to have happened almost as soon as Earth's conditions permitted) was an even bigger probabilistic barrier to hurdle than that cell eventually becoming a human being.

Religion and Law

Bullet #16 is the longest statement, and seems to be a repository for put-down phrases for anyone who does not agree with the NABT. Though the point is not worded thus, the proviso "unlike you guys, we do not" would be a perfect beginning for the actual phrases that explain what the NABT feels it does *not* do: "start with a conclusion and refuse to change it"; "acknowledge as valid only those data that support an unyielding conclusion"; "base theories on an untestable collection of dogmatic principles." The rest of the bullet basically reviews the proper steps to the scientific method, and in thinly veiled terms criticizes "churchly people" for their unscientific failure to apply them.

After all the broadsides from the first 19 bullets, the last three appear to try to make a little peace. Of course they first reiterate that any form of religion has no place in the science classroom. (Forms of religion cited include "creation science," "scientific creationism," and "intelligent design theory.") But that blow is softened with wording that says a person can still be scientific while maintaining a religion (assuming you pick your religion carefully). Now that's comforting.

In the document's conclusion, readers are reminded of two federal court cases where judges upheld an "evolution only" curriculum— *McLean v. Arkansas,* 1982, and *Edwards v. Aguillard,* 1987. Of course there is no mention of the outbreak of legal action in the last 15 years favoring Design, pressuring mainstream science to support academic openness and have the integrity to examine all points of view while in the search of the truth.* Instead, readers are admonished to "hold their ground" during evolutionary challenges because the law, science—and of course the NABT—are on their side.

The Results of the Mind-set

The NABT opens the entire document with a quote that sets the tone. They recall the 1973 words of one of history's most aggressive Darwinists, Theodosius Dobzhansky, who said, "Nothing in biology makes sense except in light of evolution." After being part of the science teacher cadre for the last 30 years, I can give you complete assurance that the NABT "Statement on Teaching Evolution" and Dobzhansky's quote still define the mind-set of public school science instruction. Therefore there can be no doubt that a preconception controls the system.

As further proof, if the school district has an overall science supervisor, he or she is sure to be of the "NABT approved" variety. Also, these supervisors and their close associates predictably adopt textbooks that strictly enforce the system. Then from a combination of agreement with the curriculum and just to ease doing the job, my experience is that the majority of teachers teach straight from the books given them.

---

* See chapter 14 for some discussion of legal cases.

This means few or no supplemental materials are introduced, and class discussions and outside homework revolve around the book's Darwinistic point of view. The bottom line? Rare is the science classroom where either teacher or textbook offers students anything other than "self-made."

Going Around in Full Circles

As a directive on how to approach science in classrooms, the "Statement on Teaching Evolution" has tremendous impact. Because of the closed fraternity of authors, science textbooks published for receptive middle-school minds, and the teachers who instruct from them, are likely to introduce the "microbe to man" theory in the sixth to eighth grades. Following that, high-school biology curricula and student learning standards predictably demand that evolutionary concepts be developed. What is more, the chapters on Darwinism are almost sure to receive coverage in high school since questions on evolution always appear on standardized tests in grades 9 through 12.

Finally, higher-education science and philosophy professors responsible for career development commonly instill evolutionary beliefs in today's collegians, who will shape tomorrow's research, politics, and public opinion. And let's not forget that the influence of these graduates goes full circle as they in turn become responsible for science-teacher preparation programs and new textbook authorship and adoption. Without question, the impact of the NATB's mind-set is far reaching.

Texts or Pretexts?

Having taught tenth-grade biology for 18 years, I know the impact the textbook has on the mind of the 16-year-old student. Except in the rare case where a teacher brings in supplemental materials, the textbook calls the shots. Consider an average high-school biology text used in innumerable schools across the country, like one that I used from 1996 to 2000 until the textbook adoption cycle replaced it with something actually very similar. The table of contents of this text outlined 11 major units containing 54 total chapters. Chapter 1 opened the book with a nice overview called "The World of Life," and chapter 54 ended the book with a valuable conclusion on "Environmental Issues." The remaining chapters covered all the prescribed curricula on cells, genetics, microbiology, ecology, plants, animals, body systems, and the human body.

So where was evolution given its big pitch? Unit three was specifically titled "History and Diversity of Life" and had four chapters. The first of them—chapter 15—was titled "Changes Through Time," and covered concepts such as how life began, chemical evolution, advancing complexity of life, and life invades land. Chapter 16 was titled "The Theory of Evolution," and covered natural selection, evidences of change, and patterns of evolution. Chapter 17 was titled "Human Evolution," and covered evolution of primates, early hominids, and the genus *Homo*. Finally, chapter 18 was titled "Classification of Organisms" and covered categories of life, phylogenetic comparisons, and how related species gave rise to each other.

> Evolution is treated as fact (no wording like "perhaps" or "thought to be"), and no counterarguments to Darwinism receive even the slightest mention.

If you pause to let the above information sink in, it is obvious the textbook endorses the self-made approach 100 percent. Also, since the unit on evolution was third in the sequence of 11 units, this pivotal content was introduced early in the school year. Then—and as might be expected—information in successive units on cells, genetics, and so on, was tailored to reinforce and re-teach evolutionary principles. What is also noteworthy is that throughout the book, evolution is treated as fact (no wording like "perhaps" or "thought to be"), and no counterarguments to Darwinism receive even the slightest mention.

The bottom line is this. If done according to the NABT's guidelines, by the end of the nine-month school year Darwinism will have taken up about one month of your son or daughter's science class. And this will be the pattern for seven straight years from middle school right up to high-school graduation, because rare indeed is the case where even teachers who profess faith will deviate from what the system prescribes.

At this point, I'm sure many science teachers would say something like, "Okay, so our minds are made up. So it's true we are in perfect agreement. What is wrong with being in agreement over the truth?" First, this book will go on to show natural evolution to be completely and unequivocally false. Second, about 80 percent of the people still do not accept what the other self-appointed 20 percent keep telling them. As proof of the dissension, Dobzhansky's words indicating that evolution reigns supreme don't seem to carry the day as they did back in 1973, when natural evolution was enjoying a virtual free ride.

Going into the twenty-first century, educators, researchers, politicians, and just common folks are speaking out against the closed Darwinistic mind-set that many now see as more philosophic than scientific from the get-go. The movement is gaining enough momentum that Design is even becoming somewhat of a household term, and types of objections such as those I noted in the 22 bullets above are fueling the movement.

The stifling influence of groups like the NABT is dissipating as valid scientific evidence clears the air. The remaining chapters of this book will lay out that evidence for all to see.

Change Is in the Air

Some individuals and organizations are already driving the newly developing paradigm of science education. For example, the International Foundation for Science Education by Design (IFSED) offers non-evolutionary instructional materials, including worksheets, lab exercises, and topical essays. They also offer non-Darwinistic teacher-training seminars and professional support for initiatives against the "evolution only" approach. (They can be reached at www.IFSED.org.)

PART TWO

MATHEMATICAL
PROBABILITIES

Chapter 5

Are Zeroes the Heroes?

Do large numbers provide refuge
for "self-made" theory?

Darwinists view huge numbers as not only a major plank in their theory, but also a refuge where the theory of natural evolution can escape when in trouble. For this reason, numbers with long strings of zeros are an integral part of the belief that life made itself. Many of these zeroes are to the "left" of the decimal point. Realizing the need to grasp the implications of those big exponential sizes, I brainstormed into a way to drive the concept home to the students in my class.

To emphasize the magnitude of a million of anything, I once asked my sixth grade students how long they thought it would take to collect a million pennies. I proposed everyone should bring in the contents of their penny jars from laundry rooms and dressers, get relatives and friends to donate theirs, and even encourage students from other grade levels to get involved. If we did these things, I asked them, how long did they think it would take to reach one million pennies? The estimates ranged from two weeks to four months, and the challenge was on.

So I got an empty aquarium, placed it in the middle of the room, and we went to work. Students made daily deposits, and after about six weeks of trying, the effort fizzled. The final tally was $314.78, and about a third of that was actually silver and a few bills. Some quick math showed the students that even though their resources were generally depleted, as was their motivation, it would take over *three-and-a-half years* of collecting change at this level of effort, day in and day out, to accumulate the value of one million pennies—which I reminded them was equal to $10,000! The point was made—a million of anything is a lot!

Now if a million is large, how much more so a billion (a thousand million)? Then a trillion (a million million) and beyond? (This can be extended to the right of the decimal point to allow evolution to factor in the ultrasmall probabilities as well—"one quintillionth" of a chance.)

Multiplication Factor	Power	Prefix	Symbol	Name in USA
1,000,000,000,000,000,000	10^{18}	exa	E	quintillion
1,000,000,000,000,000	10^{15}	peta	P	quadrillion
1,000,000,000,000	10^{12}	tera	T	trillion
1,000,000,000	10^{9}	giga	G	billion
1,000,000	10^{6}	mega	M	million
1,000	10^{3}	kilo	k	thousand
100	10^{2}	hecto	h	hundred
10	10^{1}	deca	da	ten
0.1	10^{-1}	deci	d	tenth
0.01	10^{-2}	centi	c	hundredth
0.001	10^{-3}	milli	m	thousandth
0.000 001	10^{-6}	micro	μ	millionth
0.000 000 001	10^{-9}	nano	n	billionth
0.000 000 000 001	10^{-12}	pico	p	trillionth
0.000 000 000 000 001	10^{-15}	femto	f	quadrillionth
0.000 000 000 000 000 001	10^{-18}	atto	a	quintillionth

Certainty—An Obsolete Concept

With 4.6 billion (giga) years of Earth's history to allow change, billions upon billions of incredibly tiny molecules interacting in Earth's primordial soup, and trillions (tera) upon trillions (tera) of stars in the universe with the possibility of their own planets, some scientists have called the appearance of life somewhere in space by purely natural processes not only a likelihood, but "a certainty." Nobel Laureate and Harvard biology professor George Wald said,

> However improbable we regard this event, or any of
> the steps which it involves, given enough time it will almost

certainly happen at least once. And for life as we know it, once may be enough. Time is the hero of the plot. Given so much time, the impossible becomes possible, the possible probable, and the probable virtually certain.

Now, this quote came from 1954, a time when belief in natural evolution was rising toward its zenith. It was about 100 years after Darwin's landmark book *The Origin of Species*. People like Thomas Huxley and events like the Scopes Trial had made Darwinism a household term. That era also included widespread understanding and acceptance of a supposed 4.6-billion-year-old Earth, a concept bolstered by the ideas of primordial soup, spark chambers, pangaea, mutating agents, and cavemen as a few of the necessary components. Meanwhile, Darwinists were trusting that the paleontologists scouring the world for new intermediate fossils would fill in the remaining gaps, and that astronomers were gaining a better appreciation of the size of the universe and the implications thereof. All was evolutionary bliss.

The Word from Physics

However, 1954 was before physicists began wholesale agreement on calculations that the conditions necessary for the big bang took place within a fantastically minuscule window. A prevailing view in physics today is that the balance of very technical concepts like electromagnetic forces, nuclear intensity, strength of gravity, mass of material, temperature, excitation of nuclei, and rate of expansion all had to somehow be "monkeyed" with to make the event a mathematical possibility. In fact, physicists now say that if any one of the above factors were out of proportion, the elements, especially those like carbon so necessary for life, would never have been formed, and the cosmological game would have been over. Therefore, the probability of just getting a universe solely by natural processes already puts the "lottery of life" out of reach. When I cover the myriad of incredible factors in our finely tuned universe under the second law of thermodynamics in part 4, you might understand why physicists generally make poor Darwinists.

The Word from Molecular Biology

1954 was also before the incredibly complex structure of DNA was completely identified and its role in protein synthesis was realized. Researchers have since learned the absolute specificity of the amino-acid sequences in a recognizable protein that are coded by the exact nucleotide arrangement in DNA—the sequence of "G's" bonded to "C's" and "T's" bonded to "A's" in the stairsteps of the twisted double helix.

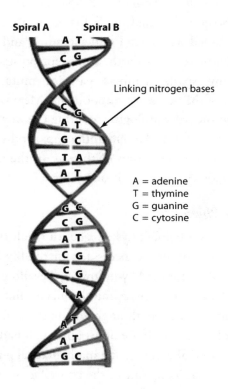

If any of the nucleotides in DNA are out of order, then the amino acids in the resulting protein are out of order, and the protein is most likely rendered useless. It then follows that if the body needs only a few specific proteins out of the unimaginable number of possibilities, an explanation must be given for how they were manufactured without the help of the DNA that could not have preceded them. When you add even more technicalities such as essential enzymes and histones, the probability of generating even *one* small protein by random chance easily surpasses the zeroes in an estimate of the number of atoms in the whole universe.

Did you catch that? Not enough atoms exist in the entire known universe to rival the number of small *useless* proteins that would be made in random fashion before accidentally getting one of the *useful* variety. (These numbers will be crunched for you in chapter 7.) For this reason, it doesn't surprise me that from the ranks of biology, molecular biologists were among the first to jump ship from the *Beagle*, the legendary vessel that carried Charles Darwin around the world.

Bridging the Gaps?

Turning to fossils, paleontologists have had about 50 years of hunting since 1954. They now know the intermediate species needed to fill in Darwin's acknowledged gaps simply and without question do not exist. Did you catch that one also? Missing links remain—missing. The obvious implication here is that Darwin's idea of gradual change must be junked, and for species to naturally advance, they must now make giant leaps forward in complexity.

But then this sticks the poor geneticists with explaining a mountain of incalculable odds if so many mutations must happen simultaneously, to the tune of some 30 million species estimated to be alive today. Is the universe capable of holding the odds of instantly generating entirely new organs that suddenly appear in the next most advanced animal? Can one swipe of the mathematical brush suddenly establish innumerable incredibly complex symbiotic biological relationships around the world, like the interdependence between bees and flowers? If natural evolution says ratlike creatures the size of a dime turned into blue whales in about the same time it took Cinderella to lose her slipper, isn't this yet another number crunch of fairy-tale proportions? ("Hopeful monster," you say? Now that's what I call faith!)

From Certainty to Futility

In 1954, Dr. Wald essentially called exponential numbers the "heroes" in the drama called natural evolution. Now, over a half-century later, Darwinists have a hard time selling that script, and many don't particularly want to audition for that role. Instead, they must struggle daily to find plausible ways to disarm the villains of time and chance, which actually *lack* the zeroes to attract today's more discriminating crowds to their one-act play. To drive this point home, the next chapter fully illuminates the futility of relying on math to underwrite the impossible.

By the way, if an evolutionist ever tries to sway you with a dazzling display of large numbers, I hope you think of all the loose change sitting in that aquarium in my classroom.

Chapter 6

A New Spin on
an Old Idea

A vastly improbable idea that makes sense

Over the years, several interesting analogies have been proposed to argue *against* the possibility of ancient inorganic materials becoming living organic cells all by themselves—for such must happen if Darwinism is to be believed. You may have heard some of them: "Consider the chances of a violent mountain rock slide constructing a medieval castle." "Imagine the probabilities of an intense explosion in an airplane parts warehouse producing a jetliner." "Calculate the odds of powerful lightning strikes at a printing business assembling a dictionary."

Like the Oparin–Haldane hypothesis of autobiogenesis (that says life self-organized in the violent, interactive chemical soup of ancient Earth), each of the above scenarios has all the necessary raw materials and an active reconfiguring force to possibly assemble them. But as the argument goes, the one missing element that makes all of these highly unlikely, to put it mildly, is absence of a guiding intelligence.

I find it strange that Darwinists can reject the castle/airplane/dictionary analogies while accepting the Oparin–Haldane hypothesis. By this I mean Darwinists always have no trouble shrugging off the first three as just plain silly while believing in the fourth as the Rock of Gibraltar. Perhaps it is the "duration" factor. Perhaps Darwinists feel the forces exerted by the rock slide, the explosion, and the lightning strikes end so quickly that there is insufficient time for randomness to complete its tasks. They would say by contrast, chemical evolution in the soup had millions and millions of years to get lucky.

Also, even if the probability of random life is called "one chance in a gazillion," I have heard people more than once counter with, "Ah, you did say 'one chance,' and that does not mean never, ever." Then let me propose a new analogy that may better highlight not the *improbability* of self-made biochemistry, but the *impossibility*. Since this analogy extends the duration of the powerful reconfiguring force indefinitely, let's see if it removes the "at least one chance" argument.

Not a Chance

Imagine a house is to be constructed and the materials have been delivered to the building site. It is all there—boards, nails, glue, windows and doors, shingles, wiring and outlets, lights, paint, appliances, you name it—and of course all necessary tools. But before the building crew can begin work, a powerful tornado hits the building site and holds its position indefinitely, throwing all items up in a continuous whirl.

It is definitely possible, perhaps even certain after 4.6 billion years of commotion, that something like two boards will meet at just the right moment and be fastened by a flying nail in exactly the position required by a carpenter. Then perhaps those two fastened boards could later encounter a hinge covered with glue that lands in just the right place so it will one day hold a door…and we are on our way. Therefore, the question becomes whether the house *could* be built given 4600 million years of swirling activity, especially if tornadoes could also happen on as many "building sites" as there are suitable planets in the big, wide universe. Darwinists have answered that not only *could* it happen, but it *did* happen—to the tune of building quite a luxurious "mansion," and right here on good ol' Earth.

A bit of elementary math may shed some light. Who could argue against the fact that destructive forces are present in the raging tornado? Identify these by the variable **D**, for destructive. But if you believe two boards could be fastened perfectly with a nail, which I see as a reasonable assumption after long periods of time, allow that some constructive forces are also at times present in the frenzy. Identify these by the variable **C** for constructive.

Now—if the forces were *equal* in magnitude (destruction taking place at exactly the same rate as construction), you would get a net result of zero by subtracting the two equal quantities from each other. This produces the simple equation **D – C = 0**, which would define activity inside the tornado if objects were being built at the same rate they were torn apart, or a neutral outcome was being caused by the violent winds.

But given the disintegration caused by tornadoes, that equality being sustained in the funnel cloud is impossible to defend. Therefore, destruction must generally be the greater value, and if you subtract the smaller construction value from it, your answer reflects that destructive forces are *greater* than zero. This means your potential house is being pulverized, and the equation **D – C > 0** applies.

How much greater would you call **Destruction** than **Construction** in the tornado? If the size of the letters were to capture the magnitude of the comparative forces, how much bigger would you make the "D" than the "C" reflecting how much more able a tornado is to destroy than build?

$$\mathrm{D} - \mathrm{C} > 0$$

$$\mathbf{D} - \mathrm{C} > 0$$

$$\mathbf{D} - \mathrm{C} > 0$$

$$\mathbf{D} - \mathrm{C} > 0$$

$$\mathbf{D} - \mathrm{C} > 0$$

If you've never really observed or experienced the power of a tornado, I suppose you could let your imagination produce some constructive results. But then ask the people interviewed on the evening news—as they sift through the rubble of their tornado-leveled house—how much larger they think **D** is than **C**. I can guarantee they won't be looking for newly constructed pieces of work performed by the storm.

How Many Ways Can You Say "Impossible"?

At this point, do you still believe a tornado can make a house? Then consider this rendering of impossible. For construction to ever proceed forward, it has to be admitted that the difference in destruction/construction magnitude would have to somehow be *reversed*, meaning the tornado is now building faster than destroying. This would be the equation $C - D > 0$. Then this amazing disparity would have to be *sustained*, and for how much time? Well, my neighbors built their place in what seemed like record time—four months. Do you get the feeling that perhaps we are asking a bit much of our tornado to have that house finished in four months?

But there is more. Who can argue that the tornado would have to assemble different sections of the house in the correct order? Ask any carpenter if windows, magically not broken, or magically glued back together after being broken, can go in before walls.

And finally, after the four months of "construction by wind," the violence would have to suddenly cease so the house is not smashed in the next instant. Will gazillion times gazillion give you sufficient odds to build the house? Can the universe itself contain the necessary probability? If you are not yet convinced, read in the next section about the universal probability concept. You will find, in all honesty, you do not even have that *one* chance to get your house...or to get your first cell.

One common objection to my conclusion of "impossible" is that trying to make one house on a specified planet is much, much more improbable than trying to make one cell on that planet where billions of chemicals are interacting everywhere. The argument is that in the oceans on ancient Earth we had unimaginably numerous sets of "building materials," greatly enhancing our ability to get lucky here. And then if you add nearly unlimited planets elsewhere in the universe with their boiling oceans...well, maybe the odds are actually rather short. The problem with this reasoning is a true lack of understanding of the nature of exponential numbers. The previous chapter already showed that, even at a glance, large numbers betray natural evolution rather than support it. When in the next section I examine exponential numbers in depth, you will realize how weak the "enough time and enough chances" argument is.

Another objection aimed at the biochemical level goes something like this. Perhaps your tornado would not give you the desired house, meaning a fully functioning cell, but you might get a usable "shack," meaning you might get subcellular components that will do "for now," until improvements come along later by the selection process. In other words, you may first get a modest but functional glucose molecule (functional for what?), and later it gets bumped up to become a DNA mansion. Or maybe you get deformed or incomplete pieces of DNA (from where?) that eventually join themselves into usefulness.

In Darwin's day, cells were thought to be homogeneous blobs of jellied protoplasm, but science has come light-years from that belief.

But there is a tremendous problem with this reasoning. At prelife levels, there is no natural-selection process to drive molecular improvement forward. Without cells to generate, protect, and utilize larger molecules, these useless and cumbersome entities are awash in a violent and toxic saline sea, where they are more susceptible to destruction than even their smaller inorganic counterparts. These are exactly the issues that must be ignored for the famous Miller–Urey experiment to remain remotely plausible, and also the reason why Miller's apparatus has never generated more than the smallest components. (The Miller–Urey experiment will be taken up in detail in chapter 8.)

Finally, it is fair game to ask if the simplest bacterial cell is more or less complicated than our fully constructed houses. If less, then making the cell becomes more believable. In Darwin's day, cells were thought to be homogeneous blobs of jellied protoplasm, but science has come light-years from that belief. Now we know there are as many as 200 separate highly complex chemical reactions required to completely catalyze just one molecule of sugar. Also coming to light is the amazing array of molecular machines responsible for a dizzying number of metabolic processes. Cell specialists called cytologists know that when you say *metabolizer,* you have said more than you can possibly imagine.

Furthermore, cells must be readied to dispose of waste, possess movement mechanisms, store food, and provide for their own reproduction—all before metabolic activities are initiated. And if you don't find cell reproduction a complicated process, first study in any biology book the ultratechnical sequences of mitosis and meiosis that allow a cell to divide. Then imagine how these processes could have been readied when as yet there was no use for them. It's almost like saying that cells were preprogrammed to exist without the involvement of intelligence, which is a statement comical in its self-contradiction.

And think of this—if the analogy were to be completely fair, the tornado would have to be spinning over a forest-covered deposit of various minerals and sand—in correct proportions—because boards, nails, and windows would have to be produced randomly as well.

So when you realize that the first developing but nonfunctional cell must somehow have anticipated all the processes mentioned above, the whole theory of self-organizing life is reduced to the same result *always* left by a tornado…utter destruction.

Mitosis   Image courtesy of The Open Door Web Site.

Chapter 7

A Sword with
One Edge

Vastly improbable *versus vastly* impossible

Do you still hold to "vastly improbable" for the first accidentally generated cell, and "highly unlikely" that this cell could become a human—but still not "impossible"? Then it is vitally important to fully comprehend the large numbers you think provide one chance for life.

Albert Einstein's words "compound interest"—his answer to what he thought was the most powerful force in the world—was more insightful than humorous. Einstein knew that a modest sum in a bank account drawing interest on accumulated interest would initially grow almost imperceptibly. However, extremely soon compared to the millennia of geologic time, the pocket change would mushroom (via the "J-curve") into a theoretical sum unconfined by the universe.

The wisdom in Einstein's answer escaped me for most of my life, even though I took extensive math courses in three different college-degree programs, taught upper-level math in high school for several years, did detailed statistical analyses for state-level government-grant programs, and helped five kids through public-school "new math" assignments. Let's see if the true power in an exponent has escaped you.

Exponential numbers written in scientific notation ("something to the something power") have the utility of expressing gigantic values (or even minuscule ones) without writing all those zeros. Ten to the third power (10^3) or one thousand (10 x 10 x 10) is easy enough to write as 1000 with three zeros. But what about writing the number of offspring a single bacterium can produce in a day-and-a-half? Unless you have plenty of time and space to write 15 zeros, isn't 10^{15} much easier?

Consider this application. Some geneticists say the odds of getting a "good" mutation, like perhaps a wing bone, are about 1 in 10 million (10^7). Then if you need a total of six proper wing bones for flight (remember, just five would be totally useless!), you need six consecutive good mutations for a working biological system of six parts. This means the math says your chances of getting that six-bone system through luck are 10^7 times six, or about 1 in 10 to the forty-second power (10^{42}) chances—expressed by writing a 1 with 42 zeros!

The Power of Powers of Ten

The problem with fully comprehending the magnitude of these numbers results from their rare use. People are much more accustomed to arithmetical increases, where a "three" is one more than a "four," and a "four" is halfway between a "zero" and an "eight." But Einstein knew well that kind of reasoning does not apply to exponents.

The idea finally struck home to me when I showed a video to my math class called *Powers of Ten*. This 15-minute feature began in a Chicago park by Lake Michigan with a frame scale one meter wide (10^0, read as "ten to the zero power," which equals one by definition), which is approximately three feet. The picture was large enough to show only part of two picnickers on a blanket in the grass. Then the camera zoomed outward by one power of ten every ten seconds. The next frame was ten meters wide (10^1), about ten yards, and you could see both picnickers, the entire blanket, and part of the park. At 100 meters (10^2), you could see the whole park and an adjoining four-lane road, and at 1000 meters (10^3) you could see portions of Chicago itself.

The picture kept widening until the picnickers were a speck beside the lake. Chicago and then Illinois melted away, Earth shrank into the solar system, the solar system shrank into the Milky Way galaxy, the Milky Way shrunk to a point of light among clusters of galaxies, and so on. The sequence stopped when the edge of the known universe was reached, and we were looking at a frame representing ten to the twenty-first meters (10^{21}) wide. The video then reversed the picture, and powers of ten reduced in two-second increments took us right back to the picnickers on the blanket. (The video then went into a picnicker's hand, down into the body, and down to the smallest reaches of the inside of an atom. Here distances are measured in "angstroms" at one ten-billionth of a meter (10^{-10}), which as a standard number is .0000000001.) However, before the narrator reversed the sequence at the edge of the universe, he reminded us that "each retraced power of ten would take us *90 percent* of the way back to the picnickers" (emphasis added).

Ponder the implications. On a scale of ten dollars (10^1) to a billion dollars (10^9), it might appear without thought that 10^5, which is a hundred thousand dollars, is halfway between those lowest and highest dollar figures. A quick examination of the three amounts—$10, $100,000, and $1,000,000,000—should easily reveal the misconception. That is like saying the weight of a football player at 10^5 grams is half way in size between a penny at 10^1 grams and a ship at 10^9 grams.

In actuality, the football player at 10^5 grams, or 220 pounds, is *900 percent* larger than a dog at 10^4 grams, or 22 pounds (100,000g minus 10,000g equals a 90,000g difference). Furthermore, the football player needs an increase of only four more powers of ten before he approximates the weight of a 1102-ton ship. Or as Einstein might have said, doubling 10 dollars to 20 dollars is indeed doubling, but the sum pales compared to the result of doubling 100,000 dollars, and fades to near nothing when doubling a billion dollars.

An Application to Origins

What does this realization have to do with the origins debate? Natural evolutionists wield exponential numbers as if they were swords that cut in only one direction. They hope to impress the unaware with the 4.6 billion (4.6 x 10^9) Earth years available for mutational change—and the trillion trillion (10^{24}) stars in the universe with possible planets where life could have also spontaneously formed. Yet those same people can look at the odds of 1 in 10 followed by an additional 41 zeros (10^{42}) for accidentally generating one organism with a biological system of six working parts, such as our wing bones...and not bat an eye. (Speaking of eyes—though ophthalmologists would laugh this off the page—you could say the eye was nothing more than a combination of lens, iris, vitreous humor, retina, optic nerve, and an assortment of muscles.)

It makes me wonder if Darwinists find ten to the forty-second power not that impressive because they see it as merely not quite double the 10^{24} stars in the universe? Do they not realize that if the odds of the six-part system were "only" one more power of ten than the number of those stars (10^{25}), it would take *900 percent more* chance mutations than all the stars in the universe to get that eye? And do they not realize there are some 30 million other indigenous Earth species (written as a paltry 3×10^{7}) whose complex working parts must also climb out of the primordial soup? What clouds the perception of people who believe math supports natural evolution?

The number of atoms to make all matter in the entire universe must truly be a colossal and impressive figure. It certainly is—a common estimate is ten followed by 79 more zeros: 10^{80}! Yet in so many texts and discourses on Design, it is noted that the odds of generating one of the smaller proteins we need of 100 specified amino acids by totally random processes is 1 in 10^{130}! Going from the number of all the atoms at 10^{80} to the numbered odds of making one small protein at 10^{130} is not just 50 more chances, but 50 increases of 900 percent each! Pause, if you would, and absorb that concept.

This also means if protein-based life accidentally organized itself on Earth after the first two billion years or so (the passage of 10^{16} seconds), nature would somehow have to be "testing out" 10^{114} new amino-acid combinations *every second* (10^{16} plus 10^{114} equals that 10^{130}) to cover all the combinations of that one small specified protein within that time frame! If you consider the estimate of 10^{80} atoms needed to make our entire universe, does it seem like there is enough matter and enough time to get that lucky? And there are still about 100,000 other more complex proteins to generate that bodies need, some with specified amino acid sequences that are not 100, but 10,000 units long! I apologize for the overuse of the exclamation point, but how else do you express incredulity that highly intelligent researchers and immensely gifted mathematicians still place their trust in blind luck? On what foundation do they rest their hope?

You Can Bank on It

Einstein's observation on compound interest shows he undoubtedly understood the nature of exponential growth. To gain my own perspective, I asked Gordon, my banker friend, what happens over time to a small amount of money at a modest rate of interest. After some figuring, he replied with this example. If you take $1.00 at 5 percent simple interest, you will have an impressive sum of $4 in 30 years. Big deal, especially with inflation. But in 200 years it will grow to $21,000, in 500 years it swells to $70 billion, and in 1000 years it explodes to $4.76 x 10^{21} dollars—working toward $1.00 for every star in the known universe! Then after doing some measurement in the street outside the bank, Gordon said this was enough money to pave 91 eight-lane highways to the Sun with $100,000 bills! From this example, you can begin to grasp why exponential growth follows what I have already identified as the "J-curve"—a line on a coordinate graph that moves out with a slow start, but then rises upward and out of sight with unimaginable explosiveness.

Finally, I asked Gordon if he could come up with a money calculation that would approximate all the atoms in the known universe. His

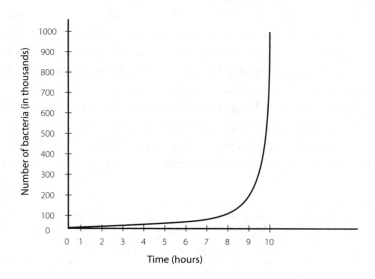

Curve of Exponential Growth

response was that if Moses had put $1.00 down at 5 percent interest (Moses lived 3667 years ago, which is a blip in geologic time), his descendants today would have 10^{80} dollars to share! That's $1.00 for every estimated *atom* in the known universe. Fun.

Surely There's a Chance?

What are the broader implications for failing to understand the exponential function depicted above? In my view, the natural evolutionist's greatest mathematical error is in thinking the smaller exponential figures they use give them leverage (age of the Earth, number of stars, and so on), while the greater figures revealed by Design theory (the making of one small protein) still give evolution a window for success.

In fact, Darwinists act as if the endlessly high exponential probabilities always still provide that one chance they need. For example, molecular biologists say that while a protein of 100 linked amino-acid proteins is on the small side, one with a string of 250 amino acids is an average size—and we know how much more useful averages are than minimums or maximums. Now there are 10^{325} ways to assemble an average-sized protein from 20 different amino acids, only one of which the body will recognize for its purpose. Thus nature's odds of success balloon to 1 in 10 followed by 324 more zeroes!*

To some, I suppose success in 10^{325} available chances remains theoretically possible because if you are allowed to give it a try, you could argue that the "one" is still tantalizingly there. However, are odds that high even possible in reality? In other words, is there an actual boundary to a probability—a number so high that beyond it, any other odds are impossible and you have reached zero? William Dembski, easily the most influential and respected writer on Intelligent Design, has calculated a number that represents the absolute limit on luck. Dr. Dembski proposes a "universal probability bound," a boundary beyond which any

---

* To be completely fair, there is the possibility that certain of the amino acids in these proteins could be "fillers" where substitutions from the list of 20 amino acids are possible. But if you consult the actual structures of these amino acids, you will see very few "kissing cousins" you could reasonably exchange for one another. Also, if you are watching the TV show *Wheel of Fortune*, how many letters in a long puzzle must be in place before a guess is even possible, and how many wrong letters in a misspelled word will you permit before you call it a mistake?

other probability is not just highly, extremely, or outrageously stringent, but "zero" for any mathematical purposes.

The "Universal Probability Bound"

Dembski's formula is actually very simple to derive, and employs only figures straight out of science. You begin with that previously used common estimate of the total number of atoms in the entire universe, 10^{80}. (For those who prefer words to digits, that's one hundred million trillion trillion trillion trillion trillion atoms.) You then multiply this value by the maximum number of possible divisions in a second, which, if you think about it, would yield the maximum number of changes in any given second that all the atoms in the universe could possibly undergo any type of transformation. For the total number of smallest possible slices in a second, Dembski uses the value of 10^{45} (or 10^{-45} seconds of time allotted to just one of these slices).* What this all means is that the highest number of change events that can take place in the universe in any given second is 10^{125} (80 plus 45), which would represent all 10^{80} atoms undergoing all 10^{45} possible changes in that one second.

One more easy calculation yields Dembski's maximum probability. Consider that science estimates the universe to be between 10 and 20 billion years old, which translates roughly into 10^{25} seconds. If you take the total number of atoms already multiplied by the maximum possible atomic changes per second, and then multiply that by all the seconds available in the age of the universe, you get math that results in the following:

$$10^{80} \times 10^{45} \times 10^{25} = 10^{150}$$

How Many Ways Can You Say "Never"?

Stop and absorb this. The final total is a probability limit that accounts for the combined chance occurrences of any one possible

---

* This 10^{45} figure is derived from Planck's constant, that long-standing bulwark in physics measured at 6.626 x 10^{-34} joules per second, which is the proportionality of the energy of a photon to its frequency. To see how Planck's constant is converted into the smallest possible division of physical time, consult Halliday and Resnick's *Fundamentals of Physics*, 1988. Here the authors dissect the derivation and explain that with any amount of time smaller than 10^{-45} seconds, present theories of physics are likely invalid.

event in any one of the smallest particles anywhere in the universe—all that can happen to anything, anywhere, anytime. What number in our present reality could possibly be larger? That also means if the probability of an event is calculated to be *over* 1 out of 10^{150} (commonly written as 10^{-150}), the odds say that it will *never* happen. Remember the odds of blind luck making that one medium sized protein essential to life at one in 10^{325} tries? To reach that value, you would have to take the probability boundary already calculated, one in 10^{150}, and increase it by 900 percent a total of 175 times to reach the 10^{320} value! (Recall, if you would, the powerful nature of exponential number increases explained earlier in this chapter by the picnickers at the Chicago park scenario.) Would you say "vastly improbable" has just become "vastly *impossible*"? I would—and if this is true, self-made life is already rendered an impotent theory. Dembski's own words make it perfectly clear:

> Implicit in the universal probability bound such as 10^{-150} is that the universe is too small a place to generate specified complexity by sheer exhaustion of possibilities.

Still, many I know cling to the "one chance" hypothesis, saying things like, "Hey, if the odds of winning the lottery are one in 10^{150}, and you get to buy one ticket, well then..." Next they will often add comments like, "Hey, if you buy all 10^{150} tickets, you *must* win." My answer?

1. If it takes 10 billion atoms to make a single ticket, and all the atoms in the world were in lottery ticket form, you could sell a maximum of only 10^{70} tickets (sell to whom?). This means while the mind is allowed to imagine with impunity, nature puts actual limits on every possible probability scenario.

2. If we remove all such restrictions imposed by reality (a Darwinist's dream) and you bought 10^{150} tickets, your "winning ticket" for the protein of 250 amino acids could still be among 10^{175} others you didn't purchase.

3. You still have thousands of other proteins, some thousands of amino acids long, to pull out of your "hat."

The bottom line? That exponential number "sword" the Darwinists try to wield ultimately has only one edge that cuts only one way—and it slashes the head off any hope for natural evolution.

What We Need to See

Another idea could be inserted here. What happens when a professor from a prestigious Ivy League university comments that there is no way to calculate the probability of the accidental construction of the human eye. Is he right? Of course he is. How could you ever quantify all the factors involved in the supposed random improvement of the eye over millions of years in millions of creatures in millions of locations?

However, can you calculate the odds of blind luck making the amino-acid sequence necessary for just one of the proteins required for that eye? Absolutely. Also, can you calculate the odds of any one atom in all the universe making any one move in all available time that might begin the construction of that protein? Yes, you can. It's in the paragraph above. Then if the former value is shown to be bigger than the latter value—which it has been—can anyone not see that the random origin of the human eye is a mathematical impossibility (or even the most primitive eye, for that matter, because they are all made of proteins)? Yet my amazement continues that many a mathematician with impressive credentials can so completely ignore the power of the exponential function.

> My amazement continues that many a mathematician with impressive credentials can so completely ignore the power of the exponential function.

* * *

If I wrote nothing further, science already has all the reasons it needs to disassociate itself from Darwinism. And yet the chapters to follow will go on to challenges in molecular biology, physics, astronomy, zoology, botany, genetics, human biology, and paleontology. However, do not think the subject of math is closed. The prohibitive nature of these exponential numbers appears time and again. If the field of science is being reclaimed from Darwinism, it follows that the tool of science—mathematics—should come along.

PART THREE

MOLECULAR BIOLOGY

Chapter 8

CELLULAR RECIPE

*The scientific requirements for making
the first cell by blind luck*

If you were not impressed by the "zero chance" mathematics of accidentally making the chemistry of life before the cells that use it, then how would you explain the advance of such chemicals? Assuming the sudden interaction of inorganic components in air and water ("inorganic" meaning nonliving) did not immediately produce that first cell, evolving chemistry must have happened via a series of developmental steps.

How many steps did it take, and did the steps lead to "floors" where you finally had a group of similar molecules at a certain level? I tried to imagine what tiers of organic components ("organic" meaning living) a Darwinist would construct, and what molecules would be in each tier according to size. Then, once these tiers were established, what mechanisms would the Darwinist say carry one group of chemicals to the next larger?

Finally, after a proposed sequence of evolving molecules was constructed, a more pivotal question would then follow: "Was nonlife to cellular life more difficult than cellular life to human life?" In other words, was it harder for random activities to make that first simple single-celled organism from inorganic molecules, or was it more difficult for that first cell to then evolve into *Homo sapiens,* whose biochemical codes are the most sophisticated on earth? Allowing that the distant past's simplest cell would be today's bacterial prokaryote—a cell with no nucleus, a single set of DNA, and only asexual reproduction by simple cell division—surely "bacterium to beast" is a bigger hurdle than inorganic chemistry to bacterium.

A Major Hurdle

However, unfortunately for Darwinists, biochemists feel that is not the case. It is a powerful statement to say that the spontaneous generation of the first cell was a bigger probabilistic hurdle than that single cell eventually turning into a person. Yet this assertion is fast becoming the consensus of molecular biologists. There is a connection here with a concept lesson I do in middle-school and high-school science classes called "Relative Sizes." The lesson's objective is to get students to grasp the extremes of "littleness" and "bigness" in the universe, and the instruction ends with students doing a poster project. Their posters must display three scaled continuums supported by a string of graphics to compare sizes of everything from subatomic particles to superclusters of galaxies.

Three "Worlds"

To give the students plenty of ideas for their poster, I start by explaining to the class the "Middle World" continuum. To do this, I draw a line across the middle of the board and put a human being on the middle of the line. Then I arrange objects on the line to the left and to the right according to size (usually living objects to catch the attention of the kids). The criterion for the Middle World is that an object must be visible to the *naked eye*—able to be examined unaided by instruments.

At the left end, I list the smallest object just barely visible to the naked eye, often choosing a single-celled amoeba. At about a hundred thousandth of a meter across, (10^{-5}m), you actually can see them in the petri dish if the light is right and you look real hard. At the right end of the continuum, I usually end with the Earth, having a diameter in the order of about 10 million meters, or 10,000,000m (10^7). If you can imagine what the students now see, you have a line on the board ranging from 10^{-5} to 10^{7}, decorated from left to right with objects like fleas, flies, worms, dogs, elephants, blue whales, aspen groves, mountains, ecosystems, and biomes. Then if you add the human at the range of one meter, or ten to the zero power (10^{0}), there we are smack in the middle of a journey that takes us through 13 powers of ten.

The next step is to draw another line above the Middle World, a second continuum that becomes the "Macro World." This line contains those extraterrestrial objects best studied with the aid of a telescope. I begin this list on the left with Saturn, whose diameter is approximately ten times greater than Earth's, measuring in the 100-million-meter range (10^{8}m). Then comes the diameter of the moon's orbit, approaching 1 billion meters across (10^{9}m). From there I take the Macro World to the edge of the known universe at over ten to the twenty-first power meters (10^{21}m), passing dizzily through stars, solar systems, comet orbits, constellations, galaxies, local galaxy clusters, and galaxy superclusters as we span another 13 powers of ten.

Finally, on a line below, the students develop the third continuum, called the "Micro World." This world obviously examines those objects whose existence was not fully known until the microscope was invented. This time I develop the line in reverse direction, starting on the far right with some groupings of cells too small to see individually taken from an algae strand growing in the class fish tank, Spirogyra, at about one-millionth of a meter (10^{-6}) per cell. This continuum ends on the left with those mysteries of physics—quarks, mesons, leptons, baryons, and so on—down to a supposed 10^{-19} meters. On that reverse journey downward through inner space we pass bacteria, viruses (viruses being on the barrier between cellular biology and molecular biology), nucleic acids, proteins, lipids, sugars, water molecules, hydrogen atoms, protons, neutrons, and electrons.

The journey through the Micro World is another amazing 13 powers of ten, and the entire three-line progression covers sizes from 10^{-19} to 10^{21}, spanning a total of approximately 40 powers of ten! What might be even more amazing is that as humans we are still right there, standing roughly in the middle, between the biggest and the smallest of what we can measure! (Allow me to say that viewing the students' completed posters, with pictures, drawings, and clippings on their three timelines, shows that the project, and the lesson, is well worth doing.)

A Biochemical Journey

So what is the connection in the "Relative Sizes" lesson with challenges to Darwinistic thinking? In the "Micro World" it highlights what very few people ever consider in natural evolution—that chemistry has to evolve forward before life can follow suit in the "Middle World." Also, in the "Macro World" we first need a miraculous big bang that didn't immediately incinerate itself or collapse back on itself (something many physicists find nothing short of astounding), and basic inorganic molecules like water (H_2O) that are properly constructed so they may properly behave (another wild stroke of fortune). Now supposing we are given all these lucky breaks, we can then go back to the original question. How many steps would there be in advancing molecular complexity to finally produce a living cell? The answer in the following information is going to be a bit technical—but then, the chemistry of life is no simple matter.

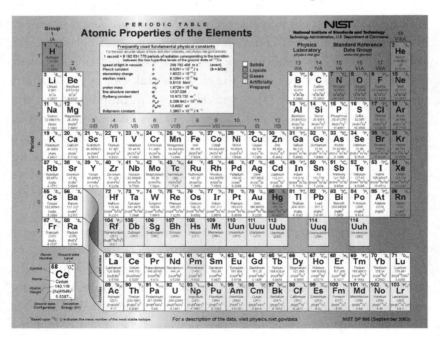

My science students should be well aware that 99-percent-plus of living tissue is composed of only 4 atoms from the 100 or so on the periodic table of elements. (Try to imagine only 4 letters out of 26 making 99 percent of all words!)

Of the four basics, carbon at #6 has top billing because all organic molecules are built on carbon chains, hence the familiar term *carbon-based life-forms*. Then come oxygen, #8, and hydrogen, #1, required to make all *carb-o-hydrates*. Finally comes nitrogen, #7, which is necessary for all 20 amino acids, the building blocks of the proteins so often mentioned in this book that make all cells. The reader should take special note here. Proteins are the life-giving structures of cells, but they are made of smaller essential units called amino acids. No amino acids—then no proteins and no life.

Beyond the "big four," we should also add two nutrients, because we need small quantities of sulfur, #16, and phosphorus, #15. Sulfur is found in some amino acids, making it necessary for all proteins, and phosphorus is an integral component of nucleotides that make DNA and RNA.

Some of the 20 main amino acids

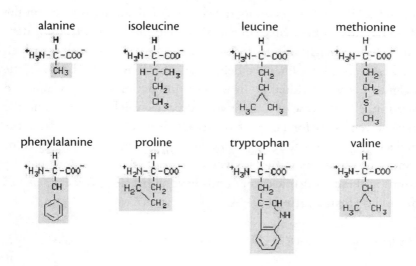

At this point, believers in the standard scientific timeline are likely to agree that these six vital elements (carbon, hydrogen, oxygen, nitrogen, sulfur, and phosphorus) were present in molecular form on our newly made and violent earth of 4.6 billion years ago. That is because molecules containing these atoms are most certainly common throughout the universe. The diatomic gases of hydrogen (H_2), nitrogen (N_2), and oxygen (O_2) can be found in large supply in many objects in space. You can find carbon and hydrogen in methane gas (CH_4), nitrogen and hydrogen in ammonia gas (NH_3), hydrogen and oxygen in water (H_2O), carbon and oxygen in carbon dioxide gas (CO_2), nitrogen and oxygen in nitrous oxide gas (N_2O), traces of sulfur in sulfuric acid (H_2SO_4), traces of phosphorus in phosphoric acid (H_3PO_4), and on it goes throughout the universe. But how do the sizes of these tiny molecules compare to a macromolecule like DNA, and what steps would it take for random processes in nature to make get that large? (For as most people know, no DNA, then no Earthly life of any kind.)

Weighty Matters

One easy way to compare sizes of these molecules is to use their atomic weights. These can be calculated from the individual molecular formulas (like H_2O) by adding the weights of all atoms as given on the Periodic Table of Elements. (In chemistry, protons and neutrons by definition have a weight of one *AMU—Atomic Mass Unit*—with the much smaller electrons not included being negligible in weight. Therefore, the weight of any individual atom is the combination of its protons and neutrons.) In the case of water, two hydrogens weigh one each, and the oxygen weighs 16, for a total of 18 AMUs. Simple calculations from the molecular formulas above yield the following comparative weights for common substances found anywhere in space. Keep in mind that the atoms in these inorganic compounds have all the necessary elements to make the organic prize of DNA.

hydrogen gas = 2 AMUs   methane = 16 AMUs   ammonia = 17 AMUs

water = 18 AMUs   nitrogen gas = 28   oxygen gas = 32
                               AMUs   AMUs

carbon dioxide = 44 AMUs   nitrous oxide = 44   sulfuric acid = 98
                               AMUs   AMUs

phosphoric acid = 98 AMUs

Now it must be stated here that these molecules above are no indicators of life. Even water, so essential to life as we know it, is not a living substance. However, as said before, these small inorganic molecules do contain all the atoms necessary to make simple organic molecules, *if* you could just get them to reorganize properly. So how much fracturing and recombining would be necessary to carry these small molecules in the weight range of less than 100 AMUs (less than 10^2) to the size of a DNA molecule on which life is built?

Well, with human chromosomes containing about 3 billion nucleotide base pairs, the total weight of our DNA is estimated to be in the ritzy neighborhood of 10 billion AMUs (10^{10}). Going back to the exponential concepts from the previous chapter, we must take something as small as water and enlarge it by 900 percent—not once, but eight separate times—to reach the requisite size of DNA. Since this size explosion certainly cannot have happened quickly, the powers of ten approach used in the Relative Sizes lesson provides a framework for going from small to large. Starting with a repeat of those simple inorganic molecules listed above—which alone are no proof of life—we have what constitutes a grouping from which to begin.

Four Groupings

INORGANIC GROUP ONE—Less than 100 AMUs each

hydrogen gas (H_2)	methane (CH_4)	ammonia (NH_3)	water (H_2O)
nitrogen gas (N_3)	oxygen gas (O_2)	carbon dioxide (CO_2)	
nitrous oxide (N_2O)	sulfuric acid (H_2SO_4)	phosphoric acid (H_3PO_4)	and so on

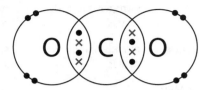

Model of a carbon dioxide molecule

To move up to molecules in the weight range of the next power of ten, 100 to 1000 AMUs, carbons would have to become chained together. This is because carbon is the "backbone" for even the simplest organic molecules. The best known example of a small organic molecule is probably a simple sugar, or monosaccharide, called *glucose,* because glucose is *the* all-important product of the carbon-linking process called photosynthesis. The molecular formula for glucose is $C_6H_{12}O_6$, for a total of 180 AMUs. If the inorganic molecules in GROUP ONE molecules could somehow be consistently fractured by natural forces and reorganized into the organic molecules, like glucose, included in the list below, that would be significant for Darwinists, because GROUP TWO molecules are the undeniable indicators of life and its related processes.

ORGANIC GROUP TWO—100 to 1000 AMU range

mono- and disaccharides (such as glucose and sucrose)	amino acids (necessary to make proteins)	nitrogenous bases	fatty acids
glycerols	adenosine triphosphate (ATP)	and so on	

Glucose molecule

If we get those introductory organic molecules above, the next reasonable step in naturally developing complexity is for GROUP TWO molecules to reorganize into GROUP THREE examples (below), which are the next highest power of ten. In that sugars and amino acids are monomers (single units) of polysaccharide and polypeptide polymers (chained units), if random forces could get them to link up, life could ostensibly be well on the pathway to the larger molecules in the next size range.

ORGANIC GROUP THREE—1000 to 10,000 AMU range

polysaccharides	polypeptides	nucleotides	lipids
vitamins	chlorophyll	and so on	

Model of a folic acid molecule

If fortuitous accidents can just produce these GROUP THREE molecules above, it appears we are at the threshold of life. Since additional polymerization still needs to take place, the presence of enzymes would be a critical step. Even high-school chemistry classes teach that enzymes are biological catalysts that speed up reactions. By providing a "template" for the joining process of *dehydration synthesis* (the removal of water), enzymes help bring two smaller molecules in proximity for bonding. This rapidly increases the rate of polymerization, where two molecules would otherwise have to move into position by "luck."

Since enzymes are proteins, and RNA itself can act as an enzyme, the formation of enzymes and RNA will initiate the GROUP FOUR level of molecules seen below. This will accelerate the progress toward other macromolecules, and perhaps the additional boost will provide all the molecules needed for life, like DNA. So if all these macromolecules complete their assembly according to evolutionary plans, it appears we have reached the threshold of a living cell. And as evolutionists will proudly point out, all by natural processes.

ORGANIC GROUP FOUR—10,000-plus AMU range (macromolecules)

enzymes	RNA	cellulose	proteins
hemoglobin	histones	DNA	and so on

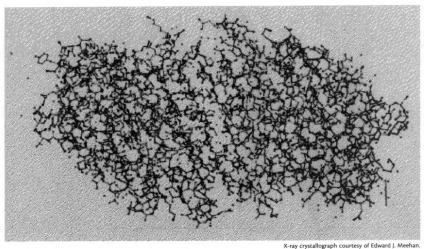

X-ray crystallograph courtesy of Edward J. Meehan.

Model of a lectin protein molecule

Help from 1953?

If you got lost in all the previous chemistry, now would be a good time to bring you back with a reality check. For this chemical growth hypothesis to be more than just a philosophic exercise, there would have to be some scientific proof. If you didn't know, all natural evolutionists turn to one procedure done back in 1953, probably printed in every biology text ever written since—the Miller–Urey Experiment.

To briefly explain the experiment, graduate student Stanley Miller, with the help of his advisor Harold Urey, put a mixture of those inorganic GROUP ONE molecules into a glass apparatus and bombarded them

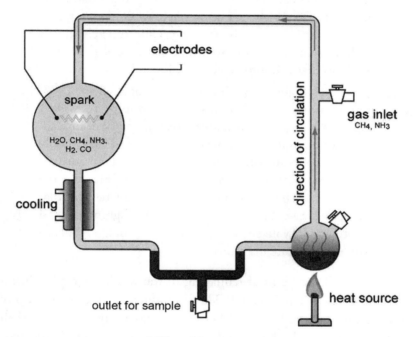

Miller–Urey apparatus

with electric sparks. These sparks were to simulate the reconfiguring force of lightning in an ancient Earth atmosphere. Reaction products were condensed in a trap, and found among expected disassembled remnants were a hodgepodge of GROUP TWO fragments—particularly some amino acids that could be used to make proteins! To Darwinists, this was the beginning and ending of all the proof one needed that molecules could become more complex all by themselves.

But before this sequential process is hailed as proof and put on the pedestal of truth, consider the following:

1. Miller tinkered with the composition of the gas mixture in the spark chamber many times before any results were achieved. In the end, the most promising mixture of gases he put into the flask has been under constant attack by even evolutionists as being totally unrealistic in regard to Earth's ancient atmosphere.

2. Science agrees across the board that oxygen gas had to be present in Earth's ancient atmosphere when these organic molecules were said to be forming. Unfortunately, this is a "death sentence" since oxygen's effect is fatal to organic synthesis that is unprotected by cell membranes.

3. Since the original experiment was completed in 1953, improvements, modifications, or extensions in Miller's approach *have yielded no more meaningful progress.* Instead, any research in this field is never publicized because it only serves to discredit Miller's hypothesis rather than advance it. (If there were any promise to put more "meat on the skeleton" of Miller's original work, you can be sure that evolutionists would be harnessing plenty of lightning—and shooting more voltage through glassware than Dr. Frankenstein did to create his monster.)

Finally, and maybe most damaging to the whole concept, reintroduction of any initial GROUP TWO products back into the top of the apparatus for another dose of electricity has always just led to their chance degradation back to simpler molecules. Make special note here: Never has there been anything close to an advancing synthesis toward GROUP THREE, which is still pitifully short of a DNA molecule in GROUP FOUR.

Further Misconceptions

How can a Darwinist think the absolute dead end of Miller–Urey provides any hope? And we are far from done with problems in accidental chemical evolution. First, in improving molecules, there is no natural selection functioning. In fact, as any chemist knows, with increasing complexity comes increasing susceptibility to disassociation instead of

Those 900-Percent Increases

I did have a student say once, "Hey, if Miller's spark chamber can get you to GROUP TWO, you're halfway there." Remember the penny/football player/ship analogy from chapter 7? The football player at a weight of 100,000 grams (10^5) is not halfway in size between a penny at about ten grams (10^1) and a ship at 1,000,000,000 grams (10^9). Similarly, a GROUP TWO molecule at maximum of 1000 AMUs (10^3) is *not* halfway in developmental weight between those in GROUP ONE at a maximum of 100 AMUs (10^2) and those in GROUP THREE at a maximum of 10,000 AMUs (10^4).

The reality is, GROUP ONE molecules would not have to double, but increase 900 percent in molecular weight to become GROUP TWO size, *another 900 percent* to make the GROUP THREE range, and as was shown earlier, undergo *six more increases at 900 percent each* to eventually reach the AMU size of DNA (10^{10}). (The DNA molecule so often pictured is said to hold as much information as all the books in 20 libraries. It's immense!) How can ballooning growth like this, without reversals, take place unassisted?

polymerization. And since there are as yet no operational cell organelles to facilitate, utilize, or protect the growth process, more complex but incomplete molecular recombinations remain useless. This "fire—aim—ready" mentality continues to be a major Darwinian misconception. Evolution assumes proteins before the DNA that must code for them, histones before the DNA they must properly coil, enzymes before the necessity of a reaction, ad infinitum. Sorry, but that's just not sound reasoning.

And there is also the massive problem of chemical *chirality.* I discussed in chapter 5 the impossibility of nature, without the help of DNA, being able to get amino acids properly sequenced to make required proteins. Then I covered in chapter 6 the unavailability of the amount of time needed to try all the possibilities. Yet I have not explained that the orientation of the amino acids *before* they are joined is yet another factor.

To catch the concept of chirality, imagine pieces from a Scrabble game dumped on a table. If we're going to string the letters together to make words, we don't even stop to think that first we must flip over those landing face-down as needed, and spin the others around to be upright as required—all by intelligent choices, of course. In like manner, we now know that correct amino-acid sequences become meaningless without proper bonding sites, and spatial and rotational orientation—the meaning of chemical chirality—must be perfect or the protein cannot fold correctly for use. Since each amino acid has a multiple number of bonding sites—and only one is correct—what's to keep a random process from turning out proteins that, though properly sequenced, are completely mangled?

> The theory of accidental organic molecular evolution will never hold water until someone starts with something like air and battery acid...and makes deoxyribonucleic acid.

Finally, it is a reach of mammoth proportions to assume that filling up a Miller–Urey flask with the most promising mixture of GROUP FOUR molecules, and bombarding them with energy—even under the most controlled and advantageous laboratory conditions—will find them combining into a metabolizer: that is, a functioning cell. Before a cell can survive, whether plant or animal, it needs a whole host of organelles—like a nucleus, ribosomes, mitochondria, Golgi bodies, lysosomes, vacuoles, membranes, and so on. And once again, even macromolecules are a long way from being these.

In 1966, the eminent co-discoverer of DNA's structure, Francis Crick, proclaimed,

> It may be some time before we could easily synthesize such an object, but eventually we feel there should be no gross difficulty in putting a mitochondrion together from its component parts. This reservation aside, it looks as if any system of enzymes could be made to act without invoking any special principles, or without involving any material we could not synthesize in the laboratory.

Now that the twenty-first century has arrived, has Crick been prophetic? Hardly. An amazing number of laboratory experiments have been done since 1966, and every attempt to synthesize just a "simple" cell organelle like the mitochondrion, though it's far from being a complete cell, has met with undeniable failure. This is not to disparage the great work being done in molecular biology, because additions to, and benefits from, biochemical knowledge have been tremendous. But every unsuccessful lab attempt to naturally synthesize any larger organic molecules beyond GROUP TWO still never starts "from scratch." Remember, researchers always begin with smaller organic molecules, like amino acids, that are *already* a product of some living cellular process. The theory of accidental organic molecular evolution will never hold water until someone starts with something like air and battery acid...and makes deoxyribonucleic acid.

———————•—————

There is a catchy phrase now being used by backpedaling natural evolutionists. It is often the answer to the common challenge that paleontology is devoid of the necessary intermediate species. That phrase is "Absence of evidence is not evidence of absence." For fossils, I think this means that until we turn over most every type of rock in every type of strata in all the Earth's crust, we cannot say for sure that the intermediate linking species we never find still do not exist. Well, okay...keep looking I guess.

But I've also heard this phrase applied to chemical evolution. The problem is, aside from the dead end of the Miller–Urey experiment, there is not even a reasonable set of coherent hypotheses, tested or untested, for how inorganic molecules organized into the first cell. Here it is a case of "Absent evidence remains evidently absent." My final take on the whole myth of chemical evolution? We need to borrow the phrase "Designer genes" from the world of fashion.

Despite the arguments above, there are still some prominent individuals who pitch the concept of "self-organizing systems"—systems they say still could have made complex chemicals. The next chapter covers the champion of such systems, Richard Dawkins, and his use of the famous line from Shakespeare's *Hamlet*.

Chapter 9

SMUGGLERS' COVE

*Finding hidden intelligence in
claims of randomness*

The last chapter outlined the most prominent challenge to natural evolution in the last decade. It has a consistent theme, a theme that has great appeal from the person with average science background to the Nobel Prize winner. The challenge is the difficulty, or better said the mathematical impossibility, of macromolecules and complex living systems being self-organized by completely random processes.

The main argument is that this level of complexity, such as seen in the wondrous DNA molecule or the incredible echolocation system of the bat, has to be a product of information. And since information can only come from intelligent intent, there has to be an Intelligent Designer responsible for, but separate and apart from, what has been made. The basic tenet is so powerful, no wonder Darwinists work hard to discredit the assertion that in nature, complexity is equivalent to Design.

Here William Dembski needs to be mentioned again.* One belief Dr. Dembski holds is that counterarguments to Design meant to explain

---

* Dr. Dembski has written several excellent books and articles defending what he has coined *intelligent design* (ID) and *complex specified information* (CSI). To understand his most cogent arguments, I recommend you read one of his books: *The Design Inference, Intelligent Design, No Free Lunch, The Design Revolution*—or all four.

self-organizing complexity often "smuggle in" intelligence somewhere along the way. Like a bootlegger sneaks in the contraband under the cover of darkness when nobody is paying careful attention, so do many Darwinistic explanations disguise the involvement of intelligence so as to hoodwink their audiences—often, in the process, fooling themselves. Though I agree in principle with Dembski, I find he is often too generous. From my point of view, intelligence is not subtly infused in most evolutionary explanations I've heard. On the contrary, I think it "walks right in and sits down in the front row."

Many, many times I have heard evolutionary arguments, or seen explanations, based on "computer-generated complexity." The case usually made is that inanimate machines like computers are quite obviously capable of "creating" unique designs, original models, and other forms of innovative data.

The Darwinist then says, "So there you have it. Innovation and advancing complexity do not depend on human intelligence." Now wouldn't it be novel if those computers could accomplish these tasks right out of the factory box without having been loaded with a program based on human engrams? (It would be even more novel if somehow the computer's circuits, monitor, and case were responsible for their own construction.) I would say the only way computer-generated complexity can be used to underwrite Darwinism is if Darwinism can also produce the computer from its raw materials, as with our TV in chapter 1. Like I said, intelligence "walks right in and sits down in the front row."

Weasel Words

Richard Dawkins is probably the most recognized Darwinist who is still garnering attention as we forge into the twenty-first century. Dr. Dawkins is well known for addressing one of the most damning challenges to natural evolution, namely trying to explain how a complex protein's exact amino-acid sequence could be constructed at random. (This was the central example in chapter 7 on mathematical impossibilities.) In his argument, Dawkins uses this line from Shakespeare's *Hamlet:*

METHINKS IT IS LIKE A WEASEL

This string of 28 characters has 23 letters and 5 spaces. Each character can be one of 26 different English letters, or a space, allowing 27 different choices in each position if chosen at random. However, Shakespeare obviously intended those letters and spaces above to occupy their respective positions. Now compare Shakespeare's intentional results to a truly random method by, say, a chimpanzee banging out characters using a keyboard. If we use the chimp's first 28 keystrokes, one possibility is seen below.

WD LDNLOTUDTJBHKWIREZLMQCYOP

The above string is one possible outcome, but how many other possibilities are there if the chimp were allowed to perform again and again? To find out, multiply the 27 (number of character choices) times itself 28 times (number of positions), and we find there are about 10^{40} outcomes. That's right. If you could just get a chimp to type 28 characters before he destroys the equipment, there are about ten thousand trillion trillion trillion different ways he could do it. So how does Dawkins explain the above "alphabet soup" becoming Shakespearean prose without the involvement of any intelligence, a method he implies would also randomly construct those pesky proteins? He applies a computer algorithm to the above character string. It works much like a slot machine.

Imagine a "window" for each of the 28 positions, and a "wheel" behind each position containing all 26 English letters and the additional space option. To start, the hodgepodge of characters above are in view in each of the 28 windows, and the "electronic handle" is pulled. The lights flash, the music plays, and the wheels turn as the spinning characters roll by the windows. Shortly, the wheels begin to stop, and characters appear one by one until all windows are filled.

In Dawkins's scheme, some correct letters and spaces are bound to appear in the right positions, even if only one or two. For example, the above random stream already has the sixth letter "N" and the eleventh letter "T" in exactly the right positions for Shakespeare's weasel line. The computer program recognizes these letters, or others that are close, and they are *held* in their respective locations. Then the handle is pulled again, and the reshuffle and resort continues. Dawkins suggests that after ten attempts you might have something reading like the string below.

BQLUSNLTDATIJKSWTKIAR ZEHYLP

The above may not look like much, but already in place are one space and four letters—the only N, the second T, the second K, and the only E. The first ten random sorts have now placed about 18 percent of the desired message in correct position! This might seem like insignificant progress because the message is still very much indecipherable, but Dawkins says after 20 shuffles, maybe some sparse recognition might now be possible. He says after 20 pulls of the slot machine's handle, 13 proper letters and 3 correct spaces are seen in position below.

MDTHENLO ITJIS WLKEAW MEACSP

This makes about 57 percent of the message now intact above, and other characters are drawing close to their proper positions. How about after 30 attempts? Then the pattern below is clearly beginning to develop with 21 total characters in the correct position, a hefty 75 percent of the message in place.

MWTHINLS ITGIS MLKE Z MEASEL

After 40 attempts, the message below is over 92 percent complete. With only two letters left to correct, Shakespeare's line is generally readable.

METLINKS IT IS LIKE I *WEASEL*

And after 43 attempts, with only a random process, success!

METHINKS IT IS LIKE A WEASEL

Dawkins's summation is that an average of only around 43 sorts is necessary to produce the target sequence from any of the 10^{40} possibilities. Therefore, if nature applies the same procedure to the 20 amino acids that are strung together to make all proteins, and you can allow millions of geologic years of primordial oceanic shuffling instead of a few computerized seconds, then why is it considered impossible for protein-based life to organize itself? Dawkins's bottom line is that random activities can change the unspecified into both the appearance, and the usefulness, of specificity.

The Smuggler Unmasked

A great many highly intelligent people have lauded Dawkins's conclusions. And yet, is his procedure truly randomized? The truth is, the "smuggled" intelligence operating here couldn't sneak past a 19-year-old mall security guard on the last five minutes of an eight-hour shift. If you would, go back up and find the italicized word that is "held" a few lines above. Here is your not-so-hidden smuggler. What, or who, knows to hold any letter or space in place when it begins to come close, or even lands in the desired position? What is to keep from sending a hopeful letter or space into reshuffle on the next pull? For certain, Dawkins's computer program has some type of instructions *intended* to recognize target letters.

In Las Vegas, if you could keep every "cherry cluster" in a slot machine window where it appeared before your next pull, legendary jackpots would hit much more often than every forty-third yank on the handle. Also, best pull up another chair in that front row for the first cousin of intelligence—"directed"—because how can a completely random process proceed toward a target sequence as if it knows where it is going? If natural evolution is truly a "blind watchmaker," how can it possibly know the preconceived destinations that perfectly make each of the approximately 100,000 different proteins that will someday have to fully interact to make life?

The truth is, for our slot-machine operator to be successful, the desired line would just have to pop up unexpectedly somewhere during those 10^{40} attempts. (There are those dratted exponential numbers again!) For example, if one readout suddenly found 42 of 43 characters were perfect, random would have no way of knowing how excruciatingly close the goal is, and all characters would be sent into oblivion on the next yank of the handle. And since Dawkins says the procedure is analogous to making proteins, the message must be perfect to the last character.

That is because just as no jackpot was ever awarded for a "nice try," so are amino-acid sequences in proteins specific to the last link.

You Can't Win for Losing

It has already been shown that there is no mathematical support for molecular evolution—none whatsoever. And as for the continued development of complex organs and organ systems farther down the geologic road, the fossil record is so devoid of transitional examples that you must sacrifice objectivity to be a Darwinian paleontologist. By default, this leaves Design as a highly attractive alternative. And yet Design comes under attack in a number of ways, mostly philosophic rather than scientific. Consider this common complaint by evolutionists as they look over the progression of life on the way to humanity. When they contemplate the vast number of extinct species in the geologic record, they have said, "If there is a Designer, He must be an incompetent one. Look how many tries it took before He got it right." In other words, for someone omnipotent, He sure was a goof up for millions of years as life suffered to extinction at the expense of so many faulty tries.

Okay then, by the same reasoning Mozart was an incompetent bumbler in his early compositions. I guess Mozart showed no promise of future success in his younger years due to his "imperfect" efforts, and therefore he is not to be given credit for even his pinnacle works. There is also a reverse accusation to the Designer's incompetence, and it goes like this. "If an omnipotent Creator just brought organisms into being with a snap of a finger, why would they bear such a striking resemblance to one another?" In other words, shouldn't life forms made "on a whim" look like the weird concoction of creatures in the bar scene of the first *Star Wars* movie?

Okay then—no bridge designer is allowed to establish and reuse sound engineering principles in his productions, and every bridge he completes should bear no resemblance to another.

In truth, both objections above are very weak. Instead of smuggling in intelligence, now the evolutionary contraband is a "grasping at straws" skepticism because, I suppose, the alternative that a Designer deserves credit is just unacceptable and unthinkable.

Based on this argument of patterns in living creatures, or lack thereof, a related point can be made. The belief in gradual evolution rests on organisms from the past, as yet undiscovered, bearing similarities to those in the present. Then explain the following sequence of the number of chromosomes in the cellular nuclei of these various organisms:

fly (12)	shrew (18)	cat (38)	wheat (42)	human (46)
mouse (46)	lizard (46)	monkey (48)	fern (72)	crayfish (200)

What is the evolutionary explanation for this complete lack of chromosomal pattern found throughout all nature? Since humans and lizards both have 46 chromosomes, are they closer in origin than a monkey, which has 48? Are we more closely related to a stalk of wheat at 42 than a cat at 38? Of course a Designer could arbitrarily select the chromosome quantities He wishes, but if the truth behind life is "descent by modification" from common progenitors, what mechanisms produced this nonsensical chromosomal arrangement?

In their lack of credible explanations, natural evolutionists seem to fall back on the "God is a bumbler" defense by saying, "What's the matter, can't God find a pattern that works best?" In my experience, this is always the reasoning of people who will defend natural evolution to the death. It shakes out like this. When life is ordered and sequential, common descent is the answer because God would have been more creative. When life is not ordered and out of sequence, it is also evolution because, after all, "God couldn't get it right." In my opinion, this "bait and switch" tactic is one way to augment smuggling operations.

Returning to Dr. Dawkins and his weasel research, I'm sure he knows the background behind Shakespeare's line "Methinks it is like a weasel." The quotation comes from act III, scene 2 of *Hamlet,* where Hamlet and his friend Polonius are "cloud-gazing" and picking out formations that appear to have a recognizable likeness. (This is an apt scenario because Dr. Dawkins holds that life on earth only gives the "appearance" of being designed.) Polonius sees one cloud bank and says, "By the mass, and 'tis like a camel indeed." Then Hamlet answers with the famous line that is the subject of this section. Now if Dr. Dawkins were cloud gazing and happened to see a cloud formation *exactly* like a weasel drawn by my son—an "incompetent" seven-year-old artist—would he dismiss the crude-looking body with two eyes, two ears, two nostrils, eight whiskers, and four (okay, three) legs, as an odd happenstance?*

No, if Dawkins saw this picture in the clouds, perhaps he would strain his eyes to find the skywriting plane. Failing that, perhaps he

would go have his vision checked or pinch himself to awaken from this strange dream. What he certainly would not do is dismiss the picture up in the sky as a product of random barometric forces.

I suppose the motivation for smuggling has always been the same, to avoid paying tribute or being in subjection to an established authority. But I'm not immune to error or preconceived biases myself. The next chapter tells the tale of a lesson I had to learn.

---

* Illustration courtesy Ethan Poppe.

Chapter 10

PLEASE EXCUSE MY PRECONCEPTION

Wherein I make an unfortunate mistake
trying to date the origin of the first cell

Without a doubt I was found to be in error, caught up in the pre-conceptions of my own mind-set. I wanted the data to reinforce a preconceived personal belief, therefore I picked the narrow scientific information that supported the generalization I wanted, and ignored the rest. That was not good science on my part.

Being raised in a religion that promoted molding, massaging, and sometimes mangling ideas to fit an *a priori* assumption, my preconceptions caused my world to remain small until I learned to be more objective and intellectually honest. So where did my error lie, and how did I resolve it? It had to do with the origin of the very first cell.

Hypotheses surrounding the origin of the very first cell go in many opposing directions. This is perfectly understandable. Our knowledge of the makeup of the cell's organic molecules and its biochemical processes, while greatly advanced in the last 50 years, is still sketchy. Also, very few pieces of actual evidence are left behind (like fossils of individual cells) to clearly explain how chemicals might have transitioned into single cells so long ago. Going back to the crime scene analogy, it is rather like a homicide investigation with no hard clues. The deed obviously has been done (life is here), but investigators must profile their perpetrator almost entirely on circumstantial evidence and supposition.

As to my belief system, I rejected Darwinism long ago. I never thought much about the challenge of chemical evolution, but the notion that bacteria could eventually turn into something like a Bactrian camel by natural means seemed like voodoo science. Therefore, I felt delaying the first cell's appearance until late in geologic history would strengthen my belief. In other words, the later the first cell appeared, the bigger the evolutionary hurdle to evolve into us—so I looked for, adapted, and perhaps even generated data to support my bias.

A One-Year Timeline

You can see my prejudices in a clearer frame of reference if you consider all of Earth's geologic history remolded into a more digestable time frame. Imagine the total existence of our planet condensed into a 365-day calendar year, with the formation of the supposed 4.6 billion-year-old Earth beginning at the stroke of midnight starting January 1.

If the end of that fictitious year is at midnight on December 31, at what day of the year have various researchers said chemical evolution successfully produced the first cell? To add perspective to this analogy, realize the following scale now applies:

- One month equals about 380 million years
- One week equals about 88 million years
- One day equals about 13 million years
- One hour equals about half a million years
- One minute equals about 8 thousand years
- One second equals about 140 years

Based on this scale, earlier studies in the 1960s and 1970s placed the advent of the first cell around April, others around June, and others even early August, the latter leaving less than 50 percent of Earth's history for a cell to produce a *Homo sapiens*. Obviously I preferred the latter scenario because it favored my beliefs, and I promoted such.

But present-day research caught up with me. Scientists investigating the possible polymerization mechanisms (how smaller molecules may have linked up), especially those theorists working with RNA as possibly the first catalyst that produced DNA, now seem to finally agree. They say the first cell appeared quite early, almost as soon as conditions on Earth permitted, after about the first 900 million years of planetary settling. That would be about 3.7 billion years ago (bya), which is around the end of February on the scale above. If so, then a scant 20 percent of the "year" produced the first cell, leaving a whopping 80 percent of the time for evolution to give us high society. This new scientific consensus sure put the squeeze on my views, and I was having some difficulty finding some "wiggle room." Was I hung out to dry?

A Worsening Problem

As it turns out, a cell appearing as early as 3.7 bya has instead put natural evolution in an incredible bind. As said before, cellular science has exploded forward from Darwin's time when he and his contemporaries believed a cell was filled with a simple homogenous type of jellied protoplasm. The mind-boggling complexities of macromolecules within even the simplest cell, the subcellular structures they create, the mechanisms that produce and transport them, and the bewildering technicalities of cell division are just beginning to be appreciated.

As a result, it continues to confound understanding how the complex informational codes in DNA were mysteriously produced from simple inorganic molecules like water, carbon dioxide, methane, and nitric and phosphoric acid in such an amazingly short time. Yet science still agrees the first cell naturally appeared almost as soon as it could stand Earth's hostile but cooling environment. That would make its origination a more fantastic event than anyone, especially myself, could have previously imagined. How fantastic? Many now say what few people ever consider—having all accidental molecules tie together to suit the needs of one living cell took immeasurably more luck than the cell ever evolving enough to wear a suit and tie.

> Having all accidental molecules tie together to suit the needs of one living cell took immeasurably more luck than the cell ever evolving enough to wear a suit and tie.

Prominent molecular biologist and origins researcher Lynn Margulis has said, "To go from a bacterium to people is less of a step than to go from a mixture of amino acids to a bacterium." (Margulis is the ex-wife of Carl Sagan, which says something!) She obviously feels there are a myriad of huge barriers to getting that first living cell from the necessary organic building blocks, and there are still additional steps that must be explained to produce those amino acids that constitute the blocks. Can the primordial soup of simple inorganic molecules changing into a fully functioning cell be crammed into one-fifth of all available developmental time?

And, of course, you could reintroduce my original assumption. Is the remaining 80 percent of time still sufficient to produce a human, especially since we don't have abundant dinosaurs until around December 18—and mammals until about December 27? (Pause and think about that one—no dinosaurs until thirteen days before the end of the year, and no mammals until four days before the New Year's ball drops on Times Square!)

Either way, natural evolution is stuck, and I'm free to err on either side of the geologic timeline.

Another fact is that if science accepts an "early" first cell, then the concept of spontaneous generation is greatly restored to prominence, though it is so ridiculed in biology textbooks because of the ignorance of the eighteenth-century scientists who proposed it. Sorry, but the 365-day timeline cannot be skewed at either end to accommodate my, or anyone else's, preconceptions. And while I've learned to be more objective, the perpetrator of our crime, namely the Maker of Life, will remain at large if sought through natural means.

———————

With the myth of molecular evolution thoroughly debunked, we can now go on to other issues demanding that Darwinists release their increasingly shaky grip on science. For instance, how did we really get the Earth on January 1, and how did we go from the first apes on December 30 at 5:00 AM to human civilizations by December 31 at 11:59:30 PM? But before I take on the fossil record in part five, let me first proceed to part four—physics and the laws of thermodynamics. This chapter introduces what might have been happening *before* January 1 with the big bang.

PHYSICS AND THE LAWS OF THERMODYNAMICS

At this point, I believe a quick recap of the first three parts is in order. Call it sort of a midterm review. Beginning with the introduction, the theme of the book is clearly stated: Darwinism no longer has any right to hold science hostage. Natural evolution's attempt to extinguish competing points of view must end.

According to the overview in part one, you cannot sit on the fence over Darwinism. Either natural evolution has the ability to provide all the origins answers over time, and its control of science is justified, or a Designer deserves all the credit for what happened instantly or gradually, and "self-made" is a failed theory. The issue is a choice of only two. The one in error is trapped in a preconceived mind-set.

Part two on math begins the proof that Darwinism is definitely the position in grave error. The three chapters here show how huge numbers, once the linchpin of natural evolution, betray it rather than support it. The bottom line is that the exponential numbers natural evolution once touted in fields like physics, astronomy, molecular biology, and paleontology have collapsed under their own weight, and it is impossible for the universe to even contain the odds necessary for "random" to be successful.

Part three then looks at the specific impossibility that molecules could organize themselves from inorganic to organic and eventually reach the sizes necessary to build a living cell. Self-organizing systems trying to justify the random origin of cells have smuggled in intelligence somewhere along the line, and the historical placing of the first cell puts a tremendous bind on either biochemistry or paleontology—or both.

With these concepts in hand, let's go on to examine what physics has to say about Darwinism.

Chapter 11

THE LONG ARM OF THE LAW

*Trying to neutralize the laws
of thermodynamics*

Allow me to back up in history a bit to look at objections levied by the first group of modern scientists to drastically doubt Darwinism. Physicists have long been aware of the laws of thermodynamics and how they prohibit the type of random improvement claimed everywhere in natural evolution. I guarantee you these laws must somehow be neutralized, or "self-made" cannot even get out of the cosmic gate.

Let me start by saying it is rather rare to hear the word *law* applied to a concept. If something is called a law, it had better prove inviolate, or someone is sure to proclaim an exception. How many laws can you name? The *law of gravity*, of course. How about the *law of supply and demand?* I've heard of something called the *law of diminishing returns*, and then there's the infamous *Murphy's law*. Any more come to mind? I know there should be a longer list, but offhand, I can't think of another.

In science, laws seem the most difficult to come by. The reason is that in science, a law must hold true in all times, conditions, and locations, and must be validated by any independent investigator with no exceptions. I would call that very stringent. Even the concept of atoms is still referred to in textbooks as the "atomic *theory*," despite the fact that the periodic table of elements graces the walls of almost every science classroom. Though all chemistry seems to operate on rock-solid principles, perhaps in its caution science will wait to grant atoms "law" status until we can examine an individual particle held in our hand.

I would say the best-known scientific law is the *law of gravity*. As long as you stay on our planet, Isaac Newton showed that what goes up must eventually come down, leading to the various laws of motion.

Moreover, Earth's gravity behaves predictably and reliably anywhere on the planet at all times. But are there any other scientific laws unerringly backed by science and never disproved by experiments, laws that are so dependable that science stands on them without even a modicum of caution? If you know your physics, you already have an answer.

The laws of thermodynamics are most assuredly written in stone, so to say. This set of laws explains relationships between matter and energy for which no exceptions are found anywhere in the universe. The first law, also called the *law of conservation of matter and energy*, basically says that the sum total of both matter and energy in the universe is always constant. In shirtsleeve English, this means that since the event that brought the universe into existence, no new matter has been generated from any other source. It also means you can't make any more new atoms, and you can never lose the old ones. True, new stars appear to be forming, but the atoms in the stellar gas clouds that condense and ignite have also been in the universe since its origin, and the rise in energy is balanced by the loss of mass.

Here is a simple example. The two hydrogen atoms and one oxygen atom in a particular water molecule of H_2O may travel the world over by condensation, precipitation, and evaporation, but it is the same three atoms. (I heard it once said that as many as four of the water molecules in each of our bodies once traveled through the body of a dinosaur.)

It is true that the water molecule may be fractured and the hydrogen and oxygen atoms become integrated into sugars, proteins, and so on, but the existence of these three atoms still coincides with the point of origin of all other particles. Furthermore, they can never pass out of existence unless a nuclear reaction changes them to energy, and then the sum total of matter lost and energy gained still remains unchanged. The first law can be summed up in three words—"creation has ceased"—and this no reputable physicist denies.

Entropy

The second law of thermodynamics is an extension of the first. It says that since its origin, the universe has been in the process of winding down to complete silence. The pathway to its death could be explained in many ways—going from ordered to random, action to stillness, diverse to uniform, dynamic to inert, or organized to chaos. Again, in shirtsleeve English this means that energy expenditures in any *closed system* (*closed* meaning a system with no additional matter or energy input) will eventually leave it powerless, and it must wear out and die. The entire concept is captured by the single term *entropy*, and the degree to which a system has lost entropic energy is measured by the change symbol Δ (Greek letter *delta*).

This one-way path toward complete confoundedness is also called the *law of universal decay*, and is frequently compared to a newly wound spring as in an old-styled watch. When the watch is fully wound (or a reaction starts, or a star ignites), the first tick of time signifies the beginning of the descent from maximum order, and the last tick means the system is now fully disordered, silent and inert, never to be started again without an outside influence. Our sun is another example of entropy. At some past point in time it ignited and began to burn its fuel. At some future point (one estimate is 500 million years), the fuel will be expended, the sun will explode or wink out, and entropy with respect to the sun will have reached a maximum state—zero activity. Whether it is watches, chemical reactions, or stars, all these one-way paths to silence are *irreversible*.

I have found a perfect analogy to explain the second law to my students. I tell them to imagine their bedroom freshly and fully cleaned. There it is—bed made, all clothes put away, and everything in its place. All is dusted, vacuumed, and spotless. Then from that point, the entropy process seems unstoppable as disorganization slowly creeps in. A smudge here, a shoe left there, and so on. If an object were never put away, clothes never laundered, a bed never made, or a surface never dusted, eventually the result would be the room's return to the accustomed total teenage chaos. As any parent knows, this is an unstoppable process unless one intervenes.

Losses Everywhere

Important corollaries to the second law abound. One is that every time you change states of energy, there is a net loss. In my environmental science class I often use this explanation for how the sun is the ultimate source for all our energy needs, and how we work hard to use its energy as efficiently as possible. Consider the case of hydroelectric power that likely supplies some of the energy needs in your house. Water vapor in the clouds has to lose energy to condense and get back into the river. It then loses more kinetic energy as it flows downstream to the dam. The water expends additional energy as it drives the turbine to produce electricity, and returns downstream where it eventually reaches the ocean where it is finally at rest. Meanwhile, the electricity that reaches your house may power a TV that gives off the last remaining power in the form of heat and light.

Now we could use the sun's energy to directly power our TV, but the size of the required solar panel makes that impractical. So instead we have to deal with the pathway by trying to cut down the energy loss at each step (more reliable turbines, more energy efficient TVs, and so on). At any rate, the final result is the same. All this radiant energy from cooling water, hot turbines, and warm TVs drifts off into the cold of space, obviously not returning to the sun. Of course, as the sun continues to churn out more energy, the water cycle continues to renew itself and our TV keeps working. And yet remember—the sun is on its own pathway to death, so the water cycle is destined to cease if time continues that far.

Another second law corollary is that heat always flows to cold. This means energy leaves a system that is more dynamic and travels to one that is less dynamic. For this reason we heat our cars in winter as the warmth escapes through the exterior and into the colder air. However, we air-condition them in summer as the heat from the summer day keeps working its way into the cab through the car's insulation.

This is also the reason animals in the food chain or web must continue to eat. Without the intake of additional calories in food, the body begins to run out of fuel and will cease to live. So tertiary consumers like the owl eat secondary consumers like the shrew, but about 90 percent of the intake of shrew biomass is lost through the owl's waste products and energy expenditures, and only about 10 percent is used to support cellular components in the owl's body. At the same time, secondary consumers eat primary consumers—such as shrews eating grasshoppers—also with a 90 percent net biomass loss; and primary consumers eat primary producers—grasshoppers eating grass—at about the same rate of loss.

At that point, scavengers and decomposers consume dead bodies and release nutrients and gases back into the system to recycle the process. But since all food chains are anchored by primary producers like photosynthetic plants, and plants need that dying sun for energy, life on Earth is also on a one-way ticket, where the energy supply at all levels is destined to be exhausted—eventual silence being guaranteed.

One final corollary to the second law is, when chemicals interact, you end with less energy than was initially present, either in the molecular bonds or in the catalyst driving the reaction. If a chemical reaction is *exothermic* (giving off heat)—like burning wood, for example—the energy escaping is obvious, and the amount of energy potential left in the ashes is certainly lower than originally in the wood. If the reaction is *endothermic* (absorbing energy)—like your freezer making ice, for example—the outside power source recycling the refrigerant is doing more work than the refrigerant did to make the ice.

And of course the freezer's power source can be traced back to the electricity running the compressor, electricity that cannot be provided indefinitely. That is because hydro, solar, wind, wave, fossil fuel, and even geothermal generating systems are all linked to that entropic sun as the power source. Returning to chemicals, once the reaction is over (like the concoction quits fizzing), and the products are generated in full, nothing can ever restart unless something outside the system re-energizes it.

Applications and Analogies

So what is the overall application of the second law to the origins debate? It is as simple as it is powerful. The second law absolutely negates any type of random improvement—the backbone of Darwinistic thinking. For example, it prohibits a series of interacting chemicals from becoming more complex, like amino acids developing into proteins, without outside assistance. In fact, the law says the reverse tendency is true. If complex chemicals could somehow be intentionally made to exist, there is no way to keep them from reverting to simpler forms without intentional assistance.

The truth is, if inorganic chemistry ever naturally evolved into increasingly complex organic chemistry, then evolved into a living cell, and finally into a complex life-form, then the second law governing all reality would have been set aside, violated, and would be no law at all. Since physics says entropy *never* works in reverse, I would agree with many who say the debate over Darwinism and Design is immediately settled because advancing life is an impossibility. Disorder *never* goes to order…unless, of course, intelligence is lending a hand. Have you ever heard the phrase "there's no free lunch" applied to the false expectation of getting something for nothing? In this case the phrase is a perfect description because life just can't organize of its own accord.

Time Enough to Monkey Around?

Perhaps an automobile analogy would help. What happens if you put this year's brand-new model in the manufacturing parking lot and wait upon the second law of thermodynamics to do its thing?

After one year, probably no observable changes. The second year, maybe a slight bit of fading paint. Five years? Cracking upholstery. Twenty-five years? Flat tires. A hundred years? Detaching parts. A thousand years? A growing pile of parts. Ten thousand years? You can't tell what model it was. A hundred thousand years? You can't even tell the pile of rubble was once was a car. A million years? Remember the song "Dust in the Wind"? Now if you were to return and find *next* year's model after the passage of any of those time frames, wouldn't that be quite a surprise?

But in all sincerity, this is not a fair analogy. Evolution is said to have a change mechanism (random mutations) and a driving force (natural selection) to retain positive changes for eventual improvement. Fine. Wheel the car onto the manufacturing floor to protect it from the elements and add a random change mechanism for mutation in the form of our old friends, once again—a band of free-roaming chimpanzees.

Then give the chimps a copious supply of all the metals, fiberglass, wires, glass, and other necessary components—as well as the tools, computers, drafting boards, and art supplies humans would need for next year's model. And to be sure to create a closed system—supply the chimps with ongoing habitat maintenance such as places to raise young, unlimited food, and waste removal. Then lock the doors. Oh, yes—to add the factor of natural selection, provide the manufacturing floor with a team of ever-watchful engineers who will rescue any improved components, correctly typed instructions, or perfectly pressed quarter panels and set them aside for later assembly when the chimps feel inclined.

Now, how many millions of years before the chimps have an improved model ready to hit the streets? Is 4.6 billion years, the supposed age of the Earth, enough? How about 13.7 billion years, the supposed age of the universe? If you are calling "foul" in this scenario, then explain how the analogy is not being true to the theory of evolution. You have a change agent, a selection method, and huge quantities of time. If nothing is missing, you must say there is at least a *slight* chance the chimps could build that car. (And maybe even place a Darwin fish on the rear bumper!)

Random Rubble

I have actually heard people try to defend scenarios that possibly reverse the second law, like the chimp/new car example. Now I don't want to seem rude, but their rambling "what ifs" sound like they have been inhaling the wrong kind of secondhand smoke. I maintain that if the above scenario, or any others like it, were tried for an unlimited number of years in an unlimited number of settings, your chances of getting that new car are zero, zilch, nada. It's the law, you know. The second law says that without outside help (in this case, intelligence), there can never be advancement—ever—only degradation.

I've seen it firsthand. I once drove through an animal theme park in Europe that had a separate section with free-roaming monkeys. As soon as I made it through the screened gate, two or three landed on my car and began to pull at the windshield wipers, radio antenna—whatever seemed loose. On the car in front of me I saw one monkey pulling off a long strip of rubber window molding. And the ground was littered with broken mirrors, strips of chrome, you name it. (One monkey even reached through the window and slapped me when I rolled it down and tried to shoo him off the hood!) No, monkeys do not improve cars.

One team of researchers sought to bring this analogy into reality. They actually placed a group of primates in a room with functional computers to see if they could ever accidentally create something on the various monitors. The best result ever achieved was that one chimp depressed one key for several seconds and typed long strings of the same letter before losing interest. But the experiment was stopped after equipment was destroyed and keyboards became nonfunctional when covered in excrement.

So my apologies, but at any location at any given time, your manufacturing floor will look like the bottom of a giant chimp cage desperately in need of a new liner. And going back to your new car on that floor, you can be sure that the chimps will beat it to rubble quite a bit faster than did the elements in the parking lot.

Printing and Pennies

If you are still not convinced, imagine a series of violent lightning strikes hitting an old-style printing business, as mentioned in chapter 6. Some say it *could* produce a dictionary as bindings, glue, paper, ink, and letter type are flying through the air. Okay, I can envision an A covered in splashing ink smacking a blank sheet and leaving an impression. I can even imagine another A hitting right beside the first letter a split-second later. Then an R followed by a D and a V and another A and an R and finally a K. There—AARDVARK—the first complete word in the dictionary, and we're on our way.

But if this doesn't exceed the universal probability boundary from chapter 7, nothing will. No, even the "chimp-made car" scenario sounds like a better bet because a dictionary, like a single cell or 30,000,000 life-forms on Earth, has more variables to account for than a car. Finally consider that both car and dictionary analogies represent just the assemblage of finished components. There has been no mention of the complexity involved in accidentally producing metal or paper—or amino acids—from their raw sources. (No doubt about it—whether it's biochemicals, books, or Buicks, any imagined probabilities are in actuality *impossibilities*.)

Perhaps the complexities of building cars and assembling dictionaries is too removed from everyday life. I suggest doing a simple hands-on experiment to test the second law of thermodynamics. Place 100 pennies on a tray, all showing heads. (Of course the first law of thermodynamics says that all the copper atoms in the pennies came into being by a one-time process.) The array of 100 heads would represent minimum entropy and complete order. Now give the tray a slight flip.

> That is about 10^{21}...To get a sense of that number, imagine flipping the tray once per second for 32 trillion years, waiting for a chance for success.

The winding down process has begun—a few tails represent a slight loss of order. Flip the tray again, and more tails appear. Now, depending on how aggressively you flip the tray, it may take as few as seven flips, certainly no more than ten, to achieve total randomness or maximum entropy, where the original set of 100 heads is completely unrecognizable. From here, more flips only give a different arrangement to the disorder.

At this point, it would be proper to note that occasionally a flip might produce a small cluster of pennies all showing heads. In fact, this not just likely, it is certain. However, this is no closer to ensuring a return to 100 heads than the few amino acids produced in the Miller–Urey experiment are sure to become a protein. Those clusters of pennies will disappear, or at best appear elsewhere, with subsequent shuffles. This would be the same result as Dawkins's weasel scenario (chapter 9) if he had not smuggled a good bit of intelligence into the computer program.

In the same manner, any amino acids in Miller's flask, or in the ancient ocean, will be fractured by the same reconfiguring forces long before they can even reach the polypeptide stage. Remember my analogy back in chapter 8, where you throw all the Scrabble letters on the table at once? Assuming they all land face-up and properly oriented—undoubtedly a huge assumption—might you find a few simple words? Of course. But if you keep kicking the table, will the words begin to get more sophisticated and then arrange themselves into sentences? Then, assuming unlimited letters, will sentences become paragraphs and finally a book? Consult the second law.

It is an unfair question, but I'll ask it anyway. Now that your pennies are in a random jumble of maximum entropy, how many flips of the tray will it take to return to the 100 heads? Give it a try. Any progress? Probabilities say that you have one chance of success only if you give the tray a fair flip 2^{100} times. That is about 10^{21}, or one thousand million million million flips. To get a sense of that number, imagine flipping the tray once per second for 32 trillion years, waiting for a chance for success. Such is the challenge of nullifying the second law for just one "small" event.

And yet the pennies dilemma is child's play compared to the odds of constructing that previously mentioned medium-sized human protein (1 in 10^{360}) out of the approximately 100,000 proteins needed in our bodies, not to mention additional proteins for an estimated 30 million species worldwide. Again, the universe itself isn't big enough to contain such probabilities.

Therefore, allow me to suggest an easier way to restore your pennies. Use the same way the cars, the castles, the jetliners, the houses, and the dictionaries—and the proteins for the chimps, aardvarks, and humans—were made in the first place. Apply intelligence and intent. For the pennies, physically turn them all back to heads. For the rest, seek to understand the Designer who is superior to the laws of thermodynamics and responsible for their existence.

———————

In summary, physics says that complete order always goes to complete disorder. And examples can be found everywhere, from deep space to your own bedroom. (Christian theology is like-minded, saying that man began in perfection only to fall into imperfection—and examples can be found in every civilization and every individual.) In contrast, Darwinists say molecules kept improving into cells, but they have no verifiable mechanisms to back that claim. Then they say cells evolved into today's modern species, but have woefully insufficient fossilized examples to provide as proof. (Just how woeful will be shown in part five.) Doesn't anyone have respect for "the law" anymore?

Moving on, Darwinists say it wasn't a big explosion at a printing press that outsmarted the law—it was a bigger explosion in outer space that supposedly blew the universe into existence. Let's take a look at the big bang.

12

Celestial Luck

A place in space for everything, and
everything in space in its place

One interesting application of the second law of thermodynamics that has most certainly occurred in a closed system is the settling of the cosmos. According to theory, the big bang of some 17.6 billion years ago started it all from a pinpoint explosion of unimaginable force, which first blew atoms into existence, and then blew clusters of matter out into the void of space. This started the expansion of celestial objects one from another that continues to this day. (To get a quick sense of this expansion, get a balloon and with a pen draw a few galaxies and solar systems on the skin. Then blow the balloon up, and as you do, you will see the "universe" expanding.)

Following that immense explosion, particle clouds with sufficient mass began drawing together by increasing gravity and ignited to become stars. Meanwhile, smaller clusters with insufficient mass began losing their heat, cooled, and became planets. (The molten inner core of our Earth is often cited as evidence that our planet was a once hot and violent place that has now been in the cooling process for billions of years.) Besides stars and planets, other big bang curiosities have randomly appeared over time, such as quasars, black holes, comets, moons, and asteroids—all in their respective and expanding locations.

It follows that if the big bang is a totally random process, then the resulting layout of the universe has to be completely accidental as well. If intelligence has nothing to do with physics, how could cosmology be anything but unplanned and therefore unintelligent? Of course this randomness has to apply to our own little corner of the galaxy as well. And yet anything less than "impossible" is too benign a term for the fact that our Earth exists as it is, and that I am here to write this, or you to read it.

An Explosion of Good Fortune

Many astronomers and physicists who have studied the big bang event, people of faith or not, have marveled that it happened at all. Hugh Ross is among those who have seriously studied the origin and settling of the universe. In his books, such as *Big Bang, Refined by Fire,* Ross gives many factors of physics so finely tuned that it shows the tenuously balanced structure of our universe. On one such list, Ross includes over two dozen "either/or" factors (either it worked or it didn't), such that if any single one were out of balance, the "bang" would have been a nonevent.

Without getting too technical, here is a sampling of the "luck" to which we owe our existence:

- If the electromagnetic forces present at the big bang were either a bit stronger or a bit weaker, any elements with more atomic mass than boron (periodic table element #5) could not have been formed. This means 96 percent of the elements, starting with the carbon, nitrogen, and oxygen in our bodies, would not exist.

- If the ratio of the mass of the electron to the proton or neutron were out of balance, either too high or too low, no atoms of any kind would have ever assembled, and obviously no molecular bonding or chemical reactions would have taken place either.

- If the ratio of the number of available protons to electrons was off, either too many of one or too few, electromagnetism would have nullified gravity, and no objects in space would ever have formed.

And once you add to the list the perfect speed of light, the exact sub-atomic decay rates, the correct distance between stars, and even the proper total mass requirements of the entire universe itself...well, you get the idea.

Here is an analogy that seems to help bring home the idea of the fantastic nature of the big bang. Who can argue that the flying of the Space Shuttle is a delicate undertaking? Any little prelaunch factor out of place scraps the countdown, and once in flight, the National Aeronautics and Space Administration, known worldwide as NASA, keeps track of a myriad of transmissions, any one of which could indicate impending disaster. It's true—the shuttle is a flying bomb with seven souls aboard riding on a razor-thin edge of safety. Physicists know that the big bang is similarly fine-tuned, miraculously having managed to avoid either fizzling to a stop or incinerating itself.

"Lucky" Breaks

However, the above list pales in comparison to factors that were necessary to form our own little solar system with our own little planet and its multitude of life-forms. This time Ross has identified 68 separate "either/or" factors, many of which are more easily understood than those governing the universe as a whole. Here are a few phenomena that could lead to either the prevention or extermination of all planetary life. These factors, some simple and some technical, are some of the blessings we take for granted every day.

It's a good thing that through random thermodynamic settling, the Milky Way galaxy attained the right size, shape, and distance from other galaxies. Otherwise, stars like our sun would never have been formed, or would have been incorporated into a different cosmic mass.

It's a good thing our sun is in a single-star configuration. Approximately 70 percent of all stars are binary, trinary, or complex systems that revolve around each other. This causes intense gravitational forces that make stable planetary bodies of any kind nearly impossible. Fortunately, our sun is one of the remaining 30 percent of "lucky" stars that exists as a single body. It is also the right size, age, location, and strength for our solar system—or else planetary orbits would be unstable, heavier elements drawn to Earth from space could have easily been over- or undersupplied, or luminosity could have been too bright or too weak to power photosynthesis. Even the gravitational forces of the other planets are necessary for Earth's stability. For example, the mass and location of Jupiter is especially fine-tuned to balance the orbits of the four inner with the four outer planets.

It's a good thing our planet revolves about the sun in a relatively circular orbit instead of an exaggerated egg-shaped one like most of the other planets. If Earth's path were too elliptical, the temperature extremes at *perihelion* (closest point to the sun) and *aphelion* (farthest point from the sun) would make it difficult, if not impossible, for life to have the necessary flexibility to survive.

The variation in orbital extremes of Earth is only about 1.7 percent from the mean, making its path around the sun a near-perfect circle. Compare that to Mars, everyone's favorite planet for extraterrestrial life, with a 9 percent variation (which is close to the average of all nine planets at 8 percent). Because of Mars' orbital elongation variation over five times as great as Earth's, NASA will have to be very careful as they develop the landing date for a manned Mars mission.

Think about it. Because of the alternating extreme closeness and remoteness to the sun in the orbital path of Mars, an astronaut in a space suit or space station would only have windows of nominal temperatures between hot and cold cycles. It should be obvious most types of Earth life would not survive if our planet were unlucky enough to have such an elongated orbit. And these extremes on Mars are exacerbated because of its slow revolution rate, making the annual trip around the sun in 687 Earth days instead of 365. By comparison, our Earth is "lucky" enough to have a near circular orbit and an optimum rate of revolution that avoid such extremes.

It's a good thing the Earth is tilted at precisely 23.45 degrees on

its axis, which gives us the perfect balance of true seasons from the Equator to the Tropics of Cancer and Capricorn, and on to the Arctic and Antarctic Circles. Imagine if Earth had no appreciable tilt at all, like Mercury at .01 degrees. We would not just lose the refreshing rotation of seasons, but hosts of species would not exist whose life cycles follow the changing climates as you go toward either pole.

What if the Earth were tilted, like Pluto, at 32 degrees past perpendicular, pointing its northern and southern poles almost directly at the sun in their respective summer and winter seasons? If Earth were laid this far over on its side, the annual melting and refreezing of both polar ice caps would play unbelievable havoc with habitats by the wildly fluctuating temperature ranges. And then imagine what would happen to levels of water in the oceans, precipitation rates, and plant and animal life cycles. The violence of seasonal extremes might even negate the possibility of complex terrestrial food webs.

Then there is one other possibility that Earth was "lucky" enough to avoid. It is the "barrel roll" of Uranus spinning on an axis parallel to its orbital plane, rather than perpendicular like the rest of the planets. What difficulties this would present to life here at home can hardly be imagined.

Finally, it's a good thing our Earth is the right size and shape, rotates at the right speed, and is the right distance from the sun. If any of these were out of proportion, a whole host of problems loom. Our atmosphere could be too suffocating or too thin, our day-to-night temperatures could be too hot or too cold, our gravity too intense or too insufficient, our wind velocities too severe or too inadequate, or our air components too heavy on some gases or too light on others.

Also, consider that Mercury completes less than one revolution around the sun for every two rotations on its axis, making one of its "days" equal to less than half of its "year." There is no reason Earth couldn't be like Mercury (though it would be disastrous to life), but instead we properly make 1/365 of our annual journey in close to 24 hours. Overall, you could say we were very "lucky" that the interplay of forces from universe to galaxy to solar system to planet were perfectly fine-tuned. To quote the late Jackie Gleason, "How sweet it is!"

Physics Did It?

Call it a case of "a place for everything in space, and everything in space in its place." I'm impressed. But I know others are not. They say with the possibility of a nearly inexhaustible supply of potential planets in the universe, physics was bound to give us one body with this combination of distance, size, orientation, and motion factors. And in the same manner, life was able to adapt accordingly and settle into this cozy "third rock from the sun." Perhaps, but if so, there are still a host of other "lucky" parameters right here on Earth that still must be perfect. While these did not necessarily govern the physics of planetary origin, they still could severely limit or deny life.

For example, earthquake activity must be within tolerable limits. Imagine if we had the seismology of other planets. Remember how the world properly agonized over the December 26, 2004, tsunami in the Indian Ocean that instantly wiped out over 200,000 lives? There is no reason why such geologic events couldn't be commonplace on Earth. Yet as devastating as it was, the tidal wave did not affect animal and plant life to a disastrous extent, only human life because of the way we live.

Just as earthquake activity typical of other planets could be knocking down our cities as fast as we build them, there is no reason why violent storms could not also make our planet a scene of constant destruction. Hurricanes Katrina and Rita in August and September of 2005 were disasters to Louisiana, Texas, and other parts of the Gulf Coast, and yet the bulk of our country experienced no change at all. However, if Earth had the same ongoing storm as on Jupiter—the red "eye" shown on almost every photograph—we would have a continuous cataclysm cutting a lethal swath across our planet. Instead, we sit rather comfortably here at home. Lucky for us.

Next, consider that Earth's water-to-landmass ratio must not be out of bounds. With the near-complete lack of moisture available on other planets, if anything, shouldn't we be one-quarter water and three-quarters land on the planet's surface instead of the reverse? In fact, we should be nearly, if not completely, bone-dry.

And this list goes on. The minerals in the soil must be optimal for all sorts of biological and commercial reasons, the Moon's tidal effects must not be extreme, ocean salinity and ion concentrations must not be unduly toxic, and…well, isn't that enough to make the point? Also consider that with respect to tolerance levels, any *one* of these factors, like those that doomed two Space Shuttle flights, could be so prohibitive to life that the rest become a moot point.

So let's apply a bit of math. If you visit the lottery Web site for multistate Powerball, you will find all the probabilities of winning those multimillions that are sure to bestow peace and happiness. Here, the odds of winning the elusive jackpot are listed as "1 in 146,170,692." You could read this as "one winner for approximately every 150 million tickets sold"—which places you in the ritzy neighborhood of 10^8 individual purchases to provide hope for success.

By comparison, if we give all 68 of those planetary criteria previously mentioned a 50/50 chance of being in a range tolerable to life—a win-or-no-win ticket—and multiply all the 1-out-of-2 odds together, you get a figure upward of 10^{22}. Once again, going back to the strength of exponential numbers, our odds of getting a suitable planet Earth are $(22 - 8 = 14)$: *14* increases of 900 percent beyond what it takes to win a Powerball jackpot. (No wonder they call the lottery a tax on people who aren't good at math.) And then after this, we must face the even *more* prohibitive odds of getting life to self-organize.

With this lottery example in mind, perhaps now the contrasts in the vocabulary I've been using will make more sense. In case the words went by too fast, let me repeat them. On the random side we have words like *unstable, excessive, insufficient, intense, inadequate, difficult, extreme, fluctuating, exacerbating, severe, unbalanced, nonexistent, fragile, erratic, freezing, boiling, prohibitive, noxious, toxic*—and, as a fitting end—*impossible.* And I dare say that if you set foot on any planet outside Earth, one, if not most—if not all—of these factors would negate the possibility of life.

On the other hand, we describe our planetary conditions with words like *proper, balanced, refreshing, optimal, flexible, correct, exact, complementary, proportional,* and—as another fitting end—*perfect.* As we stand here on Earth, we easily see how all these supposedly fortuitous accidents allow the miracle of life. In the end, how many times can the word *perfect* be repeated (perfect this, perfect that, perfect everywhere you turn) until your faith in luck runs out and you admit that Someone was tinkering with physics?

Nothing to Shrug Off

As lengthy as the list of fine-tuned factors is, evolutionists shrug them off with the same comment almost every time. Like I earlier said, they would say that instead of a Designer adapting Earth to accommodate life, life adapted to the pre-existing conditions it found on our planet. For example, if Earth had a stronger gravitational pull, our creatures would have developed lighter bodies and stronger legs and wings. Or if Earth's air were one-fourth nitrogen and three-fourths oxygen instead of the reverse, animal lungs would be restructured, plant photosynthesis would follow different pathways, and so on. In fact, they say, our present gravity may actually be deadly, and our air toxic, to life evolving under conditions on another planet.

However, such people seldom realize the depth of this assumption. The fine-tuned features in the majority of these factors are not a matter of *alterations* but *eradications*—not just conditions to adjust to but conditions that bring death under any circumstance. First of all, many of the factors from the physics of the universe could completely negate the possibility of carbon-based chemistry, and other conditions on Earth would instantly be lethal to any type of life based on the carbon platform. (The song "Nothing from Nothing Leaves Nothing" comes to mind.) Remember that we are not just talking about whether gravity and air are optimal, but whether we even have a planet, a sun, a solar system, or a universe.

The skeptics also need to realize that some of these factors are more complicated than at first glance. Okay, so the Earth accidentally stopped closer to the sun. Just imagine that birds evolved with Space Shuttle-like heat tiles on their underbellies so they also could fly in the hot sun. If the Earth stopped farther away? Imagine birds with feathers a foot thick.

Yet in what possible location would you place the Earth and still have a water cycle? How far from its present location can you move the planet before precipitation, condensation, and evaporation collapse? (Ask the life that supposedly used to live on Mars.) The amazing water molecule is so essential to organisms that it is everybody's favorite indicator of possible extraterrestrial life. But how could water complete its inter- or intra-cellular travel if it were continually evaporated or frozen? By one estimate, if the Earth's orbit averaged a half of a percent closer or farther from the sun, we would have permanent vapor or permanent ice. No water cycle, no fluid homeostasis for cellular activities—no life of any kind.

In my opinion, you *have* to accept Design, even if only by default. But I go even farther and say some "interesting touches" were added. I say there are some amazing displays of technical science included just at the Artist's prerogative. I call it His "personal signature" on a fine piece of creative work. For example, we get to see only one side of the Moon because its rotation rate on its axis and its revolution rate around

A Touch of Art

If the Moon's strange synchronous movement does not impress you, here is one you can't chalk up to anything like tidal pull. Who would not admit that solar eclipses are cool? Be in the right place on Earth at the right time and the disc of the Moon interposes itself to be perfectly congruent with the disc of the sun—a total solar eclipse. The alignment is so exact that the massive corona of the sun makes a beautiful halo, and the central darkness gives scientists the best chance to study the effect.

But isn't the perfect overlay a bit odd considering the chance sizes and distances of the two "unrelated" celestial objects? Yet the dazzling display is only possible because of the unbelievable equal ratios of diameters and distances. The Moon has a diameter of 3476 kilometers (2160 miles) and has a distance from Earth of 384,467 kilometers (239,000 miles), for a decimal ratio of .009. By comparison, the diameter of the sun is 1,390,000 kilometers (865,000 miles) at a distance from Earth of 149,600,000 kilometers (93,000,000 miles), a decimal ratio of, you guessed it, .009! In simpler terms, while the sun is about 400 times bigger than the Moon, it is about 400 times farther away—hence the stunning effect of the total solar eclipse, something that to me looks very "planned."

the Earth are exactly the same, a precise 27.3217 Earth days for both. (Check it out by going around your family globe with a ball on a stick. If you walk just as fast as you turn the ball, the "Earth" sees only one side of your "Moon.") Now it is true that tidal pull from a larger object on a smaller object begins to mitigate orbits over time, but no such preciseness exists anywhere else in a solar system filled with planets. Call it a bit of curious mystery thrown in just for fun.

A touch of art also extends to a last point. Any map of the Milky Way galaxy will show our sun and solar system to be about three-fourths of the way to the outer edge from the center of the flat spiral disc.

From a scientific standpoint, this is a stroke of "luck" that provides the perfect location for our "evolving" life-forms. If our solar system

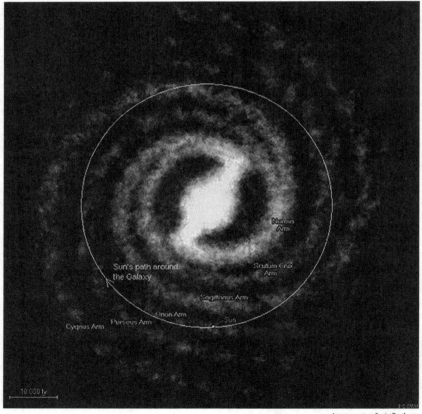

Image courtesy EnviroTruth.org.

were at the outer tips of the galactic arms, the rotational speed of the "crack the whip" effect would cause a rapid expansion of our planetary orbits, making for rapidly fluctuating conditions on Earth to which life could not adjust. If our sun were toward the center of the Milky Way, the intense gravitational attractions and the constant radiation of supernovae from so many stars in proximity would again make our Earth unlivable.

But the fact is, our sun lies not only at the proper centricity, it also lies in the open area between two spiral arms at the proper *co-rotational radius* where our speed remains relatively constant and our solar system will not be swept into either adjacent arm. Once again, we should celebrate our good fortune. Yet the artistic piece is that if our solar system could somehow survive in the galactic center or within one of the arms of densely packed stars, the cosmic clutter would prevent us from even looking out into deep space to see those distant wonders. It is as interesting as it is ironic. Darwinists use the very beauty afforded to us as we look into the heavens as justification to reduce our existence to "luck."

Tough Customers

As I said earlier, astronomers and physicists have always had a harder time buying into the random-chance scenario. Knowing what they know, they have not made the best Darwinists because of the weak philosophic argument that everything just fell into place without intelligence. Consider the well-known quote from Wernher von Braun, an astrophysicist of no small repute:

> I find it as difficult to understand a scientist who does not acknowledge the presence of a superior rationality behind the existence of the universe as it is to comprehend a theologian who would deny the advances of science.

And to show it doesn't take a "rocket scientist" to have the same opinion, hear the words of astronomer Alan Sandage:

> I find it quite improbable that such order came out of chaos. There has to be some organizing principle. God to

me is a mystery, but it is the explanation for the miracle of
existence, why there is something instead of nothing.

Or how about Princeton physics professor Freeman Dyson, who said,

> As we look out into the universe and identify the
> many accidents of physics and astronomy that have worked
> together for our benefit, it almost seems as if the universe
> must in some sense have known that we were coming.*

Here is a man of longstanding reputation who has earned 21 hon-
orary degrees by applying his knowledge of physics in almost every other
scientific discipline, such as astronomy. He has also won the prestigious
Templeton Award, given to individuals whose achievements in one professional field have simultaneously advanced the humanitarian benefits
of religion. Therefore, I would say Dyson's use of the word *almost* in
the quote above is a shot aimed at the Darwinists with whom he has
debated all his life.

To sum it up, it may take faith to "move" mountains. But so many
giants of science believe it takes much more faith to "make" mountains
through natural processes.

As Ace Ventura, Pet Detective, says, "Well, alrighty then." Let's
assume we lucked out and got a universe and a suitable planet—perhaps
several of them—ready for life. Having won the lottery for life here,
many are convinced it has happened elsewhere, and have devoted their
lives to prove it. Let's look at the ongoing search for life beyond our
planetary home to see what the experts can now say with certainty.

---

* Freeman J. Dyson, 1971; "Energy in the Universe," *Scientific American*, p. 59.

13

Are There Other Forms
of Life Out There?

*SETI-S: Searching for ExtraTerrestrial
Intelligence...Still*

Do you believe there is life on other planets? And not necessarily intelligent civilizations looking out into space for us as we are looking for them, just something else alive somewhere out there. If you do, you join the majority of people who believe in extraterrestrial life. To verify this, either consult a long-term scientific study on extraterrestrial (ET) data, or just ask a few people on the street. (An informal survey printed in the March 2000 issue of *Life* magazine said that 30 percent of Americans believe intelligent beings from other planets have visited Earth. Hmmm?)

These believers come from all walks of life, from a pre-teenager who just saw an alien-loaded fantasy movie to a scientist who has given the matter lifelong attention. Furthermore, if these ET faithful feel the alien life they envision evolved completely naturally, then according to the previous chapters, they must believe in the luck of the big bang, molecular evolution, and spontaneous generation. Furthermore, they disbelieve in the second law of thermodynamics. Are they right?

You have to admit the prospect of ET life has a tremendous bearing on the origins debate. If you do any reading about alien life, you are certainly familiar with its scientific guru, the late Carl Sagan. Sagan,

---

theophobic to the very end, was enchanted by the possibility of alien life, and made "billions and billions" of comments on the subject. For example, he agreed with MIT physicist Philip Morrison that finding life on another planet, for example Mars, would "transform the origin of life from a miracle to a statistic." Such a find would also disarm the necessity of dealing with the Design issue to a great extent, and some are obsessed with proving ET life for that reason alone.

Beyond Fantasy

So let's take an objective look at the hard evidence for the existence of extraterrestrial life-forms of any type. From here, my opinion is that Hollywood has done irreparable damage to the chance for objectivity. When the subject of alien life-forms is broached, people immediately gravitate to their favorite movie on alien or extraterrestrial life, perhaps beginning with *Alien* or *ET.* Then prepare for a stroll down sci-fi's nostalgia lane.*

But in a serious ET discussion, movie fantasies constitute a severe hindrance to what science undisputedly knows about life elsewhere. People also must get past personal UFO material, such as printed in those "newspapers" in the supermarket checkout line. (How does the *Weekly World News* get away with using the exact same alien photo in two totally unrelated ET articles?)

And there are many other ET pitfalls. I have a hard time understanding the appeal of the infamous Area 51 mystique. When the Roswell, New Mexico, "incident" ultimately led to a TV segment on the dissection of an alien body a few years ago, I wondered about the unrestrained gullibility of some folks. I just wish people would take the definition of *UFO* as intended, an *unidentified flying object.* It means someone saw something in the sky (bird? plane? Superman?) but just couldn't completely identify it (as the weather balloon, or whatever, it probably was). Then again, maybe I should just be thankful that the furor over UFOs seems to have lost commercial value for the time being.

---

* Personally, I cannot resist peeking in on the original *Star Trek* series when I see it on the dish programming guide, at least long enough to identify the episode so I can review the script at my leisure. And if the segment is "City on the Edge of Forever," I'm sure to watch Kirk, Spock, McCoy, Chekhov, Scottie, and Uhuru—and guest star Joan Collins—one more time.

So when all the fantasy is swept away, what serious information on life outside of Earth exists, and how extensive have efforts been to collect it? I suppose the best place to turn is the U.S. space program—our attempts to leave the confines of our planet and explore elsewhere. What follows is a historical look at the efforts of NASA, and its nearly half-century of monitoring the heavens and launching space vehicles.

Looking for What's Out There

On January 31, 1958, the U.S. launched its first ever spacecraft, *Explorer 1*. All it carried was a cosmic-ray detector for purposes of data collection, and it discovered the Van Allen radiation belt. After more than 58,000 orbits, it burned up in atmospheric re-entry on March 31, 1970. Four more Explorer launches followed, two never making it to orbit due to rocket failure.

The Explorer series was followed by two launches carrying satellites that were the first to leave Earth's gravitational pull. *Pioneer 3* and *Pioneer 4*, launched in 1958 and 1959, carried more sophisticated radiation-detecting equipment. *Pioneer 3*'s flight path was erratic and it was lost, but *Pioneer 4* actually survived a close pass around the moon. It is believed to still be in a dead orbit around the sun, its final destination.

Next came the lunar Ranger series 1 through 9, from 1961 to 1965. These were the first known spacecraft to make planned physical contact with another stationary object in space, our Moon, even if they were crash landings. Equipped with television cameras, *Ranger 8* was the most successful, sending back over 7000 pictures before its planned demise in the Sea of Tranquillity. The lunar Surveyor series 1 through 7 from 1966 to1968 were the first vehicles designed to make a soft landing. This highly successful line of spacecraft took more than 90,000 images of the Moon's surface with their cameras, and *Surveyor 5* through *Surveyor 7* were equipped with a mechanical scoop that brought dirt samples into a simple automated lab for analysis of soil content.

Manned Flight

All of NASA's interest in the lunar surface had an obvious purpose, in that President Kennedy had pledged to put a person on the Moon before the 1970s. The Mercury program began the odyssey of manned flight, and Alan Shepherd took our first historic suborbital space flight in his capsule named *Freedom 7* on May 5, 1961. The "straight up and straight down" ride lasted all of 15 minutes, but the race to beat the Soviets to the Moon was on. John Glenn became the first American to orbit the Earth in *Friendship 7* on February 20, 1962, and his three orbits took four hours and 55 minutes.

After the Mercury program, the ten flights in the Gemini program from 1965 to 1966 taught our astronauts how to fly, maneuver, and dock with another spacecraft, which set the stage for the Apollo program to actually go to the Moon. As most people know, a man named Neil Armstrong took that "giant leap for mankind," and he did it as the commander of *Apollo 11* on July 20, 1969. Five more Apollo missions would land on the Moon up through 1972, providing a wealth of scientific data on soil mechanics, meteoroids, seismic activity, heat flow, lunar ranging, magnetic fields, and solar winds—not to mention bringing back almost 400 kilograms (about 800 pounds) of moon rock.

Testing for Life

During all this flurry of lunar activity, NASA had not forgotten the rest of the universe was still out there. From 1962 to 1973, there were ten launches of Mariner satellites to Venus and Mercury, and especially Mars. *Mariner 9,* launched in 1971, was the first functional artificial satellite to orbit another planet, and sent back heretofore unseen close-ups of storms, mountains, and canyons on the Martian surface. It exceeded all expectations by mapping 100 percent of the surface of Mars, as well as sending detailed pictures of the two irregular Martian moons, Phobos and Deimos.

Then came two Viking spacecraft launched toward Mars in 1975, and after about a year's journey, both completed an amazing soft landing on the planet surface. Viking's onboard instruments had come a long way since the Moon's Surveyor series a decade earlier. Both Viking craft possessed a gas chromatograph, mass spectrometer, stereo color cameras, X-ray fluorescence spectrometer, and seismometer, as well as meteorological instruments for measuring weather and atmospheric composition. Finally, important to our topic, both Vikings were equipped with a more sophisticated automated lab to measure physical, magnetic, and *chemical* properties of the soil on Mars—chemical analyses that could build a case for life.

Information on Mars from Viking was augmented by perhaps the most wildly successful of all U.S. spacecraft, Pathfinder. Launched December 4, 1996, and landing using parachutes and cushioning giant air bags on July 4, 1997, Pathfinder carried a separate 23-pound free-ranging rover vehicle that deployed and operated flawlessly at a distance of about two yards from the lander. The primary lander, named the Carl Sagan Memorial Station, tripled the operation of its expected life, and the rover operated 12 times longer than anticipated!

By the time Pathfinder had made its final data transmission on September 27, 1997, it had returned 2.3 billion bits of information. This included more than 16,500 images from the lander and 550 images from the rover, as well as extensive weather data, and 15 chemical tests of rocks and soil similar to those done by the Viking craft. These tests were especially programmed to look for organic molecules related to life.

The results of all these soil tests? Here are the words of NASA from their Jet Propulsion Lab (JPL) Web-site home page.

> These experiments discovered unexpected and enigmatic chemical activity in the Martian soil, but provided no clear evidence for the presence of living microorganisms in soil near the landing sites. According to scientists, Mars is self-sterilizing. They believe the combination of solar ultraviolet radiation that saturates the surface, the extreme dryness of the soil and the oxidizing nature of the soil chemistry prevent the formation of living organisms in the Martian soil.

Looking at What's Been Found

Now stand back and consider all we have accomplished at the expense of many billions of dollars, untold work hours, and several lives. The cliché "just scratching the surface" woefully understates how few answers we have to all our questions about possible ET life, and JPL's statement above appears to negate life in the most likely place.

Granted, we do have many beautiful pictures taken with sophisticated remote television cameras and marvelous telescopes like the Hubble. We also have a wealth of weather and atmospheric data, and a reliable estimation of the chemical composition of distant cosmic objects through spectroscopy (spectral absorption and emission lines). However, all that evidence on chemistry has yielded no evidence on *biochemistry.* (Now do you see why the imaginations of Hollywood have made objectivity so impossible?)

To be fair, our spacecraft landers have only sampled a minuscule fraction of the lunar and Martian surfaces. But then again, if these landers were to test Earth soil *anywhere* (not just the most promising locations of NASA's choosing), bacterial forms and an abundance of organic chemical residue would be the results. For example, most people know that bacteria and algae live in the hottest of hot springs and the most arid of deserts. If you go to Death Valley in California, the hottest spot in North America, be prepared to see some rugged plant life, a few hardy insects, and even an occasional reptile. Or go to some of the Antarctic's dry valleys, which receive virtually no moisture year-round and where temperatures reach 80 degrees below zero (Fahrenheit).

Even though such an environment rivals places on Mars where our rovers have landed, primitive plants like lichens and other bacteria survive by living inside of rocks when Antarctic conditions are at their worst. And yet though primitive, these life-forms are true metabolizers that need oxygen and nutrition and produce waste products and residue as they live and die. In contrast, NASA has found nothing—absolutely nothing—on the Moon, or in the most promising locations on Mars, which include the polar ice caps and what are thought to be dry lake beds.

Going back to the Moon, consider how careful NASA was when *Apollo 11* returned to Earth after touching lunar soil. Did you know crew members, and any object exposed to lunar soil or air, were strictly quarantined for 21 days? This duration was chosen because it is the maximum incubation period for any Earth microorganism. During this time, thorough physicals were given to the crew, moon samples were analyzed under a microscope, and even the quarantine area's air was filtered to trap any floating particles, lest a foreign contagion should escape to overpower life on Earth. Obviously, nothing was found. Since the next two successful Apollo spacecraft, *Apollo 12* and *Apollo 14*, landed in different areas of the Moon, the same careful quarantine procedures were applied. (Remember, *Apollo 13* never made it to the Moon but did return safely after near catastrophe.)

Now the next point is significant. NASA was so convinced that the Moon was a dead object that the entire quarantine procedure was abandoned for *Apollo 15, 16,* and *17.* In other words, as soon as the hatch was opened, the astronauts were allowed to hug their families. So once again, in outer-space objects we have examined physically, mechanically, and telescopically, one might say all we have from 45-plus years of expending time, money, and lives is a little over 800 pounds of Moon rock, some comet dust from the January 2006 completion of NASA's Stardust Mission—*and not a single sign of life.* And not just the absence of cellular life, but no certain traces of organic chemistry that could have come from, or be leading to, life.

Worthwhile Efforts

Being science-minded, I am not disparaging exploratory efforts in the least. I've always been an ardent supporter of NASA. Also, I would be remiss to not highlight our Space Shuttle program. The first launch was *Columbia* on April 12, 1981—and who can forget where each of us was when hearing about the tragic loss of both *Challenger,* January 28, 1986, and *Columbia,* January 16, 2003.

Way beyond just satisfying that "need to know," these many space programs have contributed immeasurably to advances we all enjoy in technology, meteorology, communication, metallurgy, home security, transportation, environmental solutions, and medicine, and the wealth of information is sure to expand. What's more, I sincerely hope I am around for the first manned Mars shot! Yes, these efforts have been worth it all, and the fact that they have not turned up evidence of life in no way diminishes their accomplishments.

Maybe *They* Came *Here*

With respect to alien life, I guess you could say our ability to "go to them" has been extremely limited. The alternative question some people ask is whether they have come to us. (Once again, of course, we must set aside the stories of "alien abductions" of people motivated by money or those with altered mental states.)

At the risk of giving it legitimacy, I suppose I should start with a historic find of 1996, the infamous "Mars meteorite" found in Antarctica. A team of Stanford scientists analyzed the rock and soon released a story saying it arrived here about 13,000 years ago, careening to our planet after breaking off from a meteor collision near to Mars as long as 16 million years ago. The "teaser" was that trapped inside the meteorite were said to be gases resembling the composition of the Martian atmosphere found by the Viking spacecraft, and the "kicker" was that the rock looked to contain ovoid and tubule-shaped clusters of imprints in the 50-nanometer range, typical of bacteria.

Due to the respectable credentials of the Stanford investigating team, scientists around the world stayed tuned for further updates. However, in later interviews the researchers admitted the mixture of trace gases were not unique, and the shaped imprints could be the result of not biological but geophysical forces, such as that of passing through Earth's atmosphere. Also, the team could detect no evidence of organic molecular residue, and it began admitting the supposed origin of the rock was not verifiable.

Since I remember the 1996 incident well, it appeared to me that the Stanford team had to back away from earlier excitement when pressed with pointed inquiries by other scientists who seemed more objective. So, did they have something here, or did they not? I would say the best indicator that the story belongs with so many other "if—if—if" hypotheses on ET life is that it has received almost no attention since 1996. (The whole story reminded me of the ephemeral excitement over "cold fusion in a bottle," which quickly died out when the majority of scientists could not independently verify the data interpretation.)

So what other possible evidences that extraterrestrial life has arrived here on Earth are bona fide scientists investigating? Unless you go past flying-saucer sightings and "crop circles"—or any number of other "Ripley's Believe It or Not" type of unexplained phenomena—we are at rope's end. Except, of course, possible electronic signals received by a program called the Search for ExtraTerrestrial Intelligence—SETI.

SETI

Repeating thoughts from the beginning of this chapter, I'm sure certain people will forever believe we are not alone in the universe. Darwinists are just sure the process of spontaneous generation had to happen elsewhere, and others simply comment that the universe is so big we will never know what could be out there. NASA itself was intrigued by the ET idea, and in 1984 joined originator Frank Drake in a most ambitious nonprofit project, now well-known as SETI.

Having spent over $130 million in its history, and employing over 100 scientists today, SETI's mission remains the same since its inception: "To explore, understand and explain the origin, nature and prevalence of life in the universe." This grandiose mission is overseen by a "who's who" board of directors, and their efforts to find life outside of our planet have been herculean.

In 1985, SETI made operational an extensive radio telescope system called META (Mega ExtraTerrestrial Array), which simultaneously analyzed 8 million radio channel frequencies of pulses coming from outer space. In 1992, NASA helped add telescopes in Puerto Rico and California. In 1995, BETA (Billion ExtraTerrestrial Array) became operational and was so comprehensive it was termed an "all sky survey." Presently, SETI relies on a VLA (having run out of superlatives, now just a "Very Large Array") that utilizes 27 different radio telescopes in the New Mexico desert scanning space in all directions.

In addition, VLA has a laser-light decoder capability in case aliens are sending out messages through that avenue. What's more, in 1996 SETI added a program called Serendipity, offering anyone with a home computer to network with them in the search for data. Currently, owners of 5 million PCs are claimed to be in the Serendipity Network. So what are the results of such an ambitious undertaking? What has the thorough analysis of all this interstellar radio and laser traffic yielded?

"Not Yet..."

On its Web-site home page, SETI has posted a section with frequently asked questions. Can you guess what is the number-one most commonly asked question? (Like kids say, "I'll give you two guesses, and the first one doesn't count.") "Has the SETI Institute found any extraterrestrial signals yet?" I kid you not, the first word in their answer is "No," and the first two complete sentences in the expanded explanation are, "No SETI search has yet received a confirmed extra-terrestrial signal....If we had, you would know about it." Amazing!

Of course, picking up reruns of *My Favorite Martian* would be most welcome, or even a transmission where electromagnetic pulses were obviously nonrandom—like an SOS or an ordered string of prime numbers as in the movie *Contact*. (Remember that one, starring Jodie Foster? If you haven't, it's worth renting at the video store.) Yet SETI's minimum criterion is even less—to at least find a narrowband signal that could be said to be manipulated, say 1400 to 1600 megahertz wide, as opposed to the constant broadband cacophony of all cosmic noisemakers. However, after these many years there is nothing yet to report, but we all can certainly give SETI an A grade for tenacity.

On the other hand, the National Aeronautics and Space Administration grades more strictly. In 1994, after ten years of participation, NASA withdrew funding from the SETI project. Ostensibly, the reason is the same for discontinuing the unnecessary decontamination procedures after the first three Apollo flights—not to waste time and money on an idea with no supporting evidence. Since 1994, SETI has had to subsist strictly on private funds from two main endowments (founded by Bernard Oliver of Hewlett-Packard and Carl Sagan of Cornell University, both now deceased), as well as donations from interested individuals.

What more should I say about SETI? Maybe this. If any type of signal comes out of space that could be construed as nonrandom and carrying information in any way, the fervor of an organization saddled by two decades of frustration over their singular purpose would be volcanic ecstasy. Yet many of the same scientists look at a DNA molecule laden with predictable, verifiable, and unmistakable coded information and shrug it off as a product of happenstance. How can you account for such runaway incongruity? You can't...so I'll move on.

Eavesdroppers

Though there has been no contact, there is one more possibility. Maybe aliens have been monitoring our communications, maybe having even done a fly by, but have decided not to contact us...perhaps because we are too primitive or too violent. If they have caught our radio traffic, they must be living in solar systems as near as the houses next door. Otherwise, in their travels they stumbled on our radio traffic through a fantastic stroke of luck.

Take a careful look at what follows here. It is true our Earth has been sending out electromagnetic waves for eons. Earthquakes, volcanoes, meteor collisions, and the like all generate random radio pulses that have left Earth from the beginning of time itself. However, history records that it wasn't until 1887 that a fellow named Heinrich Hertz first began to "monkey" with intentional, nonrandom radio signals. (Of course Marconi found a way to send, receive, and audibilize them, and was awarded a patent for a gizmo called a "radio" in 1895.) Therefore, history says Earth has been emanating intelligence-based waves for only about 110 years.

But before you assume Hertz's first signals are still traveling out into deep space, you must realize that for only about the last 50 years have we been generating the powerful long-range microwaves used for space communication. Unlike our AM/FM radio and VHF/UHF television waves, which have obvious reception-range limitations, microwaves in the 30,000 to 100,000 megahertz range are the only ones capable of reaching deep into space.

Now ask yourself this. How far out in space have our microwaves traveled in 50 years? Is it as Buzz Lightyear said in the movie *Toy Story,* "To infinity and beyond"? To answer that, the celebrated figure for the speed of light comes into play—186,000 miles per second—the fastest known speed in the universe. I would call that plenty fast, and radio waves travel at approximately the same speed. So is Buzz right? Consider this. Our circular Milky Way galaxy is estimated to be 90,000 light-years across—a light-year obviously being the distance a beam of light will travel in one year at that fantastic speed, which can be rounded to six trillion miles! And yet at these speeds and these distances, our earliest of microwave signals would have traversed only .0006, or six ten-thousandths, of the galaxy's diameter.

Here it is in simpler terms. About 90 percent of the stars you see on a clear night (only a ridiculous pittance of the full number out there) are *still* too far away to pick up our first broadcasts of 50 years ago. And of course the emanations from the more recent 3000-plus orbiting space vehicles now actively sending signals have hardly passed the closest handful of stars.

Here is the main point in all this. If we are going to detect radio signals from active aliens, they would have to be virtually living "on our block." Then if they were, we should hear or see them as easily as the neighbor mowing the lawn. And it's the same if aliens are looking for us. Unless the Milky Way is filled with space traffic like a *Jetsons* cartoon, lonely pioneers would have to get fantastically lucky just to see our "campfire smoke."

Time and Space

The point here is that even in any unlikely intelligent ET scenario, our isolation still seems assured. Yet ET dreamers among us still dream, not grasping the vastness of space. We all need to remember that speeds of our present spacecraft average only in the neighborhood of 25,000 miles per hour. Yet even at such speeds—exorbitant by Earth-vehicle standards—getting to Mars takes about four months. Pluto? About 18 years. And these, of course, are one-way tickets.

Planning on spending the summer at the nearest star system to our sun, the trinary Alpha group? Allow about 110,000 years travel time. ("Are we there yet, Daddy?") Even if we perfected the "soon to be mastered" technology of *Star Trek's* transporter (converting matter into energy, beaming it to a location, and changing it back to matter again), it's a four-year trip to Alpha Proximus at light-year speeds. Or if you want to leave our spiral-shaped neighborhood and head toward the Andromeda galaxy across town, Mr. Scott will have to program into the transporter a trip of about 2.5 million light-years to get you to its galactic "city limits" sign. And of course, the same crushing restrictions apply to any intelligent species trying to travel in our direction.

Now at this point in the discourse, someone always says, "Maybe they are more technologically advanced than us and have mastered 'warp drive' or know about 'worm holes' or something." My first thought is to encourage that person to trust Einstein that the speed of light is a universal constant.

But my next thought is to suggest visiting a set where an alien sci-fi movie is being filmed. A change of perspective might result upon hearing the director say "Cut!" and seeing the mechanical creatures unplugged, the alien computer images turned off, the latex peeled away from the costumed faces, and the hero and villain heading to the commissary for a cup of coffee. Maybe then all the fanciful movies on aliens will be seen in proper perspective. Following that, maybe these same people will finally understand that the prospects of us going to them, them coming to us, or even us establishing any type of radio contact is an astronomical improbability—assuming also, of course, that some other planet beat the impossible odds of randomly generating life. (It seems we meet those prohibitive exponential numbers at every turn.)

Calculating ET

After all this digression, let's return to the original issue. Contact or no, do you still believe there is a possibility of more self-made forms of life out there? It might surprise you to know that someone has actually come up with a mathematical formula to calculate the likelihood. My description may give you a sense of the lengths some people go to support a pet theory.

Among James Michener's many novels is one simply called *Space*. In his docudrama style, Michener uses both fictional and historical figures to take the reader through the entire history of space travel, beginning with Hitler's V-2 rockets. Next he covers the jet-engine aircraft of the Korean War, and how these planes and their pilots became the rockets and astronauts of the fledgling NASA. Then comes background on the Cold War nuclear ICBM standoff, followed by the Soviets launching the first satellite, *Sputnik,* and the space race to the Moon. Finally, Michener closes his book with a look toward Mars.

When I first read *Space,* I still remember my curiosity over the unique ending. After 608 pages of a stimulating historical epic, Michener uses the last 14 pages for a unique change in direction. Here he presents a formula first introduced in the 1960s by astronomer and SETI founder Frank Drake, intended to actually calculate the number of advanced civilizations in any given galaxy based on its number of stars. (Re-read that last sentence if you will. This is a unique undertaking!)

The book's final scene is a fictional meeting that surely took place in some real fashion. Michener describes a panel of experts commissioned by the U.S. government to debate the possibility of ET life, and what steps to take based on the resulting consensus. Michener name-drops prominent scientists attending this imaginary meeting, including Sagan, Asimov, Cameron, Oliver, Pope, and Dyson. Then he also includes several NASA officials, and even a couple of prominent evangelists for balance. To add spice to the proceedings, any interested credentialed persons were invited to observe and make comments. (The book comes to an abrupt end when the "religious right" raises such a stink about how to proceed that the deadlocked commission sits in limbo.)

Six Limiting Factors

What I remember from that fictionalized scenario is how two "brilliant" student protégés from Sagan's Cornell University presented the panel with an equation. Though Drake himself called the formula more of a "gimmick," Michener seemed to be impressed by the equation, calling it "frightening" in his text.

Let's examine Drake's formula as Michener applied it to the Milky Way and see just how frightening are the prospects of intelligent life elsewhere in our galaxy. The equation looks like this.

$$N = N^* \, (f_p) \, (f_e) \, (f_l) \, (f_i) \, (f_c) \, (f_L)$$

The first **N** represents the objective—in any given galaxy, what is the **N**umber of stars with an orbiting planet containing civilizations that, right now, are capable of communicating with us? That number is reached by multiplying **N***, the number of total stars in the galaxy under consideration, by six fractions, the six letters **(f)** above with subscripts.

Each of the subscripts represents an exclusion factor that when multiplied will reduce the number of qualifying stars. In Michener's book, his fictitious protégés apply the formula to the Milky Way, estimated to have 400 billion stars (which seems a reasonable figure according to independent sources).

Then in succession, you begin to multiply the 400 billion stars according to the fractions of the six limiting criteria.

1. You multiply N^* by the (f_p) fraction, $(_p)$ representing the number of stars thought to have (p)lanets. This makes perfect sense, for without planets how could a star have a place for civilizations? Here Michener's estimate is that only one-fourth of all stars have planets, and ¼ of 400 billion leaves us 100 billion stars with planets that can then have civilizations. (Does this reduction process make sense? If so, let's move on.)

2. Multiply the remaining 100 billion stars by $(_e)$, the estimate of those with planets having a suitable (e)cology to support eventual life, as opposed to planets like Pluto, which are surely not contenders for life. Here, Michener's estimate is one-half, and ½ times 100 billion now leaves 50 billion eligible stars with ecologically suitable planets.

3. Multiply by $(_l)$, the remaining stars where planets with ecological potential are fortunate enough to develop any type of (l)ife at all, even if it is just algae, worms, and so on. Michener's estimate? Nine-tenths, which still leaves 45 billion star candidates in the running.

4. Multiply by $(_i)$, where that life went on to develop into (i)ntelligent forms, like mammals, primates, perhaps even hominids. Michener's one-tenth estimate still leaves 4.5 billion stars, each possessing intelligent life at one time in its existence.

5. Multiply by $(_c)$, where those intelligent life-forms would eventually acquire civilizations that would develop technology to (c)ommunicate into outer space. Michener's estimate is one-third. Pause to ponder here. If all Drake's/Michener's estimates are correct to this point, 1.5 billion stars out of the 400 billion in the Milky Way will eventually develop civilized people capable of sending

signals into space. Could it be that this estimate is a bit liberal? If not, the Milky Way should be *extremely* crowded.

6. However, Michener's last fraction pares that number considerably through an interesting concept. The sixth and final limiting fraction ($_l$) could be described as those 1.5 billion civilizations that are **(L)**ucky enough to be communicating right now. Our solar system is used as the only available example. After all, our sun does have planets, and at least one is ecological, maybe two if you add Mars. Then on the "third rock from the sun," life did evolve, later became intelligent, and finally began communicating into space. But the sixth limiting factor is that we have only been emanating extraterrestrial communications for about 50 years, closer to 45.

If you use that 45 years as a numerator, and the typically cited age of the Earth at 4.5 billion years as the denominator, the fraction says we have been communicating for only about a hundred-millionth of our planetary history. Interesting! Assuming this relative time fraction would hold for the evolutionary rate of all planets, and then multiplying .00000001 by the 1.5 billion stars still left in contention, this leaves you with just the stars having planets with intelligent, communicating life *right now*.

In the end Michener proudly proclaims the odds say we should, at this moment, have *15* communicating civilizations in our Milky Way galaxy we could hear if conditions were right! In other words, as you now are reading about the possibility that someone else is out there, in 14 other celestial locations in just the Milky Way, aliens could be reading about whether you and I are out there! Substituting all values and doing the requisite math, the formula works like this:

N (the number of Milky Way civilizations) =

$$400{,}000{,}000{,}000 \times (\tfrac{1}{4})\,(\tfrac{1}{2})\,(\tfrac{9}{10})\,(\tfrac{1}{10})\,(\tfrac{1}{3})\,(\tfrac{1}{100{,}000{,}000}) \approx 15$$

Maybe this is frightening, especially if you add that there may be as many galaxies out there as the Milky Way has stars—an additional 400,000,000 more galaxies. Then what would be our grand total of civilized planets in the known universe? Fifteen times 400 billion equals

6 trillion—6 trillion civilizations existing able to communicate with us right now if they were close enough! (Seems a bit much.)

Recrunching the Numbers

I find Drake's formula very intriguing. And you can certainly tell that Michener is tantalized by the prospect of us sharing our galaxy with 15 alien races. Furthermore, you can just "feel" the influence of the actual modern-day scientists woven into his fictional account. As with the people working in the SETI program, finding proof of extraterrestrial life would both accentuate and accelerate their professional careers and personal views. Therefore, they have always aggressively promoted through books such as these the idea that "we are not alone." However, while the approach of the formula may be impressive, I fully believe the sizes of the fractional parameters are very grossly distorted. Let's look at them one at a time.

1. (f_p)—Is it reasonable to assume that one fourth of all stars have (**p**)lanets? That's far too generous in that twin (binary), triple (trinary), and multistar systems make up approximately 70 percent of all of the night's twinkling objects. The problem here is that when two or more stars revolve around each other, the gravitational extremes created almost always negate the possibility of planets. That leaves only 30 percent of all stars in the necessary single configuration, like our sun. Then if your single star is too close to the disastrous effects of supernovae, quasars, black holes, and so on (like in the "ball" of stars in the center of our galaxy), planetary systems are also negated by such cataclysms. The Hubble Telescope with its powerful magnification now verifies only a small fraction of stars have any planets at all. Unfortunately for Michener, Hubble's information was unavailable when *Space* was first published in 1982.

2. (f_e)—Would you expect that half of all planets that do manage to exist on their single stars have a suitable (**e**)cology? If our solar system is used as an example, as Michener frequently does elsewhere, that fraction should be, at best, two-ninths (Earth and maybe Mars). And yet Carl Sagan's own independent estimate of

planets with a suitable ecology is much more prohibitive. His very educated guess is that only 1 out of 1000 stars have planets with ecological conditions capable of supporting advanced life. If we use Sagan's estimate of $\frac{1}{1000}$, the "15" civilizations drop off radar and now the Milky Way has only one chance in ten for a single civilization. (I hope that would be us.)

3. (f_l)—What about the "9 out of 10" chance that on a planet with a suitable ecology, simple (l)ife will evolve? Even the most committed evolutionists would call that estimate ridiculous. Remember the information in part four on the impossibility of random chemical evolution, and the information earlier in this chapter on the barriers of the second law? Personally, I would replace nine-tenths of a chance with "ghost of a chance" (ghosts being nonexistent), and the odds of civilizations anywhere—anywhere in the universe—shrink out of sight.

4. (f_i)—Next comes the "1 out of 10" chance that simple life will evolve into intelligent life. If this figure is right, 10 percent of the time something like a bacterium will go on all by itself and become a reasoning, problem-solving organism like the higher mammals, or perhaps some birds. Remember that molecular biologists see getting that first cell as tougher than the cell becoming us. This seems to say that, given enough time, life has a fair chance to become intelligent. Wait until you read part six on whether life could accidentally advance on our planet before you decide on this one.

5. (f_c)—Then comes the "1 chance out of 3" that intelligent life becomes electronically communicating life, complete with machinery and such. Actually, I believe that Michener's fraction for this one parameter might actually be *under*estimated. In my opinion, if we could somehow advance far enough to acquire the innate capability to communicate (and also be fortuitous enough to get our opposable thumbs), I feel the odds of something like a tomahawk becoming a Tomahawk missile are about 100 percent.

6. (f_L)—Lastly, I accept the "1 chance out of 100 million" that a technological civilization is communicating right now.

So where are we on interpreting this formula? As for me, I declare the entire equation useless in that it always yields that Darwinist's nightmare—zero. If you are brave enough to admit that bacteria turn into people 10 percent of the time, what do you do with the figure that a dead planet automatically turns into a live one 90 percent of the time? I have objectively shared Drake's original formula with many young teens, who have an uncanny ability to see subjects with fresh eyes. When I reach the 90 percent part, they always reject the figure with some rather unflattering words. ("Yeah, right." "Are you kidding me?")

I say the kids' logic and common sense are accurate. But it's not just intuition. Once again, chapter 7 showed the odds of molecular evolution to far exceed the universal probability boundary, and to therefore be zero. So if you multiply any value by zero, like Drake's entire messy equation, elementary math says your answer is zero. And that is my stand on accidental extraterrestrial life anywhere in the universe. Zero, impossible, not here, not there—not anywhere. This may put me at odds with the majority of people, but consider this. My view is perfectly in line with the facts as based on the present findings of NASA and SETI.

The Search for Extraterrestrial...Significance?

In my look at U.S. space history, I intentionally did not mention two spacecraft in the Pioneer series because they have a more important application at this point. *Pioneer 10* and *Pioneer 11* were launched in March 1972 and April 1973. Objectives? Jupiter for *Pioneer 10,* Saturn for *Pioneer 11,* and then both into deep space. *Pioneer 10* made a close pass to Jupiter in December 1973, giving us impressive close-up images from a "mere" 81,000 miles away. Then the gravity of Jupiter slung the craft to an accelerated 82,000 miles per hour, sending it in "crack the whip" fashion toward Aldebaran, the red star forming the eye of the constellation Taurus. Though the last telemetry received from *Pioneer 10* was in January 2003 and its power supply is now dead, the "ghost ship" is scheduled to arrive at Aldebaran in about 2 million years.

As for *Pioneer 11,* after taking impressive pictures of Jupiter's Great Red Spot in its flyby in December 1974, it passed within 13,000 miles of Saturn in September 1979. Here it took dazzling pictures of the massive rings and also discovered two previously unknown small moons. Its last transmission was December 1995, shortly before its slingshot pass of Saturn that pointed it toward the constellation Aquila, where it will arrive in about 4 million years. Again, to reinforce the incredible distances in space, both Pioneer vehicles have approximated only the orbit of Pluto after more than 30 years of travel.

Why mention *Pioneer 10* and *Pioneer 11* here and not earlier? Because of the identical pictures on gold plaques attached to both vehicles. Carl Sagan's name surfaces once again—as the coauthor of the plaques, along with Frank Drake. Each plaque bears a drawing of a man and woman whose dimensions and facial features are meant to be a perfect average of the world's population. They are also properly unclothed, I suppose to provide the maximum of information while not favoring any one culture. As the man waves and the woman stands demurely by his side, you can see the basic shape of the spacecraft is in the background.

> The reason for both plaques is obvious. If any unknown aliens find either spacecraft, they will know something about us, and exactly where to find us.

For reference points from the center of our solar system, the plaque also shows the position of our sun relative to 14 easily identifiable pulsars—pulsars being extra-bright cosmic "signposts" any galactic traveler would recognize. There at the bottom of the plaque, the planets of our solar system are also shown in sequence, including a small Pioneer spacecraft sketch shown leaving our Earth and traveling on a curved path around either Jupiter or Saturn. Finally, the upper-left schematic shows the hyperfine transition of a neutral atomic hydrogen, the most common element in the universe, with sufficient detail to translate any portion of the rest of the plaque. The reason for both plaques is obvious. If any unknown aliens find either spacecraft, they will know something about us, and exactly where to find us.

Maybe We're Better Off Alone

Pardon me, but does this make you nervous? Does it feel a bit like remembering you left your car unlocked and your wallet or purse on a seat that can be seen from the window? Myself, I have no dread. As I have said, all available information points to the fact we are alone. Besides, I am aware of what great distances buffer us from other objects in space.

But what about those folks who designed the plaque and took part in the construction and launch of these space vehicles? These are generally people with great faith in ET life. Don't they remember the popular movies *Independence Day* with Will Smith, or *Signs* with Mel Gibson? Did they not go to see the 2005 remake of *War of the Worlds*? (Yikes!) It seems almost every story of alien encounters ends with enslavement, not advancement. If we are any gauge, consider how Earth's civilizations have behaved when encountering less defended people here at home. Instead of giving us a cure for cancer, I would say the most realistic outcome of aliens finding us is a takeover of Earth by force. If I were Sagan or Drake and took a second look at the implications of that plaque, I would breathe a great sigh of relief to know that Drake's formula does indeed result in zero.

———•———

After reviewing content about the vastness of space, many people feel small and insignificant. Even if you have had an impressive career like Carl Sagan did, or many of the people named in this section, a human life span is still a comically brief blip on the screen of time. If your life's achievements were symbolically placed on a plaque attached to a spacecraft and you died before its journey had barely begun, life might seem like a cruel trick as it came to an end. For those who long to find intelligent life outside our planet, maybe SETI really should stand for the "**S**earch to **E**scape **T**errestrial **I**nsignificance," in that they can find no source of meaning for their lives here on Planet Earth...because they are living according to the impersonal implications of natural evolution.

But if we look at the evidence, it etches a different story on the plaque. Planet Earth is unique—and this fact points to the attentions of a Designer in the Earth's origin. Is this where we can start the search? Has the center of spiritual significance, all that really matters anyway, been right here all along?

14

How Old Is the Earth?

Thousands or billions of years?

Now then, straight to the point. No stalling. How old is our planet? Science says the big bang explosion that made the universe began about 13.7 billion years ago, and the Earth finally became a recognizable planetary mass about 4.6 billion years ago. However, some people believe very few of these lengthy evolutionary processes ever happened. Instead, they say that the miracle of creation bringing all this about was rather abrupt—happening more in the neighborhood of under 10,000 years. So there's the question—old-earth or young-earth? Which is it?

Science is almost totally unified on the old earth view, saying our tiny planet is just another unintended by-product of the big bang that made innumerable other planets as well as galaxies, comets, black holes, and so on. By comparison, many religious people believe the Earth was created in rapid fashion as an intentional and unique product of Divine activity. They claim the details are spelled out in the book of Genesis, beginning with the words "Let there be light..." Then it takes just two more chapters to outline the six days of 24 hours each in which God completes His creative work. (The seventh day was a day of rest.) The process ends with the creation of the very first human beings, Adam and Eve.

From there, the genealogies listed in the book of Genesis indicate it took less than 10,000 years for Adam and Eve's offspring to produce our present civilizations. And there you have it—about 4,600,000,000 years or about 10,000 years. That's quite a choice, and both cannot be right, because somebody errs by about 4,599,990,000 years! Because of the implications of these disparate numbers, and because of the potential consequences of being so far in the wrong, I would say it's important to get it right.

Some Good Points

It is important to know that people who support the young-earth view rely not just on Scripture, but cite a large body of scientific evidence as well. Certain creationist institutions and individuals will provide you with pages of scientific age-related factors that they believe indicate a youthful planet, and these are used to build a case that traditional geologic science is dead wrong about an ancient Earth. Here is one clear example. There is no doubt that the 1980 explosion of Mt. St. Helens toppled entire forests and rapidly entombed blasted parts of trees and animals under several feet of ash, mud, and rock. If the date of the event were not known, the results could be mistaken for hundreds of thousands of years of sedimentary accumulation containing coal, fossils, and so on.

The list of other potentially youthful scientific Earth features is long, and here is a sampling.

- It is possible that Moon dust collecting on the surface of a body with no atmosphere should be much deeper if the Moon, like Earth, were 4.6 billion years old.

- It is reported that argon gas can be trapped under Hawaiian volcanic rock in a matter of days, maybe giving the false impression of extreme age.

- Maybe the Earth should have already stopped spinning on its axis if the reported present rate of slowdown has been going on for billions of years instead of thousands.

- Radiometric dating methods such as Carbon 14 might be yielding incorrect results if radioactive C-14 concentrations in our atmosphere have not always been constant.

- If meteors reach the Earth's surface at a steady and random rate, perhaps the lack of meteorites in some sediment indicates the sediment is not that ancient.

- It is possible that piles of dead trees could be quickly buried by a relatively recent global flood caused in part by tremendous geologic upheaval, and thus deeply buried, be rapidly on their way to becoming coal deposits.

Young-earth proponents offer a great many more examples like the above, and they raise many interesting questions. In one sense I agree with such work because it helps keep the Darwinists more honest in their wholesale speculations and manipulations of what might have happened over the millenia. But again, like in the origins debate itself, the choice is only one of two. We are *old,* or we are *young.* I will tell you straight out that *only* an old-earth scenario fits the data, and I believe I can convince you of such.

Burning Issues

Earlier I brought up the concept of coal, so let's take a closer look at it. Only a touch of scientific background is needed to understand that coal is the compacted remains of billions of tons of trees and other vegetation piled on top of one another. (For pete's sake, you can still see the compressed grain of the wood in a lump of coal!) Then, after being compacted over immense periods of time, an equal weight of any grade of coal now has a greater BTU heating potential than the original wood. (According to the U.S. Geologic Survey, we have 276 billion tons of coal in proven reserves in our country. I wonder how many tons of green vegetation that equaled?)

Also, nobody can argue that some coal seams extend several hundred feet down, such as Australia's Morwell Deposit at 1500 feet deep. Furthermore, giant peat moss bogs such as those in Canada reveal slowly developing layers of accumulating dead peat being pressed into low-density *lignite* coal. Then below that you can find layers of more compacted *bituminous* coal with better heat potential, and highly purified and clean-burning *anthracite* coal at the bottom. And these phenomena are not found just in the U.S., Australia, and Canada. Every continent on the globe has coal deposits—even Antarctica. These are observations with tremendous implications.

The implications raise questions like, "How do you speed up the growth of trees?"

Available sunlight, carbon dioxide, and water govern the photosynthetic rate that produced those billions and billions of tons of coal-producing vegetation found all over the world. Of course photosynthesis is commonly hindered by less than optimal conditions, but the reaction has a maximum speed that can never be accelerated by giving a tree more and more sunlight, drowning it with water, and so on. Sure, Moon dust accumulation rates could be imagined to fluctuate at any rate to give you a desired depth, but you just can't make a tree at any speed you desire. (Would anybody fall for a TV commercial that advertises a kit for overnight growth of a mature tree—$19.95, plus $6.50 for shipping and handling, and allow eight weeks for delivery?)

In short, there is no way to produce the world's incredible amount of coal in around 10,000 years—and get it buried to those incredible depths—even by the wildest short-term botanical and geologic hypotheses. And speaking of fossil fuels, you would also have to stretch a young-earth view to somehow account for that coal in the frozen Antarctic, and all that oil, especially the deposits in northern Alaska or deep in the ocean. (The deepest oceanic oil reserve presently being tapped is Exxon Mobil's Hoover Diana Platform 200 miles out in the Gulf of Mexico in 4795 feet of water. The 300-million-barrel oil field is found another 500 to 1000 feet below the ocean floor. Furthermore, the industry talks of someday being able to tap oil fields in water 10,000 feet deep. (Two miles down? How did that stuff get there?)

More Lack of Time

The presence of oil in frozen Alaska and coal in frozen Antarctica, and the ocean depths where oil is found, creates another young-earth problem by default. Science says the reason fossil fuels are found in such inhospitable places is due to the breakup of the supercontinent Pangaea.

This phenomenon, which geologists believe began about 200 mya (million years ago) and took almost until civilized times to complete, is said to have moved land masses far from their original locations and created deep fissures that trapped substances like oil.

If the continental drift theory is true (when I look at a world map, I find the concept very reasonable) and the Earth is not very old, either it happened at "warp speed" or not at all. If at warp speed, how did Antarctica move upwards of 2000 miles, and millions of barrels of Alaskan oil get produced, in thousands of years? (And since recorded history goes back at least 4000 years when all seemed geologically and climactically quiet, this further cuts the time for such dramatic change.) I suppose there still is the "not at all" option. But that means the present shapes of the continents were created to just "look" like they would fit back together if you could rewind geologic time. Somehow I have a difficult time with that concept. (Much more information on continental drift will be covered in chapter 21—"Homologies versus Analogies" where in this case it gives a fatal blow to natural evolution.)

Though a young-earth person might call the list of rapidly occurring scientific phenomena "long," evidences for an ancient Earth are nearly endless. (Recently I visited Great Sand Dunes National Park near Alamosa. Where did all that sand come from, and how could it have accumulated so rapidly?) As I encounter science, everywhere I turn in every field I see features that speak of extreme age. And the write-up of these old-earth evidences need not use phrases containing words like "maybe," "possibly," "might," or "perhaps."

You don't have to say coal is "thought to be" in Antarctica, oil is "likely" in northern Alaska, or fossil fuels are "possibly" miles deep in the ocean. No, old-earth challenges use words such as emphasized below. "How about the *undeniable* gradual expansion rate of the universe, and the *inviolate* speed of light? What about the *documented* slow process of wood petrifaction, the *unalterable* length of rubidium/strontium half-lives, the *measurable* creeping rates of sedimentation flow, the *observable* "snail's pace" erosion process of river canyons and sea cliffs, or the *verifiable* rate of drifting continental landmasses?"

Just as natural evolutionists must have a plausible answer for every powerful challenge to the absurdity of a self-made universe and self-made life, so must a young-earth proponent constantly struggle to adequately explain away an unrelenting array of ancient Earth features. With these facts on the table, honestly ask yourself which of the two views has the best statistical "goodness of fit" to *all* the data available.

Now don't get me wrong. I've already said I'm not against calling Darwinists on the carpet over their penchant for wild hypotheses or their refusal to believe any of their self-made aging theories are flawed. But neither do I support setting aside standards such as photosynthetic rates, half-lives, and the speed of light to stuff a square-peg theory into a round hole justification. I'm just sure the audience we hope to convince about Design will not allow us the same hypocrisy of engaging in flawed suppositions as we accuse the opposition of doing.

Permit me to share a personal experience on the age of the Earth debate. One of my most treasured fossils is an inch-long shell of an extinct gastropod (snail) found by my daughter as her friend's father was digging a basement on the Colorado plains. The shell, firmly encased in sedimentary rock, was buried 12 feet down and was surrounded by flecks of quartz crystals. Now I suppose this shell could have been interred so deeply by some recent natural catastrophe, but what about fossils all over the world found thousands of feet deep such as those in the Grand Canyon?

If these are grossly misinterpreted as to age, then I suppose artifacts at lower levels of an ancient dig in the Holy Land only give the "illusion" that the civilization below was more ancient than the one built on top of it. Then allow me to mention that those quartz crystals found around the shell—crystals formed by lengthy and intensive application of heat and pressure—were also found *inside* the shell. Furthermore, the shell found 12 feet down on the Colorado plains was a *saltwater* variety, rather far away from the nearest ocean! So either extreme age is the answer, or as Ricky says to Lucy, "There's some splainin' to do."

Taking Things Literally

A friend of mine frequently states that if believers in God hold fast to the young-earth scenario, they will defeat the natural evolutionists by denying them the requisite time for their theories. However, a statement doesn't become true just because you profess it often enough. To put it more bluntly, you don't alter an error by standing on it all the more resolutely. And if you find yourself fighting to defend the unsubstantiated while dismissing the defensible, the cost is your credibility.

When creationists do this, I find it particularly sad for two reasons. First, you can see from this book that there is a colossal arsenal of other more potent ammunition available for defending the existence of a Designer. Therefore, why give evolutionists a reason to dismiss God because we insist on an unnecessary battlefield? Second (and this is so true), it doesn't take much study to find explanations that reconcile an old-earth scenario with *every* single biblical fact, while not compromising one bit on God's power and involvement.

Why, then, a young-earth view? My suspicion is that some people think to be a Bible literalist as God requires, you must keep a stranglehold on the idea that a *day* in Genesis chapter 1 has to be 24 hours. Now I personally consider myself a staunch Bible literalist. (Yes, I do—and for someone with a deep science background, I know that's extremely rare.) For example, when the Bible says Judas hanged himself,* to me it means the man was literally swinging from a rope until dead.

But the Bible can also speak allegorically, as when it says Judas fell headlong in the field acquired by his wickedness and burst open his bowels.† This is not a contradiction in methods of death—hanging verses falling—as I once heard alleged. First, the comment in Acts could still be a true statement if the body of a lonely and suicidal Judas hung there for days. But if not, it is a coldly accurate poetic description for the futility of his choices.

So am I saying the 24-hour days in Genesis could be allegorical, as well as the Garden of Eden–type events described therein? Do I believe these are possibly fairy-tale stories to make a point? Not in the least, because the key understanding is the varied meanings in the Hebrew word for *day*.

The Hebrew word for *day*—*yom*—is used over 1250 times in the Old Testament, and in only about 15 percent of the cases does it refer to an exact measure of time. In the rest of the applications, *yom* marks

---

* Matthew 27:5.

† Acts 1:18.

the beginning and end of a significant event, no matter how long or short. For example, when Joshua said, "Choose for yourselves this *day* whom you will serve,"* he was not giving the Israelites 24 hours to decide their allegiance, but seconds. And when Jacob buried his wife "and set up a pillar, and to this *day* that pillar marks Rachel's tomb,"† I have a hunch he knew her gravestone would be there for hundreds and hundreds of years.

Add to that Peter's famous New Testament phrase, "With the Lord, a *day* is like a thousand years, and a thousand years are like one *day*."‡ Here Peter is *literally* making the point that God is not controlled by time in any way. Though it would not have had meaning until the technological age, I believe Peter could have just as easily said, "With the Lord, a day is like a billion years, and a billion years are like a picosecond." Therefore, I never presume to confine God with human time—or mark His "days" strictly with a calendar, a wristwatch, or a stopwatch.

Underground Concerns

You know what? I believe we could settle this whole thing if you would return with me to the fossil quarry run by Creative Creations near Kemmerer in western Wyoming. The quarry is adjacent to Fossil Buttes National Monument on the geologic site of the famous Green River Formation. Here you and I would get down in a 50-foot hole where the cliffs above have been laid bare by heavy equipment, and we would see hundreds of horizontal layers of rock in various widths and shades of light brown. Interspersed everywhere in these layers we would see a multiple of small ultra-thin dark brown lines we would quickly learn were—fish! Then George the proprietor would take an iron bar and pry us out a section of rock shaped very much like a thick phone book. George would also give us a hammer and chisel, and our job would be to split the rock near those thin dark-brown lines to perfectly expose (hopefully) the classic Green River fish trapped inside.

---

* Joshua 24:15.

† Genesis 35:20.

‡ 2 Peter 3:8.

My first time there I learned the trick was to keep from fracturing the average six-inch specimens into a handful of forlorn pieces. Then, if you could just get a whole sample, George would beautifully frame it by cutting away any jagged rock edges with a saw. It was hard work in the hot July desert sun, but it was also absolutely entrancing. The draw for me was that the "next rock" would surely give you the perfect specimen you knew was there. My best prize? My beautifully intact eight-inch sickle-backed *Salmonoides merkus* whose general shape and jaw structure made it look like some form of extinct piranha, and I was positive mine were the first human eyes to see it!

Now for the science of it. Before we began, George gave each of us a handout detailing about a dozen different types of fish the quarry commonly yielded. The pictures looked like nothing I'd ever seen alive, and there was no doubt in my mind that we were dealing with extinct life. In real life these fish had to be at least an inch in diameter, and yet there they were, paper-thin by the millions, encased in the permanent darkness of layered sedimentary rock 50 feet underground.

How long were they there? Geologists at the Fossil Butte Visitor Center say the Green River Formation is about 50 to 55 million years old. Are they right? Let's say those experts are 99 percent wrong. That means the fish are "only" 500,000 years old. Get the point? There is *no way* (save one a couple of paragraphs below) that these fossils could be here in a young-earth scenario. If you don't like my conclusions, just wait until you see those fish in that rock wall with your own eyes.

As a major aside, maybe you would expect our host George to be a Darwinist of the first order. Hardly. His business card for Creative Creations (at least the one he gives to those occasional visitors who profess faith) has the Bible verse Hebrews 11:1 on the back. Why is he a believer in Design? As a person who deals with fossilized life every day, he sees firsthand all the inconsistencies in paleontology (about to be presented in part five) that in no way support natural evolution.

Created in Place?

Earlier in this chapter, I briefly mentioned one young-earth scenario I might be willing to endorse, one my sister Nancy and her husband, Tom, find intriguing. It is one occasionally talked about, but usually quickly rejected. Still it is quite possible that an all-powerful God just commanded that everything appear in its place, from fossil fuels to fossils. Obviously, this means those quarry fish never swam anywhere because they never existed alive, and neither did the likes of the T-rex, and so on.

If that's true, then all the evolutionary answers become as easy as "Let there be coal." Without a doubt, the Bible clearly says that God's creative powers are activated with no more than His own spoken words. (Related to that, I find it curious how some people admit that God has sufficient power to make a universe and a life-filled planet. Yet their faith in God's prowess to do the miraculous falters when they can't find a scientific method for God to use when parting a sea or moving a star over a manger.) Therefore, I have always retained illusory age as an unlikely but not impossible option.

Then again, I've never met a serious Bible student who believes that God merely made simulations that were never alive. If so, it would be the only time that God intentionally deceived believers to no constructive end, and the only unsolvable Earth-bound riddle He left us that He still expects us to comprehend. No, a catastrophic flood can happen in days, the dinosaurs can walk millions of years ago, the cosmos can be formed billions of years ago, and parts of the big bang can be measured in fractions of a second—all through the indispensable power of a Designer.

A Crucial Suggestion

Let me conclude this chapter by making clear a certain passion of mine, a bias so strong that I know I must keep it from becoming a hardened mind-set (thus losing any objectivity with those who don't agree with me). In my experience, young-earthers can introduce a piece of baggage that's tough to carry for someone searching for the truth.

I find this extremely unfortunate because at this juncture in history, I think that people of faith are in a position to unite and reclaim science from Darwinism and relegate natural evolution to the status it deserves—a historical asterisk. We just have to be sure we don't give doubters and antagonists such an easy target to attack. And there is no need for this. First, I believe I have built an overwhelming case for an old-earth scenario; and second, I will forcefully repeat that a literal

Genesis and an ancient Earth are not at all difficult to reconcile. So don't drag the conflict onto such an indefensible battlefield—there is too much at stake not to handle this correctly.

In my opinion, this insistence on including religious opinions in the origins debate is the main difficulty in trying to win legal battles to allow the teaching of alternatives to evolution in science classes. Very few people know that since 1981 there have been challenges to break the "evolution only" science curriculum in school districts in at least 34 different states. Furthermore, in 14 of these states the objections were not local initiatives at individual school districts, but challenges at the state board or legislature level and were mandates applying to every school throughout the state—with Kansas being perhaps the most well-known.

The "Dover Case"

From my perspective, every time these initiatives have faltered it is because people have introduced—either deliberately or unintentionally—religious opinions such as young-earth/old-earth into the mix. I am sure this was part of the reason the Dover School Board lost its case.

To further examine this well-known decision, on October 18, 2004, Pennsylvania's Dover Area School District board voted to specifically include "Intelligent Design" in the district's science curriculum. The following words became part of Dover School Board policy: "Students will be made aware of gaps/problems in Darwin's Theory and of other theories of evolution including, but not limited to, intelligent design."

What made the Dover initiative so unique was that for the first time, a public school board voted to *require* its science teachers to teach alternatives to evolution, such as ID. This brought legal action by eight parents, whose lawsuit, *Kitzmiller v. Dover Area School District,* specifically objected to a board-authorized statement that was to be read aloud to all ninth-grade biology students. The statement contained the four following phrases:

- "Because Darwin's Theory is a theory, it continues to be tested."

- "The Theory is not a fact. Gaps exist in the Theory for which there is no evidence."
- "Intelligent Design is an explanation of the origin of life that differs from Darwin's view."
- "Students are encouraged to keep an open mind."

While the plaintiffs were supported by the ACLU and other groups dedicated to the strict separation of church and state, the Dover Board was supported by the Discovery Institute, a Seattle-based think tank committed to challenging Darwinism over its lack of scientific validity, support of atheism, and rejection of common moral values. The Institute submitted to the court a brief prepared by over 80 different scientists who were in support of the Board, and they cited much scientific research specifically challenging self-made life.

The proceedings took an interesting twist when early in November of 2005 the citizens of Dover voted *out* of office most of those board members favoring the blend of evolution and Design. However, the judge presiding over the case, John Jones III, still rendered his decision in January 2006. He found in favor of the plaintiffs and declared the board's requirements unconstitutional. He also ruled that the little village of Dover was obligated to pay the ACLU $1,000,000 in legal fees.

Loss of Credibility

What really happened in Dover was that the board lost credibility in the eyes of both the people and the judge. Read any account of Judge Jones's decision you like, and you will see he was highly critical of the narrow religious agenda driving the former board members. While in his written opinion Jones did say, "The court takes no position on ID arguments, a proposition that may be true," he also said,

> It is ironic that several of these [former board] individuals, who so staunchly and proudly touted their religious convictions in public, would time and again lie to cover up their tracks and disguise the real purpose behind the ID [Intelligent Design] policy.

And of course, the board had already lost its case before the Dover citizens, who had voted them out of office weeks before the judge returned his ruling.

Looking back on the *Kitzmiller v. Dover* decision, which has now slipped from news into history, I find the above responses by the judge and the Dover citizenry to be incredibly revealing. First of all, the sleepy borough of Dover, Pennsylvania—population around 2000—is located in York County south of the Appalachians. Its farmland constituency is hardly a hotbed of atheism and anti-God sentiment, so there must have been something quite distasteful about the former board's approach. Furthermore, Judge Jones is a Methodist, which should be an indication he believes in a Designer of some sort. Was the age-of-the-earth issue part of the overall distaste? If so, it would be absolutely typical.

And in my experience, other religious issues often "coattail" along with the age-of-the-Earth debate—issues as unscientific as they are emotionally charged. My take is that those who want to bring Design into the classroom are destined to shoot themselves in the foot anytime they try to bring their brand of religion into what should be strictly scientific debate. When this happens, a judge (or legislator or board member) will be forced into umpiring religious squabbles instead of making scientific rulings. Then the people who should be on your side, and those whose faith you hope to strengthen—like the majority of the good people of Dover, who certainly are believers of some type—will be pushed in the opposite direction.

Problems with Religious Promotion

I am certain that a similar attempt at religious promotion became the undoing of the singular definitive U.S. Supreme Court case that semi-informed Darwinists proudly reference. It is the *Governor v. Aguillard* decision of 1987, which struck down the State of Louisiana's Creationism Act passed by the 1982 legislature. The Creationism Act required the equal teaching of creation science in the classroom if evolution was to be taught, and in this all-or-nothing policy a teacher must teach both or skip both. The highest court in the land, in a 7-to-2 vote, found the act in violation of the "establishment clause" of the First Amendment because the act "lacks a clear secular purpose."

Do I believe the justices made the right call? Well, I believe because of the way certain state senators drafted the act, and how the proponents argued for it, the Supreme Court had no choice but to throw it out.

In Justice Brennan's majority opinion in *Governor v. Aguillard,* he stated that "creation science has the distinctly different purpose of discrediting evolution by counterbalancing its teaching at every turn with the teaching of creationism." The concurring decision of Justice Powell further helped define "creationism" by referring to its beliefs in a "sudden creation of the universe, energy, and life from nothing," a "worldwide flood" and a "relatively recent inception of the earth and living kinds." So here we are again, caught up in religious squabbles and arguing over scriptural interpretations.

But Justice Brennan's biggest criticism was that the act did the opposite of what its proponents argued—it actually inhibited academic freedom. Brennan's words were, "[The Act] does not enhance the freedom of teachers to teach what they choose, and fails to further the goal of 'teaching all the evidence.'" Here I am forced to agree, and this is why. If science teachers in Louisiana are representative of the rest of the country, and I believe they are, many have no religious practices at all. And most find the tenets of evolution to be generally sound while those of creation science are at least somewhat flawed. But the act gave them just two legal choices—teach some religious content they don't believe (which they won't do), or skip an absolutely vital geological/biological topic (which they will do, but shouldn't). Brennan is right, both "freedoms" and "evidence" are lost, not gained.

The Tools Are Ready at Hand

However, a fully informed Darwinist will never mention other statements in the *Governor v. Aguillard* decision. First, in a dissenting opinion, Justice Scalia, joined by Chief Justice Rehnquist, said that after the evidence had been presented,

Infinitely less can we say (or should we say) that the scientific evidence for evolution is so conclusive that no one would be gullible enough to believe that there is any real scientific evidence to the contrary.

(I think Scalia just said that you are gullible if you think the scientific evidence for evolution is conclusive.)

But going back to the very first paragraph in Brennan's lengthy response, obviously referencing the many court cases upholding academic freedom, he said,

Moreover, [the Act] does not give schoolteachers a flexibility they do not already possess to supplant the present science curriculum with the presentation of theories, besides evolution, about the origin of life.

Here I'm certain Brennan said science teachers in Louisiana, and around the country, *already possess* the right to teach creation science, or any other alternative to evolution that is ostensibly reasonable and non-indoctrinational (two principles atheistic science teachers regularly violate with impunity).

So if you want science like Design to get a fair hearing in courtrooms and boardrooms and take its rightful place in classrooms, don't die because you "fall on the wrong sword," like that of the age-of-the-Earth debate. The science of Design is a neutral and powerful tool that can make people "think" when nothing else will. Learn it well, present it effectively, and quietly wait for opportunities to say more.

———•———

Ending part four with a discussion on the age of the Earth is a good setup for part five, "Paleontology and Genetic Change." I will show that accepting an old earth view in no wise settles the issue in favor of evolution. On the contrary, accepting an ancient planet undergoing lengthy "accidental" processes piles up an absolutely suffocating mountain of problems—both with the fossil record, and with the genetic mechanisms supposedly in operation for millions of years.

Working Within the Limitations

Darwinists continue to try to sell wording that doesn't appear in the Constitution—"separation of church and state." You know, I am quite positive our country's founders would be justifiably horrified at today's leaders who are bent on "separating" the population from any spiritual expressions in public places. (I'm sure they would scratch their heads like I do when a bunch of New Yorkers leave their $4 cups of gourmet coffee and run across the country to be sure an Alabama judge gets the Ten Commandments off his personal office wall.)

However, I also agree with the First Amendment's true wording—"Make no laws regarding the establishment of religion"—which I believe admonishes us to do what I've been saying: debate our religious opinions in religious circles.

All that said, I hope everyone truly took to heart the words of Justice Brennan I quoted above. Remember, we *"already possess"* the legal right to teach Design in public schools—*right now*. And we should spread the word with everything from technology to tom-toms. Yes, we (and Louisiana, Dover schools, and so on) will not run afoul of the First Amendment if we keep our religious opinions out of the discussion!

———•——•———

The organization I mentioned earlier, the International Foundation of Science Education by Design—IFSED—intends to act on Justice Brennan's affirmation that the right to teach alternatives to Darwinism is protected by freedom of speech and does not violate the concept of "separation." If you visit www.IFSED.org, you will find teaching materials and support services to combat the "evolution-only" approach. You can also request a free copy of the *Designated Science* newsletter.

PART FIVE

PALEONTOLOGY AND GENETIC CHANGE

The material in the first 14 chapters—math, molecular biology, physics, and chemistry—are perhaps not everybody's easiest subjects. And yet hopefully you saw in them the powerful objections leveled against Darwinism. It is especially critical to note these objections are not from religion but from science, and as I have stated, it is high time that science make a clean break with natural evolution.

It must be remembered that when Darwin first published *The Origin of Species* in 1861, physics had not developed much beyond the Newtonian variety—"what goes up must come down." Therefore, natural evolution did not yet have to answer the complications of thermodynamics applied to the cosmos in the space-time continuum, or its application to the Johnny-come-lately big bang theory. Also, the periodic table was not fully constructed, and talk of protons, neutrons, and electrons would have been words out of science fiction. More critically, molecular structures were decades away from giving up any of their meaningful secrets, especially those like DNA that made the chemistry of life.

And finally, if these challenges were not on the table, neither was the math I've used to amplify them. The point is back when Darwin's band of cohorts dreamed up self-made life, they could sell it to contemporary colleagues without having to first address the objections in this book. What's more, they have been trying to ride on that wave of ignorance ever since. In fact, if the theory of natural evolution tried to make its maiden flight today, I fully believe it would be shot down before it left the runway.

In my professional opinion, the problems with explaining precellular development, like where the first DNA came from, deal natural evolution the most painful scientific punch. When highly credentialed Darwinists eventually recant lifelong positions, I'll wager you will hear them discuss molecular complexity in their concession speeches. Here is a current example. Dr. Anthony Flew, British philosopher and distinguished atheist, championed evolution for the unbelievers for decades through highly publicized writings and open debates. But at age 81,

Dr. Flew went public with a change of mind, stating he was now a deist. In a 2004 interview with a close friend and religious apologist, Dr. Flew offered these words:

> Darwin himself, in the fourteenth chapter of *The Origin of Species,* pointed out that his whole argument began with a being which already possessed reproductive powers. This is the creature the evolution of which a truly comprehensive theory of evolution must give an account. It now seems to me that the findings of more than 50 years of DNA research have provided materials for a new and enormously powerful argument to design.

I agree with Dr. Flew. Natural evolution cannot account for creatures already reproducing, or for the complexity of the DNA molecule that allows it. It can't be made much plainer than that.

To the most investigative, exposing the myth of chemical evolution is all that is needed to dethrone Darwinism. However, with the general population I have had more success—and fun—exposing evolutionary weaknesses with discussions on the fossil record. It's hard to find people, young or old, whose interest isn't piqued by an ancient-looking shell, tooth, or skull. Besides, everybody loves a great dinosaur picture. What's more, the widespread appeal of challenges from paleontology is further enhanced by its ease of understanding. See if you don't agree as you read on.

Chapter 15

THE "ROOT OF LIFE"

*Darwin's evolutionary trees
turned upside down*

Without at least a smattering of fossil evidence, there would be no theory of natural evolution for the masses. Disagree? Then ask yourself, when evolution becomes the topic and proof is the issue, don't most people picture some prehistoric object—usually a fossil and usually of a dinosaur? If they added more pieces to the theory of self-made, they might also envision ancient shells, fish that walked out on land, feathered lizards, petrified wood, saber-toothed tigers, and, of course, prehistoric humans. And if they are really informed, they might imagine a geologic time scale chronicling the eras and periods of Earth from its ancient formation 4.6 billion years ago to today's modern times, dotted with life-forms arranged in advancing complexity.

But despite the quantity of evolutionary minutiae resulting from trying to explain the impossible, most practicing Darwinists still rely on the simple overriding premise that it is easy for life to accidentally beget more complex life. I find this strange because all it takes is a little honest digging into paleontology and genetic change to find that even here, natural evolution is much more vulnerable than venerated. So here we go.

Darwin's Tree

Bring them all back to life? Darwin hypothesized just that scenario in *The Origin of Species.* He imagined the visual impact of repopulating the Earth with all species, past and present. In other words, every creature that ever lived—on land, air, or sea—had magically returned to the planet and could be viewed in total. Darwin was positive that such a sight would quickly reinforce the process he frequently called "descent by modification." He was convinced that life slowly developed from simplicity to complexity over long periods of time, with significant extinctions along the way.

Therefore, if the panorama were reassembled, you could group them into a big "tree" with the fewer numbers of less complicated organisms concentrated toward the bottom "trunk," and the greater numbers of more complicated organisms spreading out at the top as the "branches" curve upward. If Darwin was right, and such a vast assortment as this could be organized as often depicted below, it would demonstrate his theory was true beyond a doubt.

In response, remember that paleontology was a budding field of study in Darwin's day, and most people had no idea how old the Earth could actually be. However, some biologists were already circulating the notion that perhaps many more species had gone extinct by the nineteenth century than were currently alive. (By today's estimates, 99 percent of all organisms ever to inhabit the earth have since been extirpated by a variety of causes—99 percent!) Darwin most assuredly believed many more fossils were going to be found, and they would include a dizzying array of "intermediates" that, if all alive, would validate his belief in gradual change. So what fossil discoveries have been made since Darwin's day, and if resurrected, would they support his conclusions?

What Remains to Be Found?

The real question I am asking is, How complete is today's fossil record? In other words, are any major taxa in hiding whose eventual discovery would later overturn present speculation, and are we still missing too much fossil evidence to make a call on Darwin's view?

My educated opinion here is no. Consider the millions upon millions of fossils in professional and amateur collections around the world. It means people have certainly been looking. In fact, I would say no part of the Earth even marginally accessible has avoided scrutiny to harbor great diversities of species yet unfound.

Also, consider that purveyors like the Smithsonian Institute now employ the most sophisticated and technological fossil-hunting techniques ever. But instead of constantly announcing newly found "missing links," the Smithsonian has to dispose of thousands of duplicates every year.

However, the absolute clincher is that paleontologists have not offered (as opposed to renamed) one new addition at the kingdom, phylum, or class level of taxonomy for decades. In fact, there have been only two new proposed offerings at the order level in the last 87 years. One new order has been suggested for a unique type of extinct trilobite, though it seems like I've already heard of those. The other is for an insect presently *alive* in Africa, though entomologists say it looks rather locust-like. (If you know anything about taxonomy, those who want to claim a unique discovery above the genus or species level—like at "family" or above—constantly propose new names, but they are rarely accepted.)

The point here is that by the twenty-first century, we've found most every type of ancient creature, except maybe those variations at the smallest level of classification. Therefore, if you are looking at population diversity and not population numbers, I contend that Darwin's imaginary scenario from the fossil evidence we knew in the year 1900 would not look much different from the fossil evidence we now have in the year 2000-plus.

The Tree Is Upside Down

So imagine viewing all past life that has miraculously returned. Could we use these creatures to construct phylogenetic trees made popular by Darwin—the ones with gradualism depicted by upward curved branches? Again, my educated opinion is absolutely not. Remember the words of David Raup I offered back in chapter 4? "120 years after Darwin, the knowledge of the fossil record has been greatly expanded....

Ironically, we have even fewer examples of evolutionary transition." Or consider the more recent words of Harvard paleontologist Stephen Jay Gould, who spoke out when most of his fellow professionals remained silent: "The extreme rarity of transitional fossils persists as the trade secret of paleontology."

No, instead of branching trees, what we would observe are clusters of similar plants and animals, sometimes called "nests," without transitions. It would be very much like a walk through any decent zoo—reptiles down this hall, primates in that section, fish in these rooms, and insects down the stairs. Furthermore, corridors connecting these exhibits that *should* display sequential transitional species would be, with a few remote exceptions, completely empty. This is the fact of the fossil record, with which few field paleontologists take issue.

To me, it's a classic case of double-speak. On one hand the Darwinist philosophizes that "way back when," some type of extinct nondescript carnivore evolved into a few primitive wolflike creatures, though there is no fossilized proof that this happened. (Ask a mammologist for some, because I've never seen it.) Then they say the evidence further indicates that these nonexistent wolf forerunners gradually became today's assortment of coyotes, foxes, and dogs—and then they draw paper and pencil diagrams to "prove" it. (This is *exactly* the kind of deception Raup and Gould speak out against.)

Then on the other hand, the Darwinists admit the fossil record does show that about 80 percent of the shelled creatures ever to exist have shrunk down to a few survivors, and all prehistoric humans have vanished leaving just *Homo sapiens*. If you want the best example, here is one with no dissention in the scientific community. Everyone admits the amazing proliferation of dinosaurs have been reduced to a mere handful of surviving reptiles, leaving us with just turtles, snakes, and lizards. This, folks, is what the fossil record shows over and over. And the development of life should be diagramed in this manner—as an upside-down tree where a fibrous tangle of roots converge into a few central stumps.

When believers in natural evolution admit this (for how can you escape it?), I wonder if they realize their contradictory position. Inverted trees mean diversity in species has been *lost* by the influences of natural

selection rather than generated by it. Think about that one. An associ-
ated point is that the well-known *Cambrian Explosion* of life around
450 million years ago took Earth from unicellularity to the existence
of every major phyla present today in a "blink" of an evolutionary eye.
From there, massive extinctions are said to have been a common event,
and the Earth has seen loss after loss, not gain. To be honest, there have
been some rapid surges within these phylogenetic nests. The sudden
proliferation of birds and mammals are good examples.

But the problem here is the fossil record says these "rooms in our
zoo" arrived with great diversity and complexity already intact. Darwin's
vision of a steady stream of widening and improving organisms, with
sufficient intermediate species to back it up, is only an unsubstantiated
dream.

There can be no doubt that the general theory of natural evolution, whether painfully gradual or in a series of surges, is absolutely
betrayed in the fossil record. But what about the many specific cases
of genetic change the Darwinists bandy about to "prove" the theory
actually worked millions of years ago? The next chapter examines a
classic evolutionary example—"When life crawled out of the seas and
established itself on land."

Chapter 16

The Theoretical Fish
that Took to Land

*And the real coelacanth that was subsequently
found in the water*

Back in my ninth-grade biology class of the 1960s, I distinctly
remember my textbook displaying the picture of a mysterious animal
called the "lobe-finned lungfish." This creature has been found fossilized
in every continent except Antarctica. The book boldly proclaimed these
fossils represented the evolutionary link between the Osteicthyes—the
bony fish—and the next more complex vertebrate class, Amphibia—
the animals that spend half their lives in water (larvae like tadpoles) and
the other half on land (adults like a frog).

If it could be shown that the transition between fish and frog did
pass through such a fish with both legs and lungs, this would constitute powerful evolutionary proof that chordate life escaped water all by
itself. And if this happened once, maybe life surged forward again later
to become the dinosaurs, and on and on. The artist's rendition in my
book of the "legged fish" showed the creature at the shoreline in the
backdrop of an ancient swamp, its head peering out of the water at the
beckoning land above. I can still see this "missing link" with external
breathing openings instead of gill flaps apparently heading for dry land
by crawling forward on "fins" that resembled paddle-like feet connected
to obvious knee and foot joints.

As a churchgoing ninth-grader at the time, I didn't give the implications of the walking fish that much thought. Besides, at first inspection

the picture looked convincing enough that I didn't automatically reject the notion. However, I also inherently felt God was behind the creation, so what was the big deal if He made a fish with legs along the way? But looking back now, I can understand the tremendous scientific error of "the fish that took to land" that you still see depicted everywhere today in science books and museums.

Cartoon Believers

If you want a great animated depiction of the "legged fish," please check out Walt Disney's legendary video *Fantasia*—the original 1941 version, not the recent 2000 remake. Here among fairy princesses, brooms carrying buckets of water, and dancing hippos in tutus, you will find a segment detailing with first the natural formation of our planet, and then the evolution of life itself, right up to the extinction of the dinosaurs produced by a fish that walked out of the water. For a children's video, there is quite a subliminal message here. And yet the genius of Disney explains the concept so well that I always show this to my science classes each year.

The big problem is that insufficient fossil intermediates exist between a typical swimming fish and a theoretical walking fish, as well as a walking fish and a walking amphibian for that matter. The implication is that only one or two jumps were needed to go from ordinary fish fins to extraordinary fish legs. I remember that the back legs in my book's picture had very complex hinge joints at the knees and the toes, as well as gliding joints at the ankles—quite a sudden surge forward from typical fish fins with straight ray bones.

And of course these leg bones had to suddenly appear with all the necessary cartilage and the incredibly complex musculature of many functional pairs of striated muscles. Furthermore, these two back legs must be attached to an equally complex pelvic girdle via ball and socket joints, and the entire apparatus had to be integrated into the back part of the spinal column if the "fish" were ever to hope to effectively walk. Finally, to accommodate the air vents of the creature in the book, it had to immediately exchange gills for at least a rudimentary type of internal lung structure. What an incredible redesign it would take to go quickly from gills to lungs! Sorry, you can't make that "thing" in the book with just one or two steps, or even a small handful of steps.

An Unfortunate Lack of Development

So does the evidence support the theory of gradual change? The extensive examples we do find of fossilized lobe-finned lungfish have a name. They are called the *coelacanth,* and because of the quantity of available fossil specimens, this creature couldn't have been a short-lived blip on the evolutionary radar screen. Alas, fossilized coelacanth samples found over the world and over all time show no variations. Don't you find that curious? I do. Unless the coelacanth suddenly hatched from an egg spawned by a typical fish, shouldn't it have some closely related ancestors on one side and descendants on the other? If the coelacanth is indeed a half fish/half amphibian, and we have so many of them, then where are the three-fourths fish/one-fourth amphibians? Or the one-fourth/three-fourths?

Such finds should not be too difficult since fossils of fish and amphibians are in great abundance, and these creatures supposed to soon be on land would have inhabited mucky coastal areas where interment and fossilization would be extremely likely. But unfortunately, not even a partially complete sequence between fish and amphibians has even been arranged, paralleling the staggering gaps in all other places in the fossil record that provide Darwinism with only a base of shifting sand.

> What of a replacement candidate for a plausible missing link between fish and amphibians? Such is now termed "as yet undiscovered" by those who actually work with fossil evidence.

Oh, yes. Did I forget to mention that a coelacanth was actually netted alive by a fisherman off the coast of Cape Town, South Africa, in 1938? However, back then nobody knew how important such a find would later become in the "origins" debate, and the fish slipped into legend. But then another coelacanth was caught alive off the coast of Madagascar in 1990, and this time thoroughly researched. Since then, several more identical specimens have been discovered, showing this is a true and stable species. It is now called the *Latimaria chalumnae,* and it is obviously not an intermediate.

We now know for certain the coelacanth does have monoaxial bone supports for its ventral fins to allow for greater rotation, yet the fin bones themselves are the typical straight rays as found in all other fish. Also, there is absolutely no hint of a pelvic girdle, only a typical straight spinal column; and no lungs, only gills. That's right, it's still very much a fish, and taxonomists classify it exactly as such. And for a supposedly ancient fellow, the coelacanth is more advanced than many of today's fish as an ovoviviparous *live* bearer of its young, not an egg-layer.

What's more astonishing is that its natural habitat is over 600 feet deep on the ocean floor. I would call that a long way from a warm tidal inlet where the first coelacanth/amphibian hybrid supposedly stepped out on land. Then as a final stab, researchers have actually videotaped live coelacanths, and they are always swimming, never walking, waddling, or belly crawling with their "finny legs" along the ocean floor.

Today the expert icthyologists, as opposed to the hopeful Darwinists, call it an evolutionary "dead end," meaning it gave rise to no known species. And what of a replacement candidate for a plausible missing link between fish and amphibians? Such is now termed "as yet undiscovered" by those who actually work with the fossil evidence.

———•———

As a fish story, claims made for the coelacanth before it was finally fully identified went far beyond Jonah and his fish. Yet we might be generous and cut Darwinists some slack because they say the fish-to-amphibian-to-dinosaur sequence took place between about 300 and 250 million years ago. How about a little sympathy for having to find all the necessary evidence from such an ancient time? So let's table the concept of ancient fish evolution and switch to a modern-day species often the subject of evolutionary research. Next I want to examine today's poster-child species for those who believe it is possible to accelerate genetic mutations in modern laboratories. The following chapter looks at the fruit fly.

Chapter 17

A Fly in the Ointment

*The results of all those experiments
done on fruit flies*

Believers in natural evolution put tremendous faith in a small handful
of examples of purported change in modern organisms. They contend that since these happened in our lifetime, evolution is observable
and therefore a reality over long periods of time as well. What short-
term examples are used to prove natural genetic change is possible?
From middle-school to college-level textbooks, you will predictably
find the peppered moth, finch beaks, pesticide-resistant mosquitoes,
drug-resistant bacteria, and, of course, the *Drosophila melanogaster.*

The drosophila fruit fly is the perfect specimen for research in the
hope of producing random mutations that might validate evolutionary
mechanisms. First of all it is a pest, so most animal-rights activists do
not seem concerned if you "give them the business" in the laboratory.
But more important, this plentiful fly breeds readily in confinement
and completes its life cycle in a matter of days, making experimental
results in the next generation quickly forthcoming.

In addition, fruit-fly breeding involves a wonderful array of non-
lethal recessive genes that produce "mutated" offspring with features
from deformed legs to extra nonfunctioning wings to blindness. Yet
another experimental advantage is that the six pairs of chromosomes in

each fruit fly cell are exceptionally large and easy to study for alterations. Therefore they are continually exposed to all types of genetic reconfiguring agents to see what body changes, harmful or even beneficial, might be possible.

One can only imagine the extent of experiments done on these critters. (One Web search on "drosophila" yielded a modest 627,000 hits.) They have been crossbred in every way imaginable, and have certainly been bombarded with gamma radiation far in excess of what nature could ever supply. They have also been subjected in unimaginable numbers to chemical mutagens, ultraviolet light, X-rays, and electric jolts. To that you can add everything the fruit industry has tried to rid themselves of these scourges, including pesticides and chemically induced sterility. Students in one of my college-prep biology classes even took flies from the science supply house breeding kit and placed them in near-freezing conditions for 24 hours before mating. Therefore, what are the results of this ongoing mass acceleration of Darwin's "descent by modification" mechanisms?

Predictable Results

The different types of damaged flies produced in these experiments are extremely predictable, so predictable that school-kit lab sheets actually have preset columns where students tally various deformities. Okay, that's high school—but have the sophisticated labs produced any different results? More specifically, have experts ever produced a new variation of drosophila? How about a new genus of fruit flies? Or maybe a new family of flies not of the fruit fly variety? Or most exciting, maybe a whole new order of insect? In other words, in all this concentrated effort, has anything new ever been produced by the same mechanism that is credited with accidentally producing all of Earth's species? Has anyone been able to stand up and say, "Here! Here we have finally produced a mutated fruit fly with this one great advantage that can now outcompete all other fruit flies. In fact, we must take care to prevent its escape lest it drives other fruit flies, even other flies, into extinction."

Obviously, this has not been the case or it would have been loudly proclaimed. The truth is that those flies that are not killed outright by the treatment are short-lived, never robust, handicapped, and certainly losers in the game of natural selection. Some even have that small inconvenience to survival, sterility. The bottom line is this. With the best scientific minds conducting all this intensive experimentation under the most ideal laboratory conditions for who knows how many years, how come there is not one successful fruit fly advance? And how is it possible that the luck of nature outperforms them, to the tune of generating an estimated 30 million more Earth species besides fruit flies?

If you must remove fruit flies as proof of modern-day evolutionary mechanisms, what of the other examples cited in textbooks? With respect to moths, finches, mosquitoes, and bacteria, it seems even highly credentialed scientists confuse a true mutation with an ongoing "gene sort." Whereas mutations would have to produce new genetic codes, a gene sort simply allows a rare gene expression already present to become dominant by selection pressure.

Those of you with children have almost certainly used amoxycillin, the pink medicine in the shakable bottle, to treat ear infections and other pediatric bacterial invasions. But after repeated use, the drug may lose its effectiveness, and the physician may prescribe penicillin or sulfa drugs. But when these medicines run their course, then amoxycillin may be effective again with bacteria playing "hide and seek." What has actually happened is not a mutation, but one medicine removing most of the bacterial population except for a few hardy individuals who per-haps have a recessive resistant gene. This gene, heretofore not employed and not expressed in the population, now lets the survivors suddenly flourish in an atmosphere that has exterminated their relatives. (This is why the doctor tells you to keep taking an antibiotic even if symptoms improve to kill off those robust few that may then come back with a vengeance.) And this situation can obviously reverse itself over time if another medicine kills the first survivors, but not a small remnant originally susceptible to the first drug.

True Mutations

The key point in this scenario, or one dealing with mosquitoes and insecticides, is that the bacteria maneuver only with the genes already in the gene pool, or genetic combinations normally appearing after conju-gation, and *not* with true mutations. The difference is easy to recognize because when antibiotics or insecticides have left the scene, populations return to normal gene frequencies. Like the fruit flies, no "superman" strains of bacteria have ever been produced unlike anything we have ever seen. Also consider that if these were cases of true and permanent mutations, it would take a second fantastic random mutation to reverse them back to the original—fantastic because random mutations must be completely non-directed as to destinations.

No, what takes place follows the Hardy–Weinberg law, mentioned in every biology book I've ever seen. This *law* (remember chapter 11) states that frequencies of gene alleles in a population remain stable over time, and that *natural selection actually preserves gene combinations rather than creating new ones.* Again, this has been mathematically verified in the finches and the moths that when a short-term selection pressure was removed, populations also reverted to gene percentages in the former steady state.

The term *mutation* has been sparingly used here so as not to give the wrong impression. It is a word often incorrectly applied to situations where nuclear contamination produces deformities, like the joke of the normal family living happily next door to a nuclear reactor...whose dog has grown an extra tail. Deformed flies, snakes with two heads, albino animals, children with Down Syndrome, renegade cancer cells, and so on are not mutations in the way a Darwinist needs them—in two respects. The first is the obvious. These are flawed creatures, not advanced ones to carry life forward. Second, and least often considered, damaged genes are *not* truly new genetic codes. They are nothing more than mistakes within present gene combinations, i.e., both heads on that two-headed snake look like normal snake heads.

Consider a television in optimal operating condition that you give a good stout smash with a hammer. Would you call your resulting busted TV a set of another brand? No, and neither would you have a true mutation in a creature unless something scrambled the codons in DNA and they somehow reorganized into a genetic sequence heretofore unknown.

Beyond this, I more pointedly challenge whether there has ever been, throughout all time, a *documented* "good" mutation. I've heard an analogy like this many times: "A good mutation is like taking your nonworking watch and getting it to tick again with a sharp hit." Does anyone really believe that watch has improved? If you whack your chronically cranky TV and it starts to work again, do you say, "Good as new?" (And while we're at it, will continued whacking turn your black-and-white set into a color model?) With respect to the aforementioned finches, bacteria, mosquitoes, and moths whose populations adapt to changing conditions through gene-pool sorting, neither are these mutations in the evolutionary sense.

Even the groundbreaking work on gene splicing, like adding a gene for ocean bioluminescence to a land bacterium, is just adding one existing gene to an acceptable place on another. If the Darwinists disagree, I challenge any one of them to offer an undeniable example of a mutation that has produced a new and improved species, because all the evolutionary "stalwarts" mentioned so far do not fill the bill. And yet it is the theory on which all of natural evolution hangs. Because of this lack of substantive examples, I challenge geneticists everywhere to reexamine the term *mutation* and redefine its proper use so that the rest of the world will not also jump to those wild Darwinian conclusions.

"Conservation of Information"

William Dembski, in his book *No Free Lunch,* describes a "fourth law of thermodynamics" which limits the creation of any kind of truly new information to an intelligent source. I would further suggest this fourth law—also called the law of conservation of information—also restricts the use of the word *mutation* by establishing a stringent barrier to genetic improvement. Dembski says that because information has intelligence as its origin, the best you can hope for in any random shuffle is to break even (i.e., the hammer blow didn't damage the TV). However, it is far more likely to end up with degraded information. Simply said, random *never* outperforms plain old "blind luck." Nor does it even produce faulty information that is no longer related to its original source.

And in the origins debate, here's what makes the law critical. *I will say with finality that this law disqualifies the multimillions of theoretical mutations supposedly happening in the past, and every present-day genetic example that Darwinists try to pass off as an improvement.* The fourth law can therefore be argued as the permanent barrier between a *variation,* a frequently observed and very normal modification within present genetic constraints, and a *speciation,* a supposed uniquely new genetic life form. In the origins debate, such variations are often called cases of *microevolution.* I see this as an unfortunate term because it wrongly implies even a small genetic advance. And of course speciations, which are often called *macroevolution,* are not only unfortunate but also fraudulent because these have happened only in theory, but never in reality.

Dembski's book titled *No Free Lunch* basically says that whether it's life in general or genetics in specific, you can't get something for nothing. And yet Darwinists say nature took a rodentlike creature at the end of the dinosaur period and on a silver platter handed us 25 mammalian orders in the blink of an eye—mammals that also include some 13 families of whales in the order Cetacea. The next chapter looks at how thin the evidence is for such a far-flung belief.

Chapter 18

Caution—Thin Ice

*How far out some people will
walk on uncertain footing*

It is amazing how thin the ice is under the feet of some natural evolutionists. Let me expand. In my local school district, there are three
high-school biology texts adopted for use. One is for extremely low
readers and goes into very little depth on any concepts, especially those
as technical as the origins material. It is mostly pictures and content
in middle-school level language. By contrast, our regular tenth-grade
biology text is at grade level with respect to vocabulary and depth of
information in lab exercises and such. However, for some reason it has
a rather limited section on origins. It does cover some evolutionary
terminology, but the narratives on the various Darwinian sub-theories
are couched in terms like "maybe," "thought to be," and "research suggests." For those of you who read a lot of research, you know such words
leave the door open to exceptions and do not wave the "red flags" that
elicit challenges.

However, our advanced text for college prep students is closer in
academic strength to a university's freshman biology book. That text has
an entire lengthy unit on evolution. This unit includes several extensive
chapters beginning with Darwin's voyage and going on to more history
of evolutionary theory, geologic timelines, chemical evolution, fossil

formation, natural selection, mutations, and artificial selection through breeding. Another obvious difference is when such concepts above are discussed, the change in wording says there are no other interpretations. An evolutionary point that might have been termed "maybe" is now called "certainly," "thought to be" is replaced by "is," and "research suggests" becomes "research proves."

The strength of this wording intrigued me because one co-author of our CP text has written other general consumer books on evolution, and is well known for vigorously defending Darwinism on all fronts. The slippery footing is found in one of his personal books where he adamantly supports, with very little proof, one of the most impossible cases for random mutational advancement. And then he resorts to ridicule for people who would dare ask for more specifics. The issue? Trying to defend the evolution of advanced mammals, and the argument proceeds this way.

Discrepancies Ahead!

The near across-the-board view of all naturalists is that the Cretaceous Period (late dinosaurs) of the Mesozoic Era (Age of Dinosaurs) closed about 65 mya (million years ago). At this time all dinosaurs were said to suddenly meet their end when the Earth got cold due to a massive meteor strike that covered the globe with dust clouds. This ushered in the Cenozoic Era (Age of Mammals) from 65 mya to present day. The theory adds that primitive mammals were already living among the dinosaurs, but being warm-blooded they were able to survive the short but intense temperature drop. With the dinosaurs gone, mammals (and birds and bony fish) were free to fill the void, assume control of the Earth, and develop into today's many placental species.

So what does evolution say these first mammals looked like? Most biology textbooks depict them as ratlike creatures, surprisingly enough—only about the size of a dime according to the remains of their teeth. Sidestepping size discrepancies like this is a standard maneuver for Darwinists. For example, the extinct *glyptodon* of South America—the "Volkswagen" with a heavy tail—is commonly offered as an ancestor to the Texas armadillo, our strange armored mammal that begs an evolutionary explanation.

Yet strange as it seems, no Darwinist seems to be bothered that the glyptodon was as big as a car while the armadillo approximates a medium-sized dog. Furthermore, the glyptodon and the armadillo were millennia and continents apart with no species found, fossilized or presently alive, going up through Central America to connect them.

Anyway, according to theory, these dime-sized rodents, assumed to evolve from small reptiles over time, quickly blossomed forth into the some 25 other orders of mammals that exist today—from elephants (Proboscidae) to rabbits (Lagomorpha) to solid hoofed grazers (Perissodactyla) to split-toe grazers (Artiodactyla) to felines/canines/ bears/seals, and so on (Carnivora). And let's not forget random's crowning achievement, primates, from which we would someday spring.

As an aside, presumably the more primitive pouched mammals, Marsupialia, "de-evolved" from rodents. What is more amazing, they did it twice on two widely separated continents, into the opossum of North America and the wide marsupial assortment in Australia. I don't know about you, but it seems to me we are once again asking a lot from "luck" in a very short time. It is also true that these primitive rodents would have to give us the bats (Chiroptera). Okay, perhaps not much of an evolutionary problem there because bats sure look like winged mice. (Unless, of course, you admit that ancient bats suddenly appear fully formed in the fossil record about 50 mya, and have not changed since.) But rodents also have to give us whales, and that's the chasm of untraversable width I spoke of that our author defends.

A Whale of a Tale

To make whales from rats, we need massive mutations, and we need them fast. Maybe okay for rats—"quick maturation, fast breeders, large litters, many generations, potential for rapid change." But what happens when it must slow for whales, like the blue whale, the biggest animal ever to live? "blue whales—not mature until age five, one calf every three years, world populations estimated to never be more than the low one hundred thousands." No paleontologist believes herbivorous rodents skyrocketed straight into whales. No, evolutionists say they first developed into larger land animals, like the proffered extinct hyena-like carnivorous "mesonychids." (In one science book, the caption under mesonychids was "Plant-eaters become meat-eaters.")

So did the mesonychids go directly into whales? I guess not, because if you look among today's land mammals for descendants of mesonychids that subsequently became ancestors to whales, the closest DNA match to whales is not hyenas but, amazingly enough, either hippos or cows. It would be hippos if you use nuclear or "junk" DNA as your measure.

However, it would be cows if you compare gene sequences based on mitochondrial DNA. And even though a hippo may seem a bit closer to a whale than a cow, science actually gives the nod to cows because, unlike junk DNA, mitochondrial DNA passes unaltered from female to female in clone-like fashion, not affected by male DNA influence.

If cow-to-whale is how it happened naturally, there are incredible implications. First, the herbivorous rat-types became carnivorous hyena-types, then became herbivorous cow-types, and finally found their way into the oceans to become carnivorous again as the massive sperm whale. Is it possible to bounce back and forth from a herbivorous to a carnivorous body plan that easily, that quickly, and that often—radically changing teeth, legs, digestion, eye placement, size, and many other body features? And if they did, where are the intermediate examples to document such change?

In one of his popular books, the aforementioned author identifies only one extinct fossil intermediate by name to take us from four-legged land animals (mesonychids, hippos, cows, whatever) to whales—the toothed and paddled carnivorous *Ambulocetus natans,* usually drawn to look like a large otter.

He then hints at two other intermediates that remain unnamed. (One is presumably basilosaurus.) And yet with this lack of documentation, he finds the following progression intellectually palatable: A rodent becomes a hyena that becomes a cow that becomes an ambulocetus that becomes a basilosaurus. From there, with perhaps two other possible cousins, basilosaurus becomes 13 families of various whales (toothed whales, baleen whales, pilot whales, and so on) and 22 total cetacean families (add dolphins, narwhals, killer whales, and so on)—all at that slow breeding speed. In a word, *incredible!*

At the same time, this author expresses complete contempt for a creationist book that includes a caricature of a whale with an udder. Now I have seen this picture, and I agree. It looks very, very comical. Therefore I challenge the author who *does* believe that split-toed grazers somehow stair-stepped into so many types of whales to show me a sketch of these unknown intermediates that does *not* look silly. The problem is not with the artist, but with the theory.

An Imaginative Scheme

Let me add a note of caution about the extinct basilosaurus. This huge whale-sized carnivore has recently been made famous by the Discovery Channel's highly imaginative program series called *Walking with Dinosaurs*. Here the basilosaurus is oversold as the forerunner to modern whales, yet downplayed that paleontologists consider it a *reptile*. (Like in tyrannosaurus and stegosaurus, "saurus" is Latin for "lizard.")

Its vertebral column, teeth, and nostrils much more resemble the seagoing dinosaurs called mosasaurus and plesiosaurus, and the small turbinates in the skull show it to be a cold-blooded creature. (I'm guessing this is why the textbook author was cautious enough to specifically not name this animal as a whale precursor in his book.) Furthermore, paleontologists are adamant the basilosaurus was not an intermediate in transition, but an established and permanent species in its own right that has no close ancestors or descendants.

You could say it is only its size—and, of course, the Darwinist's desperation to answer the "cow to whale" dilemma—that cause some to weakly connect it to whales by calling it *Basilosaurus cetoides*. You know how I can tell they are wrong? If basilosaurus had been about a foot long, it would only be a reptilian curiosity of the seas. But this time the discrepancy of size is used to support a wild hypothesis rather than be ignored in the face of one.

Mammalian Complications

Mammalian evolution also presents an immense time problem. When working completely within the Cenozoic Era that science says lasted "only" about 65 million years, the dilemma comes from how long a species remains unchanged to deserve a classification name. In other words, if evolution is the mechanism, how long does a life-form need to have been a stable population so it can be located, identified, and classified before it launched itself forward again? Assuming we didn't keep getting extremely lucky finding handfuls of fleeting "hopeful monsters," taxonomists call for about one to two million years of stability to warrant confirmation that a population was indeed settled and viable before it evolved onward and upward.

Now here is where the cheese binds once more. Paleontologists say split-toed grazers evolved about 50 mya and hippos 40 mya, and we had both before the close of the Eocene Epoch 38 mya. Next, paleontologists say we had at least some of today's whales by the close of the Oligocene Epoch 26 mya. Let us err on the side of caution (that phrase is found with amazing frequency in texts on Design) and go with grazers to give "nature" the maximum allotment of 24 million years (50-26) to make the cow-to-whale changes.

If we allow the average of 1.5 million years of stability before the next grazer mutation (1.5 million years being generally a standard in taxonomy), we have to get herbivorous cow-types deep in the ocean and turn them into carnivorous sperm whales in 16 mutations. (Yikes!) If carnivorous *Ambulocetus natans* was an intermediate, I guess 8 of the 16 mutations would be needed for the transition from non-toothed cow to toothed otter-type, and the other 8 from toothed otter-type to a non-toothed blue whale. (Double yikes!) Which progenitors, which whales, and which 16 total mutations, would our author—the influential molder of hundreds of thousands of students—choose? Talk about thin ice again!

Breaking Through the Ice

Trying to cram a wild theory into a preconceived mind-set can make even the most respected sources look bad. Take the highly venerated

National Geographic, to which I have been a subscriber all my life. I have tremendous respect for the investigative work they do and the awareness they foster for the need of protecting the balance of life on our planet. However, the December 1988 issue tried to document the cow/hippo-to-whale speculation with an interesting flow of pictures—that's right, not fossil samples but artist sketches. If you want comical, check the foldout called "The Land Creatures That Went To Sea" on page 883.

This spread shows how ancient rat-like creatures first became carnivorous mesonychids. Then they diverged into separate groups of split-toed grazers like sheep, deer, bison and hippos, while also becoming both toothed and baleen whales. Look at that, if you can, with "fresh eyes." My feeling is, such a layout shows how programmed some people are to automatically accept Darwinism. I guess they scan it and say, "Well, it's *National Geographic,* so okay by me," and ask no questions.

But I feel a rational person should find it disturbing that the only scientific "evidences" given by the article were comments like "African elephant mating systems are much like that of sperm whales." (Sudden herbivore-to-carnivore shift again? And why an elephant? I thought that genetically we were dealing with cows or hippos.) You can add that every time I show this graphic to high-school students, even the budding Darwinists get a furrowed brow. Personally, I think the National Geographic Society owes the world an apology.

And an apology of sorts, or at least a clarification, was offered 13 years later in *National Geographic*'s November 2001 issue. Cutting right to the chase, the article beginning on page 64 was titled "Evolution of Whales." I strongly suggest reading this article also—again, if at all possible, with a fresh set of eyes. The artist's sketches are still there, as well as the addition of a possible 65 million-year geologic timeline from the Paleocene to the Holocene Epochs.

Along this timeline are placed about a dozen drawings of intermediates between rodents and whales with exotic names like pakicetus, durodon, cetotherium, and odobenocetops, as well as the expected ambulocetus and basilosaurus. Also included are drawings as to how hearing systems transitioned from land to sea forms, how hind legs slowly shrank away to nothing more than vestigial bones under the skin, and how nostrils gradually migrated from snout to top of head. Again, all seems evolutionary bliss—that is, until some legitimate questions are allowed to be asked.

Is Any Rescue Possible?

First, is it fair to make broad assumptions that because some early forms were identified in river valleys, they were already part of, and heading into, an aquatic lifestyle? Then perhaps every rain forest mammal qualifies for the designation used in the article, "whale in progress." Next, is it fair to assume ambulocetus had webbed feet when no traces of such soft tissues ever remain? Then can you automatically assume these creatures stalked their prey in quiet estuaries, sneaking up on them in crocodilian style, which more and more bound them to a life in water until they just stayed? (There's that weird Lamarckian reasoning again. Giraffes got long necks by stretching to reach tree leaves, and ambulocetus got more and more whalelike by hanging around the water.)

Obviously you could go on and on with this "my word against your word" type of debate, but other problems in the article are tied to much more faulty science. For example, why is the *reptile* basilosaurus directly used to connect *mammalian* rodents to *mammalian* whales, this time right in the middle of the timeline at 37 million years ago? Also, how can the fossil locations shift so rapidly, with one specimen found inland at high elevations in the Himalayan foothills and the next in the deserts around Bakersfield, California? I thought gradualism was all about continuity. But if you read the article with objectivity, I'll wager you'll find it severely lacking.

Yet to me the most damning omission in the article, just like its 1988 counterpart, is a lack of presentable fossil evidence. The sketches and the names of these new intermediate creatures come at you rapid-fire, but when you step back and look, only three pieces of fossil evidence are actually shown. A nearly complete ambulocetus is laid out nicely, and it looks as plausible as, say, the stegosaurus, which also magically showed up, stayed a while without changing, and magically disappeared. So then, where are the rest?

And here's something I actually found comical. The article shows an extremely close photo of a flea-sized bone sitting on a fingertip. The tiny bone is offered as "evidence" that land mammal skull bones in the ear area were slowly adapting to water echolocation as in dolphins, but no other concrete fossilized proof is available. (Okay, I guess you could add the photo of the paleontologist sitting in an impressive-looking room full of Cenozoic Era specimens. He is examining a recent dolphin/walrus skull said to be 4 million years old, but it's not a "whale in progress" fossil example touted by the article. If they truly existed, would it be too much to ask him to hold a couple of those?)

And that's why we end up with a whale of a tale. There is nowhere near enough fossil evidence to support the premise, nor is what exists sequential. Now a professor at Northeastern Ohio University disagrees by saying,

> Whales underwent the most dramatic and complete transformation of any mammal. The early stages were so poorly known 15 years ago that creationists held up whales as proof that species couldn't possibly have come about through natural selection. Now whales are one of the better examples of evolution.

But "better" than what? Surely not better than the darling of Darwinian success, the evolution of the horse.

Classic Fiction

The great equine sequence shown in biology books for decades starts with the "dawn horse" of the Eocene Epoch, a four-toed animal looking more like a small dog. This animal marches forward with at least four more intermediates, each one bigger and closer to a solid hoof, to become today's horse. (One Web site provides much more detail, listing around two dozen different horse ancestors.)

The trouble is, Othniel Marsh first constructed the horse sequence back in 1882, when people didn't have a clue about paleontology. It finally had to be discarded late in the twentieth century when so many respected paleontologists, many of whom were Darwinists, kept raising objections. For example, when the venerated Niles Eldredge called the horse sequence "lamentable" and "a classic case of paleontologic

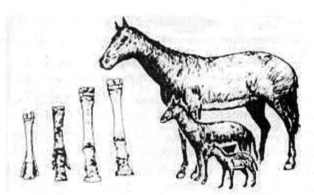

Image courtesy of Fill the Void Ministries.

The "Horse Sequence"

museology," even hardcore Darwinists had to let it go. This is why the horse sequence is actually *disappearing* from today's biology textbooks.

So here's my challenge to whale evolutionists. Assemble all your heralded evidence, and not just pictures or names but details of fossil specimens. Then like Othniel Marsh, sequence as much as you have, and put it on display for all to judge. And when you get the verdict on "one of the better examples of evolution," maybe you will be ready to question the magical development of so many other species, like whales, based on even more spurious evidence. (I am not quite done with horse evolution yet. It will be revisited in the appendix on *The Origin of Species* because Charles Darwin himself gave God the credit for the horse!)

Ignoring What's Inside

How can people with strong scientific backgrounds still believe nature produced whales in laughably short spurts of time? It further amazes me that as they fold, spindle, and mutilate data from the visible world, they totally ignore the resulting implications from the microworld.

For example, in the 2001 *National Geographic* article there is a sequence of three drawings (drawings, of course, not photos of fossils) that move the nostrils at the end of the snout of the ambulocetus to mid-skull on a rodhocetus and then to the top of a gray whale's head as a blowhole. It resembles digging a posthole whose location you don't like, so you fill it in and dig another, and then one more to get it in the right spot. What I mean is, the nostrils move just that easily in the article—assuming all necessary muscle, skeletal, and internal organ alterations incredibly kept pace.

Now what bugs me is that these scientists certainly know what redesigned proteins would be necessary to construct radically new muscle, bone, and lung structures—and how the DNA molecule itself must first be revamped to code for them all—but they ignore the implications.

Consider this specific example. Normal mammalian lungs can extract only about 10 percent of the oxygen that enters our nostrils, while whales can extract upwards of 90 percent. Therefore, whales can average an hour per dive, with the beaked whale staying under for as long as two hours! Try to imagine what *accidental* DNA changes would need to take place to produce such efficient whale lungs from cow lungs. Or take the sperm whale's incredible accordion rib cage that actually allows his lungs to *collapse* at extreme depths that would kill most creatures, only to re-inflate when he surfaces. Can this be accomplished so quickly with only a bit of DNA tinkering in such slow-breeding animals?

> With all these specimens available, you would think the paleontologists could come up with more than a flea-sized ear bone as evolutionary proof, wouldn't you?

And can such "golden" mutations occur time and again to give us 13 different whale families and 70 different whale species virtually overnight? My gripe is, scientists who believe this certainly know the inescapable role of DNA in coding for body parts. So do they simply take it on "faith" that such specified genetic complexity was quickly purchased with no effort? It is as if chapters 8 and 9 of this book, which describe the impossibility of random molecular improvement, have no bearing on paleontology. Darwinists keep trying to pull mythical rabbits out of illusory hats, and it just doesn't work.

One other very powerful argument could be added here. I have a sister who lives in Alaska. (She and her husband own a small island off the coast of Ketchikan. Lucky them!) Our family visits them as often as we can, and we once went on a two-week tour of the greater Anchorage area. Did you know artwork made out of fossilized whalebone is a huge tourist trade up there? Some larger pieces are expensive, but others are more of the "trinket" variety (choice from the basket—$5.00). The point here is that like the stegosaurus, ancient whalebone samples must be available by the ton—literally. Unfortunately for Darwinists, also like the stegosaurus, none of the samples show evidence of intermediary changes. With all these specimens available, you would think the paleontologists could come up with more than a flea-sized ear bone as evolutionary proof, wouldn't you?

———————

To close this section that mostly covered mammalian improvement, remember that I said the Cenozoic Era was also when birds really, shall we say, "took off." Is it reasonable to assume fish jumped to amphibians and then to reptiles before they became birds as well? I once had a science teacher who made it all look very believable, which natural evolution certainly can be to the undisciplined mind. Let's look at the standard pitch for the origin of birds in the next chapter.

Chapter 19

FOR THE BIRDS

What came before chickens or their eggs?

Kingdom Animalia—phylum Chordata. Chordates. Those beautiful animals with spinal cords. With vertebrae to protect the cord that leads to those highly developed brains encased in the cranium, who can argue that they are not the most complex of all animal life-forms on our planet?

When you took secondary-school courses on the living sciences (life science, biology, and so on), you may recall at least one teacher presenting a list of traits showing the sequence of naturally advancing complexity in chordates. Such was my eighth-grade science teacher's approach. She taught her students this "fact of relatedness," and you could tell it made natural evolution a perfectly valid theory in her mind. I again saw a brief list of advancing chordate traits in high-school biology, and once more in great detail in a college class. What's more, I've covered such a list with my own students more times than I can remember.

Chordates—A Darwinist's Delight

The developmental progression of chordates is a Darwinist's delight. Consider the first major type of animal with a backbone, a fish (superclass

Pisces). It is followed nicely in complexity by an amphibian (class Amphibia). If you consider the salamander, he spends half his life as a tadpole (very much like a finned fish), and the other half as a legged adult. A perfect "half-n-half." Next in development comes a reptile (class Reptilia). Consider the lizard. What could be a better "next step up" from a salamander than a faster-moving, better-sensory-equipped lizard? (In my class, my ever-present live salamanders are referred to as "lizards" so often that my classic comeback is, "Why slander a salamander?")

And, of course, smaller reptilian dinosaurs that walk on their two back legs just need feathers to start looking like birds (class Aves), and those that walk on four legs just need fur to start looking like mammals (class Mammalia). All else that is needed is a change mechanism, which we have in mutations, and a driving force, which we have in survival of the fittest, and enough time for change, which we have in half a billion years or so since the Cambrian Explosion. Things are "looking good."

There is even convenient sequential development within chordate types. For example, the simplest fish are the jawless variety like the lamprey (class Agnatha) with only cartilage for skeletons. They are followed by sharks (class Chondricthyes—often called "living fossils"), which have the same cartilage skeleton but an obvious hinged jaw. These are topped by the bony fish (class Osteicthyes), like the trout, which combine a hinged jaw with a hardened skeleton and go on to add more improvements like a swim bladder for buoyancy and an *operculum* to force water over gills so they can remain motionless.

And as a starting point for all this development, you can add the presence of today's living lancelets (subphylum Cephalochordata) that are thought to have been around over 550 million years before any other chordates. Lancelets are blind little wormlike "fish" a couple of inches long with a single tail fin, small mouth tentacles, and segmented muscles more characteristic of worms than fish. Like worms, they spend most of their time buried in the sand, but unlike many worms, they come in separate sexes. However, they draw such evolutionary attention because they also have a rudimentary "nerve cord." This cord is connected to an anterior ganglion (a type of simple brain) with a strip of cartilage running alongside that cord. The presence of that strip seems to say evolution is ready to wrap it around the cord for better protection, and did so in a time long ago to give rise to true fish. So what do we have in naturally advancing complexity? Kingdom—Animalia; phylum—Chordata; class—Pisces (Agnatha, Chondricthyes, Osteicthyes), Amphibia, Reptilia, Aves, and Mammalia.

A Slam Dunk

For believers in natural evolution, all has to be copacetic, for what additional evidence is required after more vague details are supplied, as in the time-honored lists below?

Fish:

1. Scales
2. Two-chambered heart with gills
3. Exclusively water-based
4. Cold-blooded exotherms
5. Largely instinctual; not known for parenting skills
6. External fertilization without physical contact of male and female
7. A soft gelatinous unprotected egg with inner and outer chorion layer

Amphibians:

1. Skin
2. Two-chambered heart with gills in larval (tadpole) stage, and three-chambered heart in adult stage with bellows-like low-capacity lungs augmented by epidermal gas exchange
3. First water-based, then land-based
4. Cold-blooded exotherms
5. Mostly instinctual, with traces of decision-making; occasional, but very infrequent, parental care
6. External fertilization but with physical contact of male and female

7. A soft gelatinous egg with chorion and an additional vitel-line envelope to give protection and provide a fertilization barrier to additional sperm

Reptiles:
1. Scaly skin
2. Three-chambered heart from birth with increased-capacity bellows-like lungs operated by body movement
3. Exclusively land-based
4. Cold-blooded exotherms
5. Instinctual, but show signs of decision-making; frequent parental care of nest and hatchlings
6. Internal fertilization with physical contact of male and female, some instances of courtship
7. A cleidoic (self-contained) egg with chorion, amnion, allantois, and yolk sac surrounded by a leathery protective cover

Call it an evolutionary thing of beauty how the progression above slowly advances. The sequencing also gives meaning to every example of natural selection that drove these chordates forward. For example, fish are dark on top and light on the bottom so as not to be seen by predators from above. This trait would be selected for survival by nature as soon as the random mutation appeared in the fish gene pool, and any fish not dark-colored on top would be immediate candidates for predatory extinction by removal from that same gene pool. The long sticky tongues of frogs to catch insects is another random mutation that would be immediately favored. They could outcompete and replace frogs that had to grab their prey with only their jaws. Many lizards can drop their tails when nabbed, allowing them to escape. What's more, the severed tail will still wriggle a few seconds, distracting the predator and allowing the lizard to escape.

True, there are lizards without detachable wiggly tails, but they survived the competition by compensating with better speed, vision, even poison. The more you look, the longer this list gets until you have produced—without intelligent help, mind you—every trait of every fish, amphibian, and reptile known in classification. Furthermore, it should not be too hard to mutate fish into amphibians over time because the large populations and great diversity of prehistoric fish give them tremendous genetic opportunities for chance beneficial accidents. And the resulting tremendous reptilian/dinosaur diversity that followed offers the same chances for birds and mammals to naturally develop. If you see it this way, seems like the theory of natural evolution is a proverbial slam dunk.

Volumes of Fiction?

Allow me to make a rather abrupt shift. Skeptics of the Hebrew Scriptures (the Old Testament) have long looked for historical inaccuracies, believing all it would take is one bona fide error to dismiss the whole collection. The "knife held to the throat" of the Scriptures' veracity for many years was their detailed accounts of the populous and warlike Assyrian culture. This ancient people mentioned in many biblical books, like 2 Kings, looked to have left no physical evidence, which would seem impossible. Despite its recorded location of Northern Iraq, archaeology initially could find no trace of what surely should be found.

But at the turn of the century, the ancient civilization was identified, including its capital city of Nineveh. Even its last conquering king, Sennacherib, who the Scriptures say met with a horrible supernatural defeat at the hands of an angel at the gates of Jerusalem, is verified in secular history. In fact, this king left independent mention of his crushing defeat at Jerusalem on a statue at the doorway of his throne room. So rather than being a book of fables as so many hope, to this day Hebrew Scriptures remain the most valuable reference document available for archaeologists working in the Middle East.

In contrast, Darwinists continue to hope to find one good biblical contradiction while they write detailed volumes about contradictory evolutionary theory. The difference between their volumes and the Scriptures is, immense numbers of significant pieces of evidence necessary for their position *remain* undiscovered. Compared to the few benign challenges to the Scriptures' archaeology, a myriad of undefused mines lie in the path of Darwinism, and one of the more potent ones is how to produce a bird from a reptile by only natural processes. If you think it's just as easy to transition a reptile into a bird as it was fish-to-amphibian-to-reptile, review the list of reptile traits on page 220 and compare them with the following bird traits:

Birds:

1. Feathers
2. Four-chambered heart from birth with sac-like lungs operated by body movement
3. Land-based, but many with close ties to water environments
4. Warm-blooded endotherms
5. Instinctual, but occasionally intelligent problem-solvers; great parental care often given, with even the training of young
6. Complex courtship and mating procedures, even rare instances of monogamy
7. A cleiodic (self-contained) egg giving oviparous birth, but with a hardened calciferous shell

Let me be clear on one point. In natural evolution, there is no choice but to turn reptiles into birds, for what other class of animals are better candidates? However, try to imagine the incredible numbers of oddball species necessary to bridge the gaps between any lizard and any bird. It takes a most active imagination to conjure even a hypothetical fossil record. For example, describe the anatomy of an intermediate species that transitions from cold- to warm-blooded, which a reptile would have to do en route to becoming a bird. Considering the specificities and complexities of both metabolic systems, any type of "half and half" would be something out of poorly done science fiction. (Yes, some dinosaurs have been hypothesized as warm-blooded based on the enlarged size of their nasal turbinates. However, it is still a case of were they or weren't they, and if they were, how did they become so?) If half-ectotherm/half-endotherm can't even be found in the mind, how can it be found in the "mud"? I will admit there is one decent parallel shared by reptiles and birds, and that is the amniotic egg. However, you first must convert an amphibian egg to a reptile egg, and well-known biologist Michael Denton says that there is not even a suitable *imaginary* intermediate between the chorionic amphibian egg and the amniotic reptile/bird egg. And the problems are only beginning to mount.

Saved by the Archaeopteryx

Sometimes I wonder if those who believe in Design avoid the bird issue because of just one dramatic fossil. Natural evolution does offer the archaeopteryx, and indeed offers it at every turn. *Archaeopteryx* is Latin for "ancient wing," and without this extinct standard bearer, it is hard to imagine what organism would "carry the colors" for Darwinism. The archaeopteryx is chicken-sized and chicken-shaped, and is the famed half-reptile/half-bird fossil of the Jurassic Period.

The most detailed specimen is part of an impressive display at London's Natural History Museum. Its most recognizable reptilian features include a toothed jaw, claws at the end of the toes, a long tail with vertebrae, and a pelvic structure generally patterned after the upright walking coelursaurian dinosaurs like the deinonychus. Also unlike birds, it has no deep keel-shaped breastbone, abdominal ribs, or foot bones that are not fused. In contrast, archaeopteryx's most recognizable internal avian features include a "somewhat" developed keeled breastbone (perhaps a glider rather than a true flyer?), a bird-shaped wishbone, a "back-facing" big toe on the hind feet typical of birds who grasp limbs for perching, and a pelvis too bird-like to be completely reptilian. Oh yes, and the only feature that really matters? *Feathered imprints* around the skeleton.

Obviously, these comparative traits are intriguing, and for some people, this single fossil is all that's needed to put flesh, bone, and sinew on the entirety of evolutionary theory. But does this example hold up under scrutiny? Assess the following.

Only about six specimens of archaeopteryx exist, and all come from the same general time period, the 160 million-year-old Jurassic stratum in Solnhofen, Bavaria, Germany—an area about the size of your average county in your average state. For an intermediate that is supposed to give us all birds, it had an amazingly limited range and therefore a small population at best. And if the Western European archaeopteryx has to give us all birds on all seven continents, geologists unfortunately agree that the supercontinent Pangaea had already broken up before the Jurassic Period, which certainly predates bird development.

Also, if these creatures evolved from something and then into something, shouldn't each of the six examples assumed to span perhaps 3 million years of time show evidence of some alteration? Unfortunately, like the coelacanth and basilosaurus mentioned in the previous chapter, the archaeopteryx has that never-ending evolutionary vexation of "suddenly here, no change, and suddenly gone." The only way gradual change can have happened but be undetectable is if all six lived and died at precisely the same time, and their remains were miraculously preserved in one spot while all the variations of their relatives around the world were lost. Unfortunately, that explanation backs you up against those extreme and inexplicable genetic probabilities once again. Suddenly, the archaeopteryx looks less promising as a prime example for answering one of life's big questions.

More Explorations Needed

And the deeper you dig, the more the ground for establishing a foundation for bird evolution becomes quicksand. If the archaeopteryx did manage to give us chickens and other fowl in the order Galliformes, what about the other 23 bird orders that inhabit our world, taking us from eagles to albatrosses, herons to woodpeckers, swans to penguins, and condors to kiwis? And the big flightless birds must be explained as well. What caused ostriches to lose the tremendous advantage of flight and revert to wings not functional?

The only other option is that the ostrich's wings are "on the way in" and someday he will fly. Weird! Again, where are go-betweens in the fossil record for any of this, and what intermediates could even be possible? For example, what type of alterations would nature have to make in any existing bird species to produce the physiology of those magicians of flight, the order Apodiformes, or hummingbirds?

If an imaginative evolutionary artist were to start with the next closest bird, such as a diminutive sparrow (order Passeriformes—perching birds), and was given free rein to restructure the sparrow into any species of hummingbird, what could the sketches possibly resemble?

To accept that the archaeopteryx transitioned into such birds without connecting fossil evidence is analogous to believing the hot air balloon directly gave rise to all forms of bicycles. Then, if anyone challenges the reasoning behind the balloon-to-bicycle theory, the indignant response would be something like, "Hey, they're both forms of transportation with a basket."

Actually, the entire bird issue may soon need revising anyway. This is because many paleontologists also accept as legitimate the mixed reptilian/avian fossil called protoavis, found in Texas. The dilemma is that protoavis appears more birdlike than archaeopteryx, though it predates the more celebrated "missing link" by about 30 million years. Many Darwinists are quick to refute the find, perhaps out of necessity, saying that no skeletons of protoavis have been found where the bones are as nicely attached as the London archaeopteryx.

There's irony in this. Many evolutionary paleontologists are notorious for reconstructing an entire skeleton from a single bone or bone fragment, and then providing an artist's representation of the completed hypothetical animal living in a supposed suitable habitat with others of its clan. (The television series *Walking with Dinosaurs* that was mentioned earlier has mastered this form of imagination.) Yet as to the protoavis, Darwinists say it should be rejected because the bones were not found attached, only scattered around in the same location. I call this a classic case of speaking from both sides of the same mouth.

Whence Mammals?

Before leaving the birds, the final step in complexity, class Mammalia, deserves mention. After all, mammals need a mechanism or a theory for how they arose from reptiles as well because it would be ridiculous to say our ratlike creatures evolved from birds. Listing mammalian traits as done above results in the following:

Mammals:
1. Fur
2. Four-chambered heart with bellows-like lungs operated by a diaphragm muscle

3. Mostly land-based, but one of the most advanced orders, the Cetaceans or marine mammals, found their way back into the water

4. Warm-blooded endotherms

5. Instinctual, but intelligence and problem-solving are common, and reasoning can even override instinct; excellent parenting, often protecting offspring until they can live independently

6. Complex courting procedures and mating rituals; often monogamous during parenting; fighting for territory, dominance, and status within a population

7. A viviparous live birth, usually with a placenta

From this list, one would have to say that mammals share far more traits with birds than with reptiles, and yet no serious origins scheme has ever had mammals evolving from birds. Therefore, converting reptiles into mammals looks to be a bigger hurdle than converting reptiles into birds. But because of the "ancient winged one"—the archaeopteryx—Darwinists remain convinced of the mechanism, view the theory as secure, and go on to imagine mammals just "happened" by the same process producing birds.

Speaking of imagination, what if the duck-billed platypus was known only through fossils and not through live specimens? In other words, just imagine giving a starving Darwinist a *fossil* example of a milk-producing egg-layer. Without the constraints of reality imposed by the platypus's actual existence, I can guarantee the "ancient furred one" would supplant archaeopteryx as the definitive example of Darwinism in action. If not that, perhaps fossilized platypuses might be used to redraw a major branch of "Darwin's Tree." When unfettered imaginations are put into play, it's hard to tell the outcome.

Mincing and Mixing

For people who are determined to exclude Design from the origins game, there is one haven of potential safety—*cladistics* and the generation of *cladograms*. Cladograms are like single branches of Darwinian trees that follow the increasing complexity of a single trait or handful of related traits, but are not encumbered by the messy need to attach the rest of the organism to the tree. As an example, imagine a tree branch following, say, the development of a bird's ability to fly. I suppose we could start with the dodo, the flightless bird that went extinct around 1680. Then could come today's flightless birds, like the Australian emu whose wing-to-body proportions aren't quite as ridiculous, followed perhaps by the pheasant, a poor flyer that seldom goes more than 100 yards. Then go with the duck, a fair distance flyer that still hops from pond to pond, followed by the Canada goose, a longer traveler, and end with the arctic tern, the champion "frequent flyer" that migrates from the Arctic to the Antarctic. Call it nice progression of development in true evolutionary style that starts with a pathetic non-flyer and gradually reaches an aerial ace.

Most of the cladograms done by Darwinists are more sneaky. Yet the problems with the most cleverly devised cladograms are the same—other features must be ignored that don't follow in lockstep order. Take the bird cladogram above. How would you also chart the walking speed of each of these birds that starts with slow (the dodo) and goes to extremely fast (the emu) to extremely slow (all the water birds)? If you try, any sequencing is immediately lost. Or how about intelligence in this six-bird sequence, which goes from dumb to cagey back to dumb

> When Darwinists play the game of cladogram, they deal from both the top and bottom of the deck.

to smart to extremely smart to average? And how would you make body shapes sequential without changing the order in speed of flying? (Also, Darwinists say dodos and emus lost wings they once had, so I guess you would need fossil evidence going in the reverse—where something like a tern eventually became a dodo.)

As you can see, the illusion of continuity is quickly lost if you try to simultaneously sequence more than a trait or two at a time. By selective inclusion or exclusion, Darwinists sure can make square pegs look remarkably round. And if a trait, or an entire organism like protoavis, appears much earlier or disappears much later than your cladogram suggests, then you simply restructure the *clade*. If that doesn't work, choose different traits for your clade, or maybe leave a large gap and assume that additional fossil discoveries will eventually augment what you believe is missing.

Obviously, the key ingredient here, once again, is a vivid imagination. Cladograms are especially useful for misrepresenting birds because you can successfully mark the development of traits like toe numbers (two to three to four), the size of the eye orbits, or the wingspan, and so on, while ignoring other static or "de-evolving" features like regressing maneuverability or parenting skills. But in reality, if an animal marches through time with an increasing breast keelbone, don't you think it must drag the rest of its body along?

To be completely honest, the sequence of characteristics given earlier for fish, amphibians, reptiles, birds, and mammals were themselves cladistic in nature, ignoring a trove of inconsistencies. To give a few examples, certain fish like the bettas have elaborate courtship procedures, detailed nest-building activities, and excellent parenting that exceeds certain birds. In contrast, certain birds like the mourning dove seem completely oblivious to good nest construction and danger to its young. Why does the avian eagle have vision with tremendous acuity, while the mammalian rhinoceros can barely see? What allowed the reptilian crocodile, a living fossil in its own right, to fight with extreme aggression to protect a nest, while a mammalian rabbit will run from its babies in the warren like, well, a scared rabbit?

Obviously, examples of this type have no end, and if you review the five lists of fish, amphibian, reptile, bird, and mammal traits, I'm sure you will come up with your own set of surges, retreats, and reloopings that were ignored to build the original case. However, when Darwinists play the game of cladogram, they deal from both the top and bottom of the deck. They will defend certain anomalies such as the above, calling them expected in a random process, but will reject other anomalies, and especially absentees in the fossil record, calling them, amazingly enough, insignificant.

Assigning Credit

Cladistics, hypotheses, imaginations, and personal biases aside, is it fair to think that the archaeopteryx is a "one size fits all" example that proves the entire evolutionary process? Okay, maybe in the name of fairness we should spot Darwinists the archaeopteryx as an animal you could call a half-and-half species. But for Darwinists to be fair, they have to concede that the list of missing links compared to "found links" is so horribly skewed as to be laughable, and that trying to imagine some intermediates, much less find them, is a totally impossible task.

And what of the argument that natural selection will only produce beneficial traits while eliminating harmful ones? (I'm still trying to convince my wife that my superior channel-surfing skills with our TV remote are due to our prehistoric past. You know, while her hairy female forerunners had to concentrate on keeping the all-important cave fire burning, my male counterparts had to constantly scan the horizon for potential food or danger.) Try applying the "survival of the fittest" reasoning to singing birds. You could construct quite a large clade of birds that sit and sing for no reason that would otherwise be impossible to sequence. Yet there they are, chirping their heads off, wasting time and expending valuable energy while drawing the attention of predators to themselves, even their nests.

It makes no sense—in natural terms, anyway. I suggest doing this. Watch one singing bird for a few minutes with solitary attention, and then try again to explain how such a "ridiculous" activity became highlighted in the gene pool instead of leading to the extinction of that songbird's species. Since there is no scientific reason for birds to randomly sing, and every reason for them not to, I will give credit for beautiful birdsongs, as well as my capacity to enjoy them, to their Designer.

For all its talk of gradualism and cladistics, natural evolution also has to ignore that the fossil record shows new organs and organ systems arriving complete in some species with all necessary modifications. For example, when the first hummingbird showed up, well, it was just there, right down to the heart rate of hundreds of beats per minute to rotational wings that allow it to fly backward. And yet when pressed, Darwinists sometimes try to explain how chance could make individual organs slowly improve over time. Let's apply their reasoning to what has to be the most complex organ of them all—the eye.

Chapter 20

THE BEAUTY IN THE EYE
OF THE BEHOLDER

*Can the world's most complex organ
have a natural explanation?*

Imagine yourself commissioning two different artists, each one to paint a unique canvas with the theme entirely of their own choosing—no restrictions. First, you make sure that your randomly chosen painters have never met, in fact have no knowledge of each other, their assigned tasks, or their respective art styles. Then, tell each that you will provide them with any required supplies, and that they are completely without time constraints, as long as you get regular updates on progress.

Eventually, you get your two commissioned pictures, but the sequence of events leading to the completion of each was remarkably different. One artist's progress was incredibly rapid. Almost overnight he was able to complete several different products, and while most were unimpressive and with minimal value, you recognized one as a masterpiece and an absolute act of genius. In fact, it was proudly hanging on your wall for all to see, so soon that it almost defied belief.

In stark contrast, the other artist's progress was agonizingly slow, spanning months that stretched into years. Forthcoming drafts were laborious and sporadic, sometimes marked by long periods of stagnation. Some attempts were even disappointing regressions in quality from earlier works. To be sure, there were occasional drafts showing a glimmer of promise, but they also seemed to have a dead-end aspect that could not be improved even with drastic modifications. Finally, when it seemed the second half of the project was doomed, the artist said there was a stylistic breakthrough. He claimed to have produced a design that had all those illusive intangibles, and after a few more modifications, he delivered the second picture at long last.

You decided not to look at the second portrait, and just hang it covered next to the first masterpiece until a gathering of your closest associates could be assembled for the unveiling. When the shroud was pulled away from the second, all in attendance, most notably you, were dumbfounded when the two pictures were almost identical! And while you were absolutely sure collusion between the artists was impossible, that very fact would be impossible to sell to your friends.

A person who would have been very interested in this analogy was the late Stephen Jay Gould, the late twentieth-century paleontologist deserving the highest respect. His work in the field tended to follow the children's tale I've mentioned before: "The Emperor's New Clothes." Though he had great respect for the emperor of natural evolution, he had the courage to tell all that his highness was in fact naked. To explain, Gould did not hesitate to say that fossil intermediates necessary for gradual neo-Darwinian evolution were just not there, and that different and credible explanations for self-made life had to be found. He also pointed out many of the assumptions casually pitched by Darwinists that needed to be corrected, such as evolving life somehow knowing where it was going.

As a shining example, Gould's overall theme for his book *Wonderful Life* is mirrored in the absurd outcome of my story of the two artists. Consider his following quote from that book.

> The various pathways evolution took were completely unpredictable, having no end results in mind. If the entire process were to be restarted, the forms of life produced would no doubt be markedly different, and the more com-

plicated the feature, the less likely it would be to appear a second time.

Gould's argument is powerful. Without preset goals, "recapitulations" of ultracomplex structures, such as eyes, would be ultra-fantastic occurrences. In other words, how could genetic destinations in the future ever govern random mutations in the present that would have to be built on mutations from the past?

Let's go back to the two pictures by the two artists. In evolutionary history, the first one rapidly completed is the eye of an octopus, and second by the lengthy process is the eye of a human—two creatures on vastly separate branches of the supposed evolutionary tree. As comparative anatomical drawings reveal, the spheroid of both eyes have an outer cornea, lens, and iris, and an inner three-sectioned retina separated by liquid vitreous humor. The retina is packed with pigment rods to regulate light intensity (cones added in humans for true color differentiation), and interacting neurons that sharpen boundaries between shades. Lastly, but certainly not finally, both optic nerves leave the back of the retina and connect to a brain with an *amazing* intelligence level to interpret the signals.*

Of course, the "frame" the first artist put around the picture of the octopus eye is certainly not as ornate as the one given to the human eye. After all, the octopus is a member of the invertebrate phylum Mollusca, and apart from the incredible nervous system, its body is vastly much more like a clam, an oyster, or a snail than a human. Yet evolutionary theory says the incredible octopus eye appeared along with the very first forms of multicellular life, that is, ancient cephalopods thought to be from over 500 million years ago.

By contrast, evolution says the human eye appeared a few ticks before the clock strikes midnight, after millions and millions of years of ocular development—development that started with light sensitive

---

* Back in my ninth-grade biology class, I can clearly remember viewing an old filmstrip sequence of a small octopus in an aquarium with a smaller corked glass jar containing a live shrimp. The series of frames showed the octopus circling the jar inspecting his intended lunch. Finally, the octopus climbed on top of the jar, and with his tentacles he slowly loosened and removed the cork. Then he squeezed himself through the jar's small opening, dined, and curled up for a well-deserved nap. I would call that intelligence!

chemicals in single-celled creatures and then went through regressions, novelties, and dead ends, until finally the mammalian breakthrough. Call it two wandering blind and deaf travelers—one on a very short journey and the other on a very long one—arriving unassisted at the same destination.

Would Darwin Reconsider?

More than once I have considered the wonder of sight. Imagine, if you will, the blessing of being able to see our world so we may fully comprehend it. Charles Darwin acknowledged the miracle of the eyes in his book *The Origin of Species* in a section titled "Organs of Extreme Perfection and Complication." Here are his own words:

> To suppose that the eye, with all its inimitable contrivances for adjusting the focus to different distances, for admiring different amounts of light, and the correction for spherical and chromatic aberration, could have been formed by natural selection, seems, I freely confess, absurd in the highest possible degree.

Re-read that again for effect. Those who reject natural evolution have often raised this quote as a way to show Darwin's own doubt in the theory that would some day bear his name. However, to be fair Darwin's very next sentence shows the basic reasoning for all those who place their faith in the power of randomness.

> Yet reason tells me, that if numerous gradations from a perfect and complex eye to one very imperfect and simple, each grade being useful to its possessor, can be shown to exist...then the difficulty of believing that a perfect and complex eye could be formed by natural selection...can hardly be considered real.

But let's remember that Darwin's words were first published in 1859. I wonder what his opinion would be if he could have read the following passage in *Darwin's Black Box* by biochemist Michael Behe published in

1996. Here Behe describes the biochemical sequence of what happens on the retina to allow vision.

> When light first strikes the retina a photon interacts with a molecule called 11-cis-retinal, which rearranges within picoseconds to trans-retinal. (A picosecond is about the time it takes light to travel the breadth of a single human hair.) The change in the shape of the retinal molecule forces a change in the shape of the protein rhodopsin, to which the retina is tightly bound. The protein's metamorphosis alters its behavior. Now called metarhodopsin II, the protein sticks to another protein, called transducin. Before bumping into metarhodopsin II, transducin had tightly bound a small molecule called GDP. But when the transducin interacts with metarhodopsin II, the GDP falls off, and the molecule called GTP binds to transducin. (GTP is closely related to, but critically different from, GDP.)

This section in Behe's book continues through four more similar paragraphs before the retinal process is complete and all chemicals are recycled and ready for reuse. A count of all five paragraphs reveals that the exact sequencing of *16* different and highly specific proteins and enzymes is required (as well as the presence of two minerals) if the process of vision has a chance to succeed. (Which chemical could you omit, and which order would you change, in the "nothing works until everything works" point of view?) And, of course, this is just the process on the retinal surface. What other majesties must take place in front and behind the retina before your brain beholds the face of a friend or your beautiful son or daughter?

Now think. If Behe's process were available in 1859 for Darwin to examine, I imagine this man of obvious intelligence could fully grasp the complexity at work, and I'm betting he would have stuck with that phrase in that first quote—"absurd in the highest possible degree." Then if Darwin could have known the octopus performed much the same miraculous vision process 500 million years earlier, almost as soon as science says multicellular life appeared in the seas, I truly believe he would have junked the whole natural selection idea.

Backward Perfection

As a closing point in this chapter, consider the comments President George W. Bush made in August 2005. In a press conference he said that alternatives to natural evolution, such as "Intelligent Design," have a place in public-school science classes, where students should be exposed to more than one narrow system of thought. Obviously his comments created quite a firestorm. Now, remember that professor mentioned in chapter 7 who said you could never calculate the odds of making an eye? As a fitting answer to President Bush's comments, he also said that it was a naïve impression to believe it took a designer to make something even as complex as the human eye. After all, he observed, some quirk of nature allowed our retinas to be installed backwards, on the behind side of where light actually strikes the back of the eye.

You know, I have heard this "backward retina" business a few times, and though my eyes seem to work well enough, I have always wondered what it meant. So I called my friend Dale, who is an MD and an eye surgeon. Though he had no immediate response on the phone, a couple of days later he had it figured out. You see, he said even though our retinas are paper-thin, they are made of ten layers of cells. The cells that pick up the light waves, the cones and rods, actually *are* at the back of the retina, and light must pass through the first nine nuclear layers before it strikes these photosensitive cells. Surely this must reduce our visual acuity, like a film over a glass window, right?

Hear the rest of Dale's explanation. The cones and rods are the most active part of the retina by far, and require a great amount of circulated blood nourishment via many small capillaries. If this blood had to come in from the front of the retina to supply the cones and rods, Dale said it seems we would be trying to stare through our own capillaries, and our vision would be clouded by a film of red! Instead, the blood comes from *Bruch's membrane,* which is behind the cones and rods where there is no interference. Furthermore, this membrane is coated with a pigmented epithelium, a dark layer, which helps absorb the light rays from the back.

Are the other nine layers still a hindrance? Not at all, Dale explained, because they are not *medulated* (coated) with any fluids, so they are completely transparent. He went on to say this ingenious setup is part of other perfections, like the right 5-to-1 ratio of cones and rods to nerve cells, and the optic nerve connection on the retina at a perfect 12 degrees on the visual axis so we encounter no "blind spots." No, the "backward retina" is the only way it *can* work, and this came from a doctor who had no stake in this issue but to tell the truth. All I could answer was, "Cool!"

It is worth noting here that the professor making the "backward retina" comment was not an eye surgeon or even a mathematician. His degree was in psychology. Now Dale the MD would never pretend to be an expert at psychology. Yet what makes a psychology professor feel he's qualified to speak as if he's an eye surgeon? I'd say this is a perfect example of a closed mind-set, which I wrote about in chapter 3. It shows how someone can cling to a preconceived belief and not even make a simple objective investigation of facts I found readily at hand.

And in my experiences with evolution, this happens constantly. Just as a practicing psychologist is now an eye surgeon, an accomplished mathematician is also suddenly an expert molecular biologist. Then a molecular biologist becomes a licensed physicist, a physicist becomes a certified paleontologist, and a paleontologist (removing bones) becomes a professional orthopedist and orthodontist (reconstructing bones). (I also love it when someone with no formal scientific training at all becomes an expert at all the above.) It just shows the desperation Darwinists are feeling now that the sand is slipping through the hourglass.

Though the human eye and the octopus eye are miraculously similar in their specified complexity, they have to be considered *analogous,* meaning they came from two different sources. (*Homologous* would mean they were somehow related, but that's impossible due to the time frame and the other huge list of human/octopus differences.) This comparison is often followed by mention of another set of irreducible features that also must be analogous—wings. Flight is an incredibly technical and delicately balanced accomplishment. And yet as I observed earlier, we have flying insects, birds, and mammals—even reptiles (pter-anodons)—even fish! But according to Darwinism, the development of all necessary wing, lung (gill), bone, and muscle structures required for flight has to be unrelated and therefore analogous, as then are the myriad of necessary proteins and enzymes to produce these parts.

After two different artists both developed an "eye" in evolutionary history, a process Gould ironically saw as "blind," could five more artists also independently draw wings? Or does it make more sense to believe an Artist of unimaginable craft and power foresaw the end results of all these long before He made them? In my opinion, Gould was absolutely right. Evolution needs a more credible explanation.

And yet nature does provide many other duplications and parallels. Are Darwinists able to account for these? The next chapter examines their arguments.

Chapter 21

HOMOLOGIES VERSUS ANALOGIES

*Are similarities between species caused
by genetics, environment, or...?*

Here is an important question that becomes an irritating rash on the thin skin of natural evolution. It goes like this. Are scales on a snake from the same genetic origin as scales on a fish, or did similar features from dissimilar genetic paths both select scales for their obvious protective advantage? In other words, are likenesses in nature produced by reused DNA patterns—a "homology"—or new DNA patterns produced by environmental selection pressures—an analogy? Darwinists try to play it both ways, and both ways fail.

A Textbook Case

I covered homologies and analogies so many times in my biology classes that I could almost arrive at the correct pages by letting the textbook fall open. In the first section, the left side of the page showed the comparative chordate bone structures and pentadactyl (five-fingered) arrangement in the front limb of a frog, a lizard, a bird, a human, a cow, a whale, and a bat.

Homology

On the right side of the facing page (ostensibly to present the most convincing evidence last) were the comparative chordate embryos of a fish, a salamander, a turtle, a chicken, a pig, a cow, a rabbit, and a human. The section was titled "Homologous Structures," and the over-riding message was that since both picture sequences showed remarkable similarities (which of course they did), these had to be evidence of "common ancestry" (that is, "natural evolution had taken place").

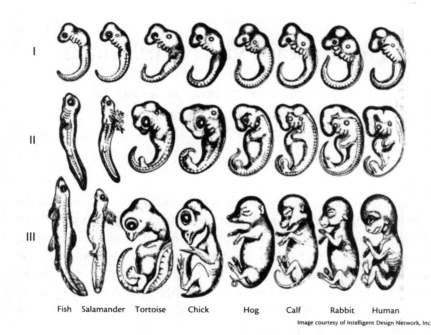

| Fish | Salamander | Tortoise | Chick | Hog | Calf | Rabbit | Human |

Image courtesy of Intelligent Design Network, Inc.

The textbook's term for common ancestry such as this was "divergent evolution." This means that some ancient ancestor, most likely now extinct, first exhibited the basic forelimb plan of upper arm (humerus), lower arm (tibia and fibula), wrist (carpals), fingers (metacarpals) and fingertips (phalanges). Then, all the limbs pictured on the page were simply "diverged" improvements produced over time from the original via mutation and natural selection. ("See?" they would say. "Even the bat wing had four fingers, and a tiny thumb top center.")

In the case of embryonic chordate development, the plan for the unborn began in fish because they were first backboned animals to appear in geologic time, but then this plan was later extended to all future chordates. The inference in the text is that at one point, the tail, pharyngeal slits, and eyespots made even human embryos look like little bug-eyed "minnows" a few weeks after conception. ("See?" they would say. "Humans used to have a little tail too!") Then only later do we diverge into the fetuses and then the newborns that evolution made us.

Ernst Haeckel, who first made public the comparisons of the unborn in the 1860s elaborated the concept in his well-known biogenetic law that states "Ontogeny recapitulates phylogeny" (embryological development retraces evolutionary development). In other words, the changes undergone by one chordate from zygote to live birth are a reflection of general evolutionary patterns of advancing chordate complexity over millions of years. All looks rather convincing, yet there's more.

Analogy

After thorough coverage of homologous structures, the biology textbook in short order presented a second natural pathway for how organisms could develop an unmistakable resemblance: *analogous structures*. Once again, using the "a picture is worth 1000 words" approach, there was an atlantic salmon and a blue whale side by side. Though obviously not exactly duplicates, both had streamlined bodies with a pointed snout to allow minimum resistance and therefore swift passage through the sea. And though fins and flippers were placed in different locations and at different angles, both were obviously necessary to propel them through their watery world. Here the term for the process was not divergent but "convergent evolution," meaning these body features came from different genetic origins. And yet due to the need to swim, and swim well, salmon and whales took on much the same look as they evolved over time.

Making the Distinction

To better understand this game of look-alike, here is a clear distinction between divergent and convergent evolution. The *divergent* process is based on genetic patterns that nature reuses, occasionally several times over, because of their potential for success in the competitive world of "who eats and who gets eaten." Science has even identified what it calls basic genetic patterns for certain body structures, like limbs and eyes, that are passed on up the evolutionary tree as a quick "recipe" to which only modifications need to be made. Called *hox genes,* these recurring DNA patterns are thought to be responsible for organs like eyes and ears that appear and reappear all up and down the scale of complexity. You could say transferred hox genes mean species are rather "predestined" to bear a resemblance.

By comparison, the *convergent* process says the environment puts selection pressure on all species to adapt to conditions. Therefore, as random mutations throw out all sorts of variations through accidental births, the "good accidents" that give a competitive edge allows an organism to outcompete. Then he or she will eventually sire or raise young with these advanced traits while the others die out. And since comparative organisms are adapting to the same conditions, as in the case of swimming through ocean water, again you could say they are "predestined" to look alike. In either situation, Charles Darwin would likely approve, in that both convergent and divergent explanations ulti-mately rely on his favorite phrase for how all species were produced, "descent by modification."

With explanations like these, who can argue that to many, natural evolution is "love at first sight"? But what happens when you take a second look and the problems bubble to the surface? For example, the mammalian ear is quite a feat of engineering. The combination of tympanum or eardrum, cochlea, auditory nerve, Eustachian tube, and semi-circular canals are rather far removed in similarity from any other organ set in any other class of animals. Furthermore, none of the above structures would have any use without three bones, the smallest in all the body, that occupy the middle ear—the malleus, incus, and stapes (hammer, anvil, and stirrup, respectively).

So how does science say such an apparatus evolved on so many mammals, not once but on both sides of the head? Evolutionists offer an answer from homology—that our ears are modified lizard ears—but see if it doesn't stretch the credibility of the homologous process way beyond the breaking point.

At the very back of the reptilian skull are two bones, the *quadrate* and the *articular.* Their sole purpose? To fit the jaw together. They provide for hinged mandibular movement, like chewing, not exactly a feature analogous to hearing. And yet because these two bones are located close to the reptile's own single malleus ear bone, natural evolutionists currently believe the quadrate and articular were significantly reduced in size, drastically reshaped, and then remarkably relocated from the back of the reptile skull to both sides of the mammalian ear to become the incus and stapes. Then both sets of bones somehow joined forces with the aforementioned inner and outer ear parts—parts apparently waiting patiently for their arrival—and the completed system was finally able fill our brains with enticing auditory signals.

So how does science say this magnificent transformation of delicate bones occurred? Apparently not through divergent homologies like hox genes because the two designs are way too dissimilar to call it an information transference. So it must have been a lucky break in DNA reorganization, a *massive* rewrite of DNA codes that caused the two pieces of a reptile's jawbone to reduce, reshape, and relocate—jaw movement now being analogous to hearing. Talk about between a "rock and a hard place"!

Of course there is that other constantly nagging problem. Either the homologous or the analogous approach should have left us examples of some fossilized or present-day intermediate creatures with ears under such reconstruction. But you can be sure they are unavailable. If they were, I dare say pictures of these transitional ear designs would grace the pages of the biology textbooks right after forelimbs, embryos, fish, and whales.

But What About...

There is a veritable mountain of similar physiological examples whose explanations must suffer through the same reasoning above. And the problems still aren't through. For a confirmed Darwinist, it must be difficult to run into hypotheses built on hypotheses at every turn—these "what about" dilemmas found everywhere in this book.

The Rhea and the Emu

For example, nearly all of science believes in the breakup of the supercontinent Pangaea, but "what about" the headaches this theory poses for the Darwinists? The eastern coastline of North and South America was thought to have drifted over millions of years from the western coastline of Europe and Africa, and if you could put the geologic VCR on rewind, they would rejoin. Other features say if you could nudge the Arabian Peninsula a bit to the left, you could re-close the Red Sea, and if you could spin Australia upside down, you could refit the gap on Australia's under side to the bottom point on India. As to a time frame, geologists agree this breakup began about 200 million years ago.

Well then, "what about" the rhea of South America and the emu of Australia?

These birds are so close in appearance that unless you were an expert, it would be hard to match them with the proper continent. If these two species graced the same continent, no biologist would ever dream of doubting that divergence through homologies produced two variations of the same bird. Yet their amazing similarities *must* be considered converging analogies because the two birds are oceans apart on continents science says separated (continental drift, and Pangaea) long before birds evolved.

I would compare these two birds to finding an identical sport played by both an Australian Aborigine tribe and an Amazon rain forest tribe using the same-shaped ball and the same rules. If two such sports were found, you would have to just scratch your head and call it a *Twilight Zone* coincidence because of the distance in space and time.

The Tasmanian Wolf

Then "what about" the now extinct Tasmanian wolf? These predators indigenous to Australia once ranged across much of the continent, but were killed off by settlers until only a remnant population existed on the island of Tasmania. Here the last one died in a Hobart, Tasmania, zoo in 1936. Despite the yellow tint and the obvious stripes that caused some to call it the Tasmanian "tiger," the animal was very much wolflike, with a skull design nearly interchangeable with that of the timber wolf only found halfway around the world. What is odder, the Tasmanian wolf also somehow "became" a marsupial just as many other homologous Australian mammals. It had premature babies that it carried in a pouch between the back legs just below the anus. (No kidding—look out below!)

So what possible explanation can the Darwinist give for the natural origin of the Tasmanian wolf? Once again, continental distances dictate that the skull similarities between the Tasmanian variety and the timber variety have to be analogous, meaning these two wolves developed from entirely different ancestral lines. What a stroke of luck to end up looking the same! However, the marsupial pouch in the rear would certainly be homologous to that of a kangaroo—if the kangaroo just had the decency to walk on all fours and be a predator. Analogous heads and homologous rears? I'd say those explanations fail at both ends.

So if you rule out the kangaroo as an ancestor, where did this one wolf come from, a single species of wolf on an insolated continent? (Unfortunately for the Darwinists, we know too much about these animals to engage in wild speculation. Going into the 1900s, the Tasmanian government still found enough wolves to trade as zoo specimens with other countries.) The obvious evolutionary answer has to be from other Australian canines, of course—except there are no other indigenous Australian dogs. And be careful here to say "what about" the Australian dingo dog? The dingo is an import, thought to be introduced to the continent by the first Asian visitors about 3500 years ago.

Even the dingo is shrouded in mystery. Traditionally the dingoes have been linked to the feral dogs of India and Southeast Asia because of similar appearances, but a mitochondrial DNA study by Swedish molecular biologist Peter Savolainen shows the dingoes are more closely related to the dogs from northeast Asia that range as far north as the Arctic Circle. Nope, the Tasmanian marsupial wolf is out there all alone, so alone that a researcher from the University of Michigan called it "a stunning example of convergent evolution." "Stunning?" That's all? To call an animal with no imaginable explanation for its origin "stunning" is like saying the *Titanic* encountered a "slight difficulty" on its maiden voyage.

Australian Marsupials

Speaking of marsupials, "what about" Australia's wide assortment—not only kangaroos but also wallabies, wombats, numbats, bandicoots, bilbies, gliders, moles, and koalas—and another unique carnivore called the Tasmanian devil? Science has a great marsupial explanation in the breakup of the supercontinent Pangaea. They say global torsions caused Australia to leave as early as 400 million years ago, when the rest of the continents did not disperse until after 200 million years ago.

Then this prolonged isolation of the entire Australian gene pool allowed random evolution to take its own path and produce its myriad of unique species. However, for some unexplainable reason (and with evolution, "random" never requires an explanation), much of the entire continent just quit evolving—staying stuck in the more primitive mammalian birthing form of a pouch. Here the highly premature marsupial babies that must crawl from vaginal opening to the pouch, and then latch on to a teat for several weeks before they reach the normal fetal birth size of all other mammals. Who knows? Come back to Australia in another 100 million years and all marsupial species may have advanced to join the present populations of regular placentals, like the Aborigines themselves.

Well, okay. Australia left early and didn't evolve at the same rate as the rest of the world. But then how do you account for one other marsupial found way across the seas in North America. "What about" the opossum mentioned earlier? If all mammals around the world descended from rodentlike forms whose fossils resemble regular placentals, why does one species from our own U.S. also exhibit that truly oddball and more backward birthing method? Did the opossum "de-evolve"? Its pouch has to be homologous to the kangaroo's, but it simply can't be because of Gould's correct statement—evolution has no idea where it is going. So you have to call it yet another weird analogous situation. (Yet if you are playing the card game named Rook and one person keeps getting the all-powerful "Rook wild card" out of a deck of 57 deal after deal, at what point do you call the game a cheat?)

Cytochrome-C

If you want a little more technical science, consider that these wild similarities mixed among stark differences even extend to the molecular world. "What about" a form of the protein *cytochrome-C* that is found in all metabolizers—from bacteria to barn owls—as a necessary catalyst to control the final steps of food oxidation after digestion? Because evolution says animals diverged over great time spans, one should expect the amino-acid sequences in cytochrome-C to differ slightly from animal to animal to animal, and generally they do just that.

But how do you explain cytochrome-C in a wheat plant, an organism you could say was rather remotely removed from a chordate? While other plants go off the chart, the amino-acid sequence in wheat varies by only plus-or-minus 1 percent when compared to the nice grouping of a carp, a tuna, a frog, a turtle, a penguin, a chicken, a kangaroo, a rabbit, a horse, a pig, a monkey, and a human.

The point here is that Darwinists say from the left side of the mouth that general cytochrome-C sequencing is proof of divergence during common descent, and something like wheat has no place in this list of animals. But when wheat does show up on the wrong list, the Darwinists speak from the right side of the mouth saying it is convergence because random can occasionally give you wild statistical results beyond the expected. "What about" convergence or divergence? When you only have two choices and neither provides an adequate explanation, which is true and which is false?

Pandering to the Lack of Evidence

If you have not yet figured out how Darwinists use homologies (divergence) and analogies (convergence), it is like a boxer's bob-and-weave tactic of ducking and slipping as many punches as possible. If an animal or plant has a closely related species living nearby, the explanation is *homology,* and the more complicated species naturally diverged from the simpler back in time. Or if an animal or plant looks very much alike another, but has no proximity in time, location, or genes, then it is *analogy,* and the species naturally converged on the demands of its environment. So if one explanation doesn't pan out, the familiar dodge is to switch to the other. The trouble is, both processes get a major sucker punch when you add the paradox of the Chinese pandas.

It is probably an eye-opener to find that many scientists classify the giant panda *(Ailuropoda melanoleuca)* not as a bear, but as, of all things, a raccoon. According to one side of the homology argument, the panda as a raccoon makes no sense. The giant panda has the general size and build of a bear, wide paws and long claws, and maxillary dentition and cranial structure more suited to bear design. Also, China has long had substantial populations of Asiatic black bears that overlap giant panda range for possible evolutionary ancestors, while the nearest and only raccoon relatives are found in North America.

So why not confidently place the giant panda in the bear family, Ursidae? The problem is evolutionary science must also explain the origin of a smaller version of the giant panda, the lesser or red panda *(Ailurus fulgens),* which shares the identical giant panda habitat in China—of medium altitudes, temperate climate, and mixed deciduous and coniferous forests where bamboo grows in the understory.

Beginning with appearance, we are all familiar with the lovable black-and-white giant panda. In contrast, the dog-sized red panda has pointed ears, a slender face, "mask marks" under the eyes, and large bushy ringed tail, all absolutely typical of the raccoon family, Procyonidae. (What else would you dare call it?) But homologies literally force the red into some type of link with the giant because the red (the raccoon) shares with the giant (the bear) this incredible combination of traits. Both have

- a shortened muzzle with widened posterior jawbones and massive premolars
- a completely vegetarian diet based solely on bamboo shoots
- stomach, intestine, and liver structures more similar to raccoon design than bear
- an amazing "sixth finger," an extended radial sesamoid bone that functions as a type of opposable thumb to strip bamboo leaves from their shoots
- a specialized tendon from the abductor muscle attached to the sesamoid bone for manipulative movement of the thumb
- no aggressive tendencies, only bleating sounds instead of growls, barks, or roars
- no hibernation

In genetic comparisons, the giant panda has 42 chromosomes per cell while the red has 36—making them a closer match to each other than all true bears who have 72.

It would be ridiculous to say this laundry list of similar traits was simply the luck of randomly produced analogies. But then which way do you take the forced choice of homologies? Pull the red panda into the bear family, though it has no other connections, so at least you have a bear ancestor in the vicinity? Or pull the giant panda into the raccoon family, where any possible ancestor is half a world away raiding grain bins in the U.S.? Interestingly enough, taxonomists who assign classification names are nearly evenly split over which of these two poor choices to endorse. Homologies? Maybe. Analogies? Perhaps. But is it fair to evoke both for the same two pairs of animals when neither is anywhere near a consistent fit? In the end, the panda dilemma takes our Darwinist boxer and leaves him "on the ropes."

Neither Flesh Nor Fowl

Without the help of a Designer, all the world's creatures have to be naturally produced by one of these two methods. Unfortunately, neither works when you have to flesh out the theories with real details. You would be a con artist's dream target if you believe so many analogous body features spread all over the world were the result of accidental DNA codes. At the same time, the homologies approach is not underwritten with intermediate examples, and is often rigged to the point of being fraudulent.

Earlier I mentioned Ernst Haeckel's embryonic comparisons, a pictorial you can still find in almost every science book dealing with origins. Unfortunately, Haeckel's biogenetic law is now more infamous than famous. There is no doubt Haeckel altered what he actually observed while doing his embryonic sketches, and arranged some drawings out of developmental sequence. He also changed the sizes of others to make them appear more identical, and conveniently omitted other chordate embryos like frogs and sharks because they couldn't be stuffed anywhere into the sequence.

Charges of fraud abounded even in Haeckel's lifetime, and his work had no remaining scientific credibility by the 1920s. Here is how you can tell. Though you can still find the embryo pictures in today's science books, the discredited Haeckel is never mentioned. In the rare case that names of scientists are cited (like Karl Ernst von Baer, a contemporary embryologist who refuted Haeckel), the pictured embryos are not an historical fit with the work of the researcher mentioned.

If the highly esteemed paleontologist and confirmed Darwinist

> Various bird beaks compare to various pliers in the average toolbox...The problem evolutionists have is the obvious implications. Who is imitating whom? Who is the copycat, and who had the original idea?

Stephen Jay Gould said, "The biogenetic law fell only when it became unfashionable," why is the idea still printed in textbooks? In my opinion, since no reputable scientist can be given credit for the theory, nobody can be exposed as responsible for the error. Also, since Darwinists keep losing moths, whales, finches, wolves, horses, pandas, lizard-birds, fruit flies, and spark chambers as evolutionary proof…well, they have to print something, don't they?

The previously mentioned diagrams of animal forelimbs and embryos, and the arguments of the presence of rudimentary pelvic leg bones in some whales and snakes, are standard to Darwinian pitches. It is almost impossible to imagine a biology book without them. And yet rare is the science book that displays human skeletal joints compared to mechanical ones, or common hand tools compared to bird beaks. You cannot find a more educationally sound scientific concept than the drawings of how various metal joints operate with the same plane of movement as human joints. For example, a human ball-and-socket joint works with the same 360-degree rotation as a standard gear shift.

Very similar to this is how various bird beaks compare to various pliers in the average toolbox. For example, curved needle-nose pliers exert the same type of force as the beak of a *Pinaroloxias inornata,* a Cocos Island finch.

These comparisons are not only very scientific, they are right out of the homologies playbook. So why aren't they in science books? The problem evolutionists have is the obvious implications. Who is imitating whom? Who is the copycat, and who had the original idea? Of course we can't give credit to God, so do we just acknowledge that wonderful catch-all but still totally random entity called Mother Nature? My response is that if you answer "yes" to random origins of human joints and bird beaks, then I should be allowed to say that all these metal joints and tools were made by a random explosion in a metals foundry, and as they lay there on the ground, someone walked by, picked them up, and said, "Hey, I can use these."

In that chapters 15 through 21 offer no hope that animals could have evolved, maybe we'll have better luck with plants. Besides, it's time this oft-ignored kingdom gets some deserved attention.

Chapter 22

PLANT EVOLUTION

*This kingdom finally gets some
deserved attention*

Little-League coach:	Son, you're the best power hitter we have on the team, and this year we need you to hit as many home runs as you can.
Player:	I'll do my best, sir.
Coach:	What you need is a goal. We have 32 games in the upcoming season, and I would like you to hit a home run in each of them. If you do, you'll finish the season with 32 home runs, a higher total by far than anyone else has ever hit.
Player:	Gee, Coach—that seems like a lot. Nobody has even come close to that.
Coach:	Look, son—all you have to do is average one home run a game. Heck, you even hit two home runs in a couple of the games last year. You have to admit it's theoretically possible. You just have to believe. Have faith!

Player: Well, okay. You've been doing this for years, and I guess you know what's best.

(The next day.)

Coach: You know, son, I've been reconsidering this deal about hitting 32 home runs this season.

Player: Thank goodness! I've been worrying about it all night.

Coach: Yeah. I'd like you to do it in the first eight games. After all, you are up to bat on the average of four times a game.

When was the last time you entered a discussion, or even read about, plant evolution? With the possible exception of single-celled photosynthetic organisms, it's the animals—dinosaurs, woolly mammoths, saber-toothed cats, prehistoric humans, and so on—that get all the press when it comes to the issue of self-generated life. Is there not enough plant evidence for Darwinists, or even Designers, to build a strong case for their beliefs? If it were a subject better processed, who would win the debate with the most credible explanations? In my view, the problem an evolutionist experiences trying to prove that plants also naturally made themselves is akin to the Little-League scenario above.

Animal Review

As with animals, the route to understanding plant evolution must pass through taxonomy, the seven-step naming system for all life forms. And again as in animal classification, plant taxonomists agree on many designated names. Yet it is not an exact science because there is also an ongoing debate over what certain plant species should be called, what plant groups belong at a certain taxonomic level, and which plants are more closely related. First, returning to kingdom Animalia, scientists vary on how many phyletic names are necessary to cover all basic animal types. Some classification experts list as few as 30 phyla, others as many as 34. However, there is near-complete agreement that the body plan of phylum Porifera, or the sponges, begins the list as the most simple of all animals.

Sponges could be described as little more than sessile hollow tubes possessing no complex body systems or organs of any kind. (One sample sponge I show my students is so amorphous that they always call it a plant.) Their life consists of filtering seawater so that about five different types of cells can breathe and eat independently. As to reproduction, they possess the asexual capability of regeneration typical of a simple creature, and the sexual reproduction process is the haphazard reliance on randomly swimming gametes.

At the opposite end of the continuum, the phylum Chordata always represents the height of complexity. Chordates are complex organisms with specialized cells, tissues, and organs incorporated into all ten classic body systems—nervous, digestive, respiratory, circulatory, muscular, skeletal, excretory, glandular, reproductive, and integumentary (skin).

In a simpler view, we go from unaware animals with no brains all the way to mammals with complex brains with incredibly complex sense responses. To bridge this huge gap between sponges and mammals, we do have present-day or fossilized representatives of about another 30 animal phyla, where we encounter jellyfish, three different types of worms, clams, octopi, starfish, lobsters, spiders, insects, three different types of fish, amphibians, reptiles, and birds along the complexity journey. Other more obscure phyla contribute little wheel-shaped animals called rotifers and moss-shaped animals called bryozoans. But as it has been pointed out repeatedly, there are nowhere near enough living or extinct intermediates to connect the phyla in the animal kingdom in a nice developmental sequence from simple to complex. "Missing links" necessary to bridge the 32 animal phyla remain just that—undeniably missing.

Is the situation in the kingdom Plantae any better? Actually, it's much worse than in animals, and here's why. Constraints of classification must again be satisfied, and depending on which taxonomist you consult, the number of plant phyla (often referred to as "divisions") range from a low of seven to a high of about ten—call it an average of about eight.

As with animals, there is agreement on where to start the game of plant complexity. Phylum Bryophyta, such as the mosses, are every-body's most primitive plant. These have no true roots, stems, leaves, or flowers, must live in or near water, have the haphazard reproductive method of blindly swimming gametes, and cannot grow more than a few centimeters because they have no vascular or support tissues for water carrying or food storage. As far as complexity, they are just a blink above algae—your classic green pond scum. However, mosses are definite photosynthetic land plants. On the other end of the continuum, phylum Anthophyta, the flowering plants or angiosperms, crown the list of plant development. Possessing definite roots, stems, and leaves that have some incredibly clever adaptations, these plants can survive in even the harshest conditions. And, of course, anthophytes possess a flower, that sexual reproductive marvel of beauty and intricacy.

"Escape from Water"

One way to better understand plant diversity is to look through the eyes of an evolutionist and call it an "escape from water." Algae are very much plantlike with their photosynthetic process, but alas, they cannot leave their watery world. But if algae did mutate into bryophytes over 400 million years ago, as science says, and established themselves at shorelines, then the race inland was on. Phylum Pterophyta, or the ferns, became an improvement over mosses due to rudimentary roots, stems, and leaves, as well as some height and transport capabilities provided by support and vascular tissue. Ferns are not directly tied to bodies of water, but as every horticulturist knows, they still need very moist environments. And with no flowers, the asexual sporophyte fern plant is more prominent in a primitive life cycle called "alternations of generations" than the sexual gametophyte stage.

Then comes the phylum Cycadophyta, the cycads, the primitive species with palmlike leaves, whose stems/trunks have some woody tissue, but with no real density to produce lumber. The water factor is still in play because these rain-forest species do not have sufficient complexity in either root, stem, or leaf to survive in dryer climates.

Next in complexity is the plant kingdom's "living fossil," the phylum Gingkophyta, or the gingkoes. Said to have appeared in the fossil record about 270 million years ago during the Permian Period, there were once as many as 18 gingko species having the characteristic fan-shaped palmate leaves, but only one Chinese species has managed to survive to present day. The gingko is a true tree able to live with moderate annual rainfall, but it still has primitive characteristics, like separate male and female gametophytes that develop from spores much like a fern. It does produce a true seed, but they grow in pairs on a dwaft shoot and look more like naked berries, uncovered by any protective structure.

So far, these first four plant phyla (Bryophyta, Pterophyta, Cycadophyta, and Gingkophyta) have covered species not well known by the general public, but not the next one. The next major group is well recognized all over the world, phylum Coniferophyta—the cone-bearers. They are also know as "evergreens" since they only shed about one-third of their needles in any growth cycle compared to deciduous trees, which lose all their leaves in the fall.

Here the escape from water is near-complete because the ever-greens—pines, firs, spruces, larches, and junipers—grow well in high mountainous areas that are often subjected to long dry spells. The adaptations to roots, stems, and leaves are impressive. The roots can penetrate rock and spread out near the surface to catch available short-term water. The stems are trunks with thick protective bark, efficient transport tissues, and deep heartwood with supportive fibers that allow for great heights. (Giant sequoia redwoods grow to 350 feet, and redwoods in general have great dry-rot resistance for lumber in that outdoor deck of yours.) And the leaves are exchanged for needles to reduce water loss, shed heavy snows, and allow potentially damaging winds to pass through. With all this complexity in conifers, why are they not considered the most complex plants? Simple. They have no flowers.

Conifers reproduce sexually as is fitting for an advanced plant. But having no flowers to attract pollinators, and pollen and ova on different cones, conifers usually produce tremendous quantities of pollen in wasteful fashion, and rely on the luck of blowing winds to carry them to the right location. (Hay fever, anyone?) Furthermore, though the cone functions as a container for the seeds, they are still nearly as unprotected as those of the gingko, for when the cone dries and opens, the seeds fall to the ground. In fact, trees in this phylum are frequently referred to as *gymnosperms,* which means having "naked seeds." Despite the complexity of conifers in many categories, their unrefined and wasteful pollination process, and the lack of seed protection, should engender an appreciation for that flower found on our most complex plant group, phylum Anthophyta.

Difference in the Sexes

There are many stark contrasts between a plant and an animal, but one of the most important very few people realize. In animals, complexity leads to separate sexes, but in plants, complexity means sexes are conjoined. For example, when you find a chordate, or many lesser animal species for that matter, you automatically expect to find either a male or female. But when you examine an anthophyte flower, you are looking at both sexual organs.

The term "hermaphroditic" means same sexes on both bodies (as in sponges, some worms, and so on.), and in animals this signifies a lack of reproductive sophistication that may limit the opportunity for variations, and therefore adaptability and survivability. But the same term is seldom applied to plants due to the negative connotation. Instead they are referred to as *self-pollinators* or *cross-pollinators,* the latter being considered the developmental advantage that allows species a better chance to change, adapt, and therefore evolve.

The *self* and *cross* terms are descriptive in that the pollen from the flower's "male" anthers can either self-fertilize the ova at the bottom of the corresponding "female" pistil, or it cannot. If not, pollinators like insects must cross pollen over from other plants if fertilization is to occur. (Many purchasers of fruit trees have become disappointed by not planting *two* cross-pollinating varieties. Unless there is another suitable tree in the neighborhood to provide pollen for the cross, fruit yields upon maturity in a single tree could be nonexistent.)

In contrast to the cone-bearing gymnosperms (seeds produced by chance wind pollination contained in open cones), flowers of *angiosperms,* or "covered seed" plants, have more dependable animal pollinators and produce seeds surrounded by a "fruit" for better protection. (There they are, at the center of your apple covered by a fleshy ovary.) The advantage of covered seeds and increased adaptability through cross-pollination has allowed anthophyte numbers and varieties to explode forward and dominate the planet. (I've often told students that just because the flowers of the grass on your lawn aren't colorful and fragrant doesn't mean they aren't present.) The covered seed, and other adaptations, have also given flowering plants the victory in the "escape from water" contest. Consider the cactus, which could be viewed as the plant equivalent of a primate in animals.

Cacti have very complex water storing tissues, highly specialized roots to anchor and absorb in such a harsh environment, and a thick waxy cuticle on all parts to neutralize water loss. In addition, they have adapted leaves into the shape of needles to further conserve water and provide protection from herbivores, allowing them to live in the most arid and inhospitable climates. (To make prickly pear cactus jelly, wait until the pretty yellow flowers drop off and the "pear" or ovary with seeds swells to a purplish color. Then burn the needles off with a blowtorch, squeeze the juice out of the cooked pears, and then proceed with a normal jelly recipe.) At any rate, a cactus is about as complex as a plant can get, and actually prefers arid climates lethal to other plants. And when you place cacti on a geologic timeline, like primates, they are thought to have been on our planet only for the last few million years.

A Natural Development?

In case you did not notice, my description of how plants escaped from water included terms like "variation," "adaptability," and, of course, "evolve." As when used with animals, these terms always convey the belief that the plant changes from simple to complex were natural and done without assistance. And at first glance, this might seem a reasonable assumption with plants as well, but does it square with the facts? Ask the Little-League kid in the 32-home-run dilemma. Looking earlier at the range of animal development between Porifera (sponges) and Chordata (vertebrates), we did have about 32 steps to reach the top of the complexity staircase. Still, from rookie biologists to seasoned veterans, objective Darwinists cannot begin to find sufficient intermediates in the fossil record to prove this actually happened.

But contrasting animals to plants, it only took six plant phyla mentioned in the preceding five paragraphs to cover nearly all plant species, far short of 32. It is true that an obscure and more primitive type of fern, the whisk fern, does have its own phylum name, as does a variation of regular mosses, the club moss, and the horsetail. However, some botanists group these with their closer relatives. You can also add the phylum of gnetophytes, another type of obscure plant that has a flower structure but swimming sperms, but that's about it.

So there you have it. To traverse the complexity of animals, you have only 32 phyla to make the impossible jumps from sponges to the creator of Sponge Bob, and with plants, you must cover the same distance in a maximum of *eight* jumps! No wonder the Little-League kid was distressed at having to hit a home run every at bat, and the experienced coach should have known better than to suggest it.

The Eight-Step Program

Having only eight steps to convert green algae into cacti poses a passel of difficulties. Fortunately for Darwinists, all eight plant phyla didn't seem to have appeared all at once, as did the 32 animal phyla in the Cambrian Explosion, an event that evolutionists still should find incredibly horrific. But extending plant evolution over time produces its own set of problems. If charophytes (green algae) appeared as algal mats in the Silurian Period 430 million years ago, as paleogeologists say, and flowering anthophytes arrived around 130 million years ago during the Cretaceous Period, how do you cover 300 million years of improved plant features in just eight strides? If nature somehow spots us an alga with its complex cell organelles and chloroplasts that accomplish the miracle of photosynthesis, then the incomplete list of complex plant structures below still have to make a sudden and fully functional appearance somewhere along the way:

- *swimming gametes*—the motile sex cells that at least allow primitive sexual reproduction
- *vascular tissues*—the specified *xylem* and *phloem* cells that carry water and dissolved food and nutrients, and the *cambium* that produces all new cells within the stem
- *support tissues*—fibers and epidermal cells that allow for upright growth and protection
- *meristems*—areas of new growth at tips of stems and roots that allow a plant to elongate in both directions

- *venation*—veins in leaves connected to stems that allow transport of food and water to and from leaf layers
- *hormones*—powerful chemicals that influence plant tropisms and reproduction
- *stomata*—those complex leaf openings controlled by guard cells that allow for gas exchange
- *seeds*—not just asexual spores, but true seeds as the result of pollination, pollen that is as specific in shape to its own plant as a key fits a lock
- *taproots*—an advanced root system for exceptional anchoring and storage
- *flowers*—the exquisite and alluring structures that leap onto the scene and quickly dominate the world

And remember, just like animals, fossil specimens once again do not show these structures developing on intermediates.

If the most overused euphemism for a Designer, namely Mother Nature, suddenly did toss in such nifty plant features, "she" sure was working abruptly at various intervals over those 300 million years. But she did her best work in the last 100 million years or so with the spread of anthophytes.

Currently, about 250,000 different species of angiosperm flowering plants are found worldwide compared to about 30,000 species from all other plant phyla combined. To get a mental picture of the diversity and dominance of flowers, visit a florist, or better yet, visit the rain forest. Unlike animals, most fossil examples of prehistoric plant species can be found still living in present-day times. Yet the eight or so plant phyla on our planet are so completely "nested" that once again even a vivid imagination has difficulty drawing, say, a transitional tree between an evergreen like a pine and a hardwood like a maple.

Also, it's "fortunate" that the pollinators necessary for anthophyte survival, like insects, co-evolved nicely…which is a big stretch because Darwin was adamant (this time correctly so) that the evolution of one organism could not possibly influence the evolution of another. Nope, plant evolution is a hopeless mess. I suppose I should have been more sensitive when criticizing Darwinists for believing animals could make it here in 32 steps, but I knew luck would have to hit "home runs" four times as fast for plants.

An Example of Diversity

To close with something of an afterthought, several years ago I built my first and only home out of logs. Knowing nothing about construction, I solicited advice from any and every source possible to help me through each phase of building. (My favorite line was, "Hey, I'm really skilled at something the *second* time I do it.") Being such a novice, I was amazed as I learned how many different types of wood were necessary, and how the different attributes of lumber allowed for different applications.

- *Engelmann spruce logs for the main structure*—They were natural dried beetle-killed trees that made for beautiful tongue-and-groove 8-inch logs with tremendous strength and a high R-factor for insulation.

- *White fir studs for unexposed inner walls*—Though they weren't pretty, their trees grew fast. They provided inexpensive lumber that still supported sufficient weight, were easily shaped, and readily took a nail.

- *Red oak for the kitchen floor*—Though it was hard to saw, shape, or nail, once in place it looked beautiful. It could withstand great impacts and abrasions and not leave a mark.

- *Knotty pine for the vaulted ceiling*—It couldn't take much abuse, but then it didn't have to. It was easy to shape, bend, and nail, and it gave a rich look overhead.

- *Cedar for the shingles and exterior trim*—Not exactly pretty and not exactly strong (too easily split). But once in place, it could stand the beating of a four-season Colorado climate and maintain its integrity for 25 years.

- *Ash for posts and beams*—They had to be strong, and they weren't cheap, but this was no place to scrimp.

• *Redwood for decks and foundation plates*—If this beautiful wood was more plentiful and less expensive, it would get used everywhere. It was easy to shape, saw, and nail, weather resistant, and absolutely impervious to dry rot. I wonder how we could ever build without it?

Of course the uses of wood do not stop here. Our family is especially fond of the rich hues in the cherry cradle made by a friend that held all of our kids. And after the use of wood in furniture and decorations come the more important plant uses of medicine and clothing. Also, I guess you *might* say the food we get from plants is worth mentioning, as well as their contributions to food webs as mentioned earlier. But though it is probably a lesser reason, the woods that made my family's house gave me a deeper sense of "designer plants." I have no doubt plants on Earth were readied with a dual use in mind—one ecological to support life, and one domestic for the people who would one day inhabit the planet.

As we near the end of part five on paleontology, I hope my prediction was accurate that challenges from the fossil record would prove as interesting as they were powerful. Yes, I know there has been little mention of the evolution of humans, but that's for another book. For now, allow me to say that scientific evidence for monkeys naturally turning into us, unlike it is always presented by Darwinists, is so flawed that it is laughable. Still, there is one more chapter on general paleontology to present, and it explains a recent evolutionary theory that actually doesn't ignore the facts of the fossil record.

Chapter 23

HOPEFUL MONSTERS AND PUNCTUATED EQUILIBRIUM

*Did bizarre births over millions of
years stair-step us to today's species?*

All throughout part five on paleontology, indeed throughout this book, I have leveled the same criticism. There are woefully lacking fossilized intermediate species to support the Darwinian interpretation of natural sequential change. Like where are the creatures that gave the dinosaur called ankylosaurus his famous "tank with the clubbed tail" design?

The experts know transitional forms are, in general, a myth. And sometimes, as in the case of Stephen Jay Gould, they even admit it. So has any evolutionist ever offered an alternative explanation for accidental life that would actually fit the fossil record? The answer is yes, and Gould was the main guy. The two key terms are *hopeful monsters* and *punctuated equilibrium,* and together they say that bizarre births in large stair-step fashion over millions of years give us today's species. Let's see if this alternative explanation works.

Once again, the year was 1859, and the book was *The Origin of Species.* Charles Darwin had just published this landmark book explaining how naturally advancing changes in species were possible. The impact was huge. In scientific circles, "descent by modification" was quickly embraced, and natural selection and survival of the fittest were expected

260 PART 5—PALEONTOLOGY AND GENETIC CHANGE

to stand the test of the developing fossil record. In philosophic circles, many orators quickly modified Darwin's work to take God out of creation. Finally both science and philosophy had in custody a prime suspect for the origins caper, and all that remained was to gather evidence to build an airtight case.

As I have stated before, paleontology was rather in its infancy in Darwin's time. As a result, the general public was only beginning to understand that fossil finds were leading scientists to think the Earth was older, much older, than anyone had imagined. And if all this were true (that is, if life did develop by gradual and accumulating changes over millions of years), surely the prime suspect would have "left his driver's license at the crime scene" in the form of a dazzling array of fossilized creatures each showing some slight modification.

Such was Darwin's belief when he said in his book,

> The number of intermediate and transitional links, between all living and extinct species, must have been inconceivably great. But assuredly, if this theory be true, such have lived upon the earth.

Unfortunately, as explained in chapter 17, Darwinian "trees" have never materialized. So while paleontological science searched and dug, scraped and reconstructed, and compared and classified, evolutionary science waited for the results. And waited, and waited, and waited.

A First Try

The year was 1940 and the book was *The Material Basis of Evolution*. The author was an evolutionary geneticist named Richard Goldschmidt who had already made his successful flight from Nazi Germany to the United States. Continuing his work at UC Berkeley, Goldschmidt wrote the book to explain that huge gaps did in fact exist in the fossil record, and contrary to Darwin's anticipation, they were not being filled. He had enough integrity to admit that fossilized species found in various geologic strata did not change gradually over time, but would rocket forward virtually overnight and be replaced by more advanced species.

And this was not a localized phenomenon, but was generally true of ancient life across the world and across time.

But because he still believed life had naturally made itself, Goldschmidt realized that the only possible explanation was that life surged forward in giant leaps. To fit with this view, Goldschmidt decided creatures in the distant past somehow gave birth to a new species very much unlike themselves—"monstrosities" if you will—so different that they could not mate with others of the parent species. He then added that such a new mutant could not be severely handicapped, as the vast majority of accidental births are, or it would never survive. In fact, it had to be *superior* to the parent species, or it would be unable to compete and its revolutionary new gene sequences would die with it.

Therefore, the monstrosity was "hoped" to be an improvement, and if it was, the advance was another small piece in the puzzle that produced today's species. At least Goldschmidt had a theory that was finally in accordance with the undeniable fossil record, therefore (violà!), the term *hopeful monster* was born. However, Goldschmidt was not well known in scientific circles, and since his unorthodox theory was devoid of supportive mechanisms, it was summarily discarded, making very few waves.

Gould and the Truth

The year was 1989, and the book was *Wonderful Life: The Burgess Shale and the Nature of History.* The author was the accomplished professor of paleontology, Stephen Jay Gould, from Harvard University. Since Gould also served as curator for Harvard's Museum of Comparative Zoology, he came to realize, like Goldschmidt, that gaps in the fossil record *still* existed 50 years later, and now had no hope of ever being filled. Therefore, Gould proposed an alternative theory called *punctuated equilibrium* to replace *phyletic gradualism,* the now-favored term for the slow Darwinian process. Though Gould had earlier books to his credit, this volume caught more of the general public eye because it applied punctuated equilibrium to an actual site of fossil richness, Canada's Burgess Shale deposit.

Much can be said about the life and times of Stephen Jay Gould. He was a prolific writer and speaker, and was well connected with other paleontologists like Niles Eldredge who also embraced punctuated equilibrium (now referred to as "PE" by supporters and "punk eek" by detractors). Though a confirmed believer in natural evolution, Gould was a man who thought "outside the lines." He had the integrity to adhere to the truth of the fossil record—that intermediate species in Darwinian explanations did not exist—and he did this to the chagrin of most Neo-Darwinists. As a substitute theory for phyletic gradualism, punctuated equilibrium as seen by Gould can be described as follows.

Stair Steps, Not a Ramp

Though PE is dressed up with the latest scientific argot giving it an esoteric feel (*neontology, cladogenesis, peripatric speciation, stratigraphy,* and so on), hopeful monsters are still at the heart of Gould's view. Reaching as far back as the very first prokaryotic bacterial cells 3.5 billion years ago, PE said life stumbled forward in stop-and-go fashion, like going up a staircase one step at a time, to eventually reach the most complicated organism at the top, namely us. At most times, species would tend to remain at rest with very little changes, a period called *stasis,* but then the equilibrium would be dramatically shattered by a "monstrous" surge forward in life's complexity, a *saltation,* and we would take another step up the stairs. Here new species on the next higher step, perhaps large groups of them, would suddenly appear and do a wholesale replacement of the previous life-forms on lower steps, which sometimes were driven to extinction.

Perhaps the best way to explain PE is a visual modification of any Darwinian evolutionary tree. You can tell Darwinian trees by their developmental "curved" lines representing gradual change from one recognizable species to another. To convert to PE, replace these curved lines with straight lines "punctuated" by sharp 90 degree angles that drive change forward. The difference can be seen in these two ways hominid development has been depicted.

As you can see, the first schematic implies that changes over time in hominid ancestors were gradual. A slight modification here, a small mutation there, and they eventually add up to a new species. Punctuated equilibrium completely rejects the curved-line approach for any type of species because it assumes a slow rate of change, and PE says these

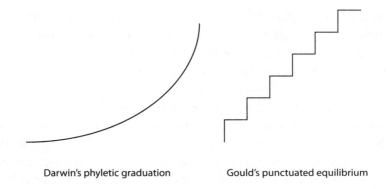

Darwin's phyletic graduation   Gould's punctuated equilibrium

must be discarded as inconsistent with the fossil record. Instead, the second graph shows the stair-step approach where a type of hominid (or any other species) is not here—then here—and then gone again. The schematic also shows a species does not change during its tenure, and though it can often coexist with others, will eventually be replaced by something more advanced. (Note also that while both views can start and end with the same species, the supposed journey toward complexity is markedly different.)

You can use PE to put all of life on one huge staircase, or you can use several small flights of stairs to track individual types. (If you wanted to track just mammals, imagine an egg-laying platypus at the bottom, a marsupial kangaroo on the next step, a placental mouse on the next, and so on, with whales and primates up at the top.) In any case, you go from bottom to top, step by step, through saltation and stasis, saltation and stasis, saltation and stasis. Also, to be standing on any individual step is to be looking downward at plateaus of decreasing simplicity, and upward at plateaus of increasing complexity, all initiated by hopeful monsters in their own time.

Consistent with the Fossil Record

At last—in punctuated equilibrium we have an evolutionary theory that actually fits the fossil record! Think about it. If a type of animal or plant kept *slowly* moving forward, how could you tell what type of fossil you had unless it stopped changing long enough to establish itself as an historical entity? PE provides this plateau of steadiness through stasis, and helps explain why the stegosaurus remained unchanged for 60 million years. (The minimum time PE says a species must remain unchanged before it can surge forward is about 1½ million years. If stasis is much shorter, a species comes and goes too fast to establish its presence and leave its fossilized mark.)

The saltations in PE also work well with the number of mass extinctions science says has hit Earth over the millennia. The sudden loss of all the dinosaurs—the famous extinction at the K-T Boundary by the supposed massive meteor strike 62 million years ago—is a well-known example. Also, the frequency of reported ice ages that number at least six and maybe as many as two dozen could account for the sudden loss of the stegosaurus, the woolly mammoth, and so on. Whatever the true number and nature of these cataclysmic disasters, the PE theory uses these massive change agents to suddenly and significantly improve life upon reaching the other side.

With PE's stability, extinction, and surge features now explained, we can say "so far, so good." All that is still needed is a not-so-monstrous explanation for the saltations that made such life-forms as the stegosaurus. In Gould's view, paleontology (supposed changes in ancient life) paralleled neontology (observable changes in modern life). To restate, the mechanism for macroevolution (*speciation,* where new forms were said to have appeared) can be understood by studying microevolution (*variation,* where present species have undergone small adaptations). As PE believes, it is hard to dispute that a modern species can adapt to a set of local conditions on the periphery of the main population, and so become a daughter species now distinguishable from the parent species.

The two versions of the American elk, the western elk of the Rocky Mountains *(Cervus elaphus nelsoni)* and the eastern elk of the Appalachian Mountains *(Cervus elaphus canadensis),* are good examples. Though early settlers hunted the eastern elk to extinction in the 1700s, it is virtually certain the two closely related species should be able to interbreed. The eastern elk would have to be the predecessor of the western elk by virtue of inhabiting the more ancient mountain range. Also, since elk in recent times have been found as far west as Iowa, an offshoot "plains elk" remnant must have made it all the way to the

Rockies to reestablish itself as a "high mountain version." And now that the eastern elk is gone, there is no chance of interbreeding to blur the lines between the two subspecies.

Therefore, the gene pool of western elk will now progress independently and they should become more and more unrelated to what was the eastern elk. In fact, if the two elk gene pools remained isolated, the separation would continue even if the eastern species were still alive. PE now says that if any major genetic improvements suddenly appear in one elk species, they cannot be shared, and one species steps forward. Finally, if the same mechanism keeps repeating, major leaps strung together can make change look to happen rather quickly. The end result could be a whole new species, and though not observable in our short time frame, perhaps someday the western elk could *not* interbreed with the eastern.

However, the true "magic" in punctuated equilibrium says that in the past, the change process was often *immediately* driven forward when one fortuitous hopeful monster radically improved the gene pool in one swipe. Using the term *peripatric speciation,* Gould says that such a wild birth accident caused a daughter population to instantly spring up in a geographically peripheral part of the ancestral range. Since the differences between ancestor and daughter populations are so great, interbreeding was immediately precluded, which lead to reproductive isolation. From that point, separate ranges would likely be established if competition did not drive one to extinction, and life has, in the snap of a finger, "surged" onward and upward. In addition, if perchance the organism did go through any intermediate stages before the new daughter population is established, PE says these species are unstable and ephemeral and therefore leave no fossil record.

A Prime Example

Now all that is needed is a specific example of macroevolution the PE way, as we had with the elk in microevolution, and it's a done deal. Well, here's as good an example as any. Staying with the wildlife theme, the brown trout is known the world over. They are also called German browns, German trout, English brown trout, Von Behr trout, and

Lochleven trout, but taxonomists the world over refer to them as *Salmo trutta,* another salmon-shaped member of the family Salmonidae.

Holding nicely with microevolution, there are many variations of the brown trout, some found in deep lakes, some found in high-mountain beaver ponds, some in fast-moving streams, and some in the warmer, lower reaches of large rivers. Though the coloration and average size does vary slightly from location to location, they are the same species because they are able to interbreed freely. (Analogous to this is that from poodles to pit bulls, the differences in domestic dogs are cosmetic because the *Canis familiaris* is another single species that readily interbreeds.)

Since the brown trout goes back before recorded history, there is no doubt it is a distinct and established species just like our elk. Proof of its individual identity is that it cannot even interbreed with other trout members of the Salmonidae family like rainbows and cutthroats, even though they share the same stretch of water. Also, as bona fide paleontologists like Gould will admit, there are no connecting fossil intermediates between the above trout species. (If you can't get a brown from a rainbow or a cutthroat in the same family, don't expect it from a fish in a different order like the perch, or a different fish class like the shark.)

So without connecting ancestors in its own habitat, from whence did the brown originate? Since Darwin's slow phyletic gradualism cannot explain brown trout origin, what is punctuated equilibrium's answer?

It goes like this. The *Salmo trutta,* brown trout, has one close relative. The brown's genus and species name means the "salmon trout" because the nearest closest relation is the Atlantic salmon, or *Salmo salar,* itself another distinct and long-standing species.

> With all the billions of salmon being born in all the millions of years...all it takes is that one good mistake. You know, the idea of hopeful monsters seems almost like a certainty, doesn't it?

Differences between the two species include average size, breeding seasons and reproductive patterns, fresh as opposed to saltwater habitats (causing a significant impact on internal anatomy), number of bone rays in fins, and, always the deciding feature, absolute inability to interbreed. So if the brown and the Atlantic salmon are still considered closely related, which would have to come first in evolutionary history to give rise to the other? That's easy. The Atlantic salmon, because it's *anadromous,* meaning it spends its life in the salty ocean *but must swim up into freshwater streams* to reproduce. The obvious answer? One Atlantic salmon suddenly gave birth to a brown trout in the quiet nesting pools of some nondescript stream. Ta-da! The Earth has a new species.

Sound far-fetched? First hear the details. Most likely during the Pliocene Epoch a few million years ago, somewhere on the periphery of the Atlantic salmon's range, genetic mistakes have taken place. A school of these salmon have completed their life cycle by returning from the ocean to the same remote creek beds where they once began their lives. Collectively, the salmon school laid about 1,000,000 eggs (that would take about 30 to 40 females, and the males to fertilize them), and in due time the eggs hatched into "sac fry."

Now here is where the math of PE comes into play. Odds say that 999,000 of the new hatchlings are going to start out fine and healthy, and begin the perilous journey back to the ocean where only about one in every 5000 will survive to become breeding adults. However, 1000 tiny salmon have severe mutations. This is reasonable because there is expected to be about a tenth of a percent (.01 percent) of noteworthy birth mutations in fish hatchlings. Since *almost* all mutations produce negative results, let's say 999 of these unfortunate sac fry have hopeless deformations and will never survive.

But "hope" springs eternal in the previous word *almost.* The radical mutation in that one rare baby salmon produces an improved "monstrosity"—a true one in a million—that results in an improved species. (Depending on which geneticist you consult, one beneficial mutation out of 1,000,000 appears to be a ballpark figure.) Ladies and gentleman, the brown trout has entered the world. His previously mentioned differences allow him to take up permanent residence in fresh water, so he stays in the stream, carves out a niche, and survives to establish a new population the world has not yet seen.

To many, the above scenario has a credible ring. The mutation rate is probably analogous to those 1000 defective TVs out of a million that do not work coming out of the box. So what do you do with yours? Same as everyone else, give it a good hard slam. In 1000 repeats of this situation, 999 nonworking TVs are likely worse off. But in that one in a million instance, you actually knock something into place, and your TV starts working—maybe even better than expected! And with all the billions of salmon being born in all the millions of years (or all the TVs sold), all it takes is that one good mistake. You know, the idea of hopeful monsters seems almost like a certainty, doesn't it?

Hopeful Dinosaurs

I'm a dinosaur devotee, and my favorite is the stegosaurus. The stegosaurus is a favorite in the whole Colorado area because more partial or complete skeletons of this guy have been found than any other dinosaur. He is unique with his low-slung small head, armor-plated humped back, and spiky tail. Now science says that as a Jurassic sample, the stegosaurus lived from about 208 mya to 144 mya—a total of 64 million years. And here's where the rub turns into a blister. All stegosaurus fossil specimens show *no* variations, whether they are found early at 208 mya or late at 144 mya. We know this is certain because we have found so many samples. It's like a spaceship dropped them off, they successfully populated the Earth for 64 million years, and then the aliens came back, rounded them up, and took them away.

When you add that they have no dinosaur ancestors remotely looking like them before 208 mya, and no descendants looking like them after 144 mya, that kind of throws phyletic gradualism out the window, doesn't it? But the goofy PE alternative says that some unrelated dinosaur gave birth to a "weird baby stego"—in fact, two of them, male and female, they survived, and so on. This strange scenario would have to be happening not just with dinosaurs like the stegosaurus and T-rex, but constantly throughout all time with all life-forms. Sorry, but include me out.

Where It All Falls Apart

So what's the problem? "One is the loneliest number," as the song by the Three Dog Night says, and herein lies the hopeless paradox of punctuated equilibrium. Whether male or female, *this brown trout needs a mate!* So exactly the same monstrous event must happen twice—hoping, of course, the second monster results in the *opposite sex,* or the game is over. Also, these mutations better not happen in two different locations along the Atlantic Seaboard, or the two new male and female browns still cannot hook up and mate, and once again we are kaput.

But even if the two new fish are in the same general area, that's just a start. Then these two "lucky" sac fry must both survive the perils of infant mortality, disease, predators, and accidents to become breeding adults. (Remember the 1 in 5000 odds?) Finally, since there is no motivation to stay together, they must later find each other in that river drainage system, successfully mate, and establish a population.

"Finally," did I say? Didn't I point out that the brown trout naturally inhabits many different river drainages? Did this new trout population do the salmon routine by going out in the absolutely toxic saltwater ocean to travel to the mouth of many new rivers, or did paired brown trout mutant "monsters" appear in all those many different rivers? When do the conjectures stop? Well, they'd better not stop here, because PE has approximately 29,999,999 more distinct forms of life to produce. Now what sounds fetched from afar?

So what do supporters of punctuated equilibrium say about these challenges? Usually the same derisive but weak-kneed response. They will cite the many types of parent species, such as those of salmon and trout, in their many locations over millions of years that will piece everything together over time. But even if you cloak PE in vocabulary and mechanisms with the feel of weighty expertise, the bottom line is that one species must still suddenly give birth to a creature it resembles, but with which it cannot breed. Otherwise PE is no more than dressed-up phyletic gradualism.

That means somewhere and somehow, changes like the following must have suddenly taken place: Hawks vaulted into eagles, salamanders jumped up to lizards, and sharks switched to bony fish, flowering shrubs converted into cacti, and on up the PE stairs. And those are the easier transitions. What were the organisms that launched themselves into a bat, a narwhal, a hummingbird, or an evergreen? Here such "parent species" are not only nonexistent in the fossil record but elusive even in the imagination. (Do an in-depth study of a hummingbird with its unique physiology and life cycle. Then try to imagine what bird took such a surge forward.) Therefore, in the final analysis, it is safe to say "punk eek" is replete with "ifs," and has far more holes than a sack full of colanders.

People of faith tend to discard punctuated equilibrium and its celebrated hopeful monsters as a ruse to circumvent the truth. However, I see PE as the one evolutionary theory that tries to remain true to the fossil record. In fact, I welcome most of what people like Stephen Jay Gould have to say. They definitely keep the rest of the evolutionists from completely running away with wild fantasies. For example, neo-Darwinists have an amazing way of treating natural evolution as if it knew where it was going, and though the idea of *predestination* may be subtle in evolutionary writing, it appears with amazing frequency.

Gould reminds us all that if natural evolution could be allowed to happen on Earth all over again, the life-forms we now see would be entirely different. How true if there were no Designer and it was all a random happenstance. And yet as has been already mentioned, wouldn't that make it amazing for evolution to give us the complexity of wings so many times? But remember, the main collapse in PE is its absolute inability to effectively account for the saltation of species that miraculously come in proximity pairs, then somehow reach breeding size, and finally luckily establish populations that have traveled the world.

Darwin's gradualism stood for a good 100 years, which is amazing in that it absolutely violates the fossil record. So why did science not seek an alternative until punctuated equilibrium finally got a full hearing in the 1980s? Perhaps all that was needed was one peg on which to hang an agnostic or atheistic hat. Well, Goldschmidt, Eldredge, Gould, and other followers of PE, though they will remain a statistical minority, have given the faithless a second option. This makes me wonder if another alternative for self-made life will ever come to light, and if it will be as indigestible as the other two.

To close, I agree with staunch Darwinist Richard Dawkins, who said life on Earth gives the "appearance of being designed." That is correct, just as your car gives such an "appearance." As I have said over and over, it looks as if a plan has been carried out, but whose plan? Did an extraterrestrial UPS driver drop off a DNA molecule that was ready to surge forward? Was it some intergalactic zookeeper who made regular deliveries? What *is* the answer to the fossil record dilemma, as well as the challenges from math, molecules, and motion? After all these questions, isn't it time I provided some answers?

PART SIX
WHERE DO WE GO FROM HERE?

Chapter 24

THE ANSWER

Arriving at a tough but workable solution

O n the TV game show *Who Wants to be a Millionaire?* Regis Philbin is always extra-careful to make sure the contestant's response is his or her "final answer." With the whole world watching and all that cash at stake, I guess there can be no uncertainty, no gray area, on the contestant's response. It is the same here. When you clear away all the smoke, our existence is a choice of only one of two views—either "He" did, or "He" didn't.*

In this book, you may have noticed there have been almost no quotations of the Bible. That's very consistent with my approach. English teachers will tell you that when defining a word, to use a form of the word is not allowed. For example, you cannot define *equilibrium* by using the word *equal.* I find that most proper. Similarly, I believe most people do not accept proving the Bible by quoting the Bible. I mention the Bible as the most universal of all sacred writings. Of the five major religions in the world, two of them have no true "origins" story (Hinduism and Buddhism), and the other three accept the validity of

---

* I find I can never enjoy a conversation with those who play the "alien" card. These people avoid making that choice by removing the origins scene to the safety of some unknown place, and now are free to make the wildest of suppositions that cannot be examined. My only response is to suggest they familiarize themselves with the distances and difficulties of space travel from chapter 13.

the Bible—at least the Old Testament through Genesis (Islam, Judaism, and Christianity). So if you plan to consult any mainstream sacred writings on the subject, you have no other place to go.

There are three other reasons Scripture quotations are not exactly appropriate in this book. First, these debates are all about science and math. If my arguments have proved in your mind that natural evolution fails, then find your own source for details about who He is, how He did it, and how it applies to you.

Second, personal experience has shown me that as soon as you quote Scripture to some people, their personal preconceptions shoot to the surface. Then the honest exchange immediately ends as they pigeonhole you with a negative impression.

Third, my personal religious views are at best only a small subplot in the book's main theme of reclaiming science, and the only reason they are here is to answer the atheism of strict Darwinism, which is itself a powerful religious statement.

Fourth—and less critical but still a factor—I don't want this book to end up in the quasireligious shelves of bookstores. (When I once bought William Dembski's powerful book *No Free Lunch* at a prominent media outlet/coffee bar, I found it on the psychobabble racks along with, I kid you not, books like *Witchcraft for Dummies*. That's unconscionable.)

On what shelf will this book be found, and in what venues will it be discussed? With the present biases in the media, it's hard to tell. But by avoiding Scripture quotations at least I have a chance to confine this volume to the realm of math and science. Seriously, can anyone look at the book's content so far and say it is not about science? And this is precisely why the desperate Darwinists cannot be allowed to stop such material from coming to public-school classrooms. So disagree, vigorously if you want, with the math and science in it. Debate the sources, challenge the facts, and argue over the points, but don't call it "religion" or "psychology."

As a personal reflection, I would say the many years and countless hours I have spent working on Design have equaled a "second major" of sorts to go along with my degree in biology. In the state of Colorado, teacher recertification every five years is based on completing six credit hours of approved university work—the equivalent of two semester-long classes. However, you can also apply for "alternative certification" if you complete an equivalent numbers of hours of independent work directly related to your area of expertise and your teaching assignment.

My efforts in Design, and the compilation of this book, outdistance *by far* other independent work hours for which I have been approved. But when you are dealing with a state institution, and an educational system that seems to accept Darwinism almost without question, my chances that this work will be approved for licensure are not promising.

And there are a whole host of other issues in public schools certainly tainted by Darwinism. Such as, no more children singing Christmas—okay, okay—"holiday" songs about the "baby in the manger," no more team prayers before athletic contests, no more Pledge of Allegiance to avoid the phrase "under God," and no more baccalaureate ceremonies at graduation time. Such are the many related issues at stake other than scientific academic honesty, and that's what makes recognizing Design for what it is—science—and Darwinism for what it is—philosophy—so critical.

But now comes my opinion. Whether you accept Scripture or not, I find the answers most compatible with *science* come in certain biblical texts. Try adding the involvement of God at each of PE's stair steps, and see if all doesn't fall together with the big bang, geologic timelines, and fossils. If you have become overfamiliar with the first chapter of Genesis, try the lesser-known account of creation in Psalm 104. Here you read again about the stabilizing and forming planet Earth and the establishment of all types of species—all complete and in the order presented by Genesis.

- For example, when Psalm 104:2 says, "He wraps Himself in light as with a garment, he stretches out heavens like a tent," it isn't verbatim "Let there be light," and "Let there be an expanse"—but what else could it be? (I like the "stretching" part. It's perfectly compatible with the expanding universe of the big bang.)
- The rest of Psalm 104 takes you through the separation of water and land, the adding of the solar system, and the bringing forth

of vegetation, animals, and man. The only major piece missing is the cumbersome 6-day/24-hour restriction that, I believe, was never meant to be taken literally (see chapter 15).

• If PE is the "law" of the fossil record, which it is, and creatures remain stable for long stretches of time, which they certainly appear to do, who does the psalmist say supports life during periods of stasis? Get a load of Psalm 104:27-28: "These all look to you to give them their food at the proper time. When you give it to them, they gather it up; when you open your hand, they are satisfied with good things."

• Why does the geologic record say some species subsequently go extinct in rapid fashion? Hear the next verse, Psalm 104:29: "When you hide your face, they are terrified; when you take away their breath, they die and return to dust."

• What is behind the forthcoming saltation where something new is suddenly on the Earth? Psalm 104:30 has the answer. "When you send your Spirit, they are created"—and let me emphasize this last phrase: "*you renew the face of the earth.*"

Yes, PE is compatible with the pattern of the fossil record, but Psalms explains Who is behind the stair-steps. Can it be any clearer?

Having worked with science-minded people all my life, allow me my opinion of the overriding difficulty some people have in accepting creation of any kind, such as that mentioned in the preceding paragraph. Basically, I feel it is easier for a science mind to believe in a virtual impossibility that nonetheless lends itself to measurement than to accept a likelihood whose essence cannot be captured by numbers. This means scientists might feel more comfortable with a faint star millions of light years away that they can at least quantify than an entity perhaps positioned next to them that no instrument of any kind could ever detect. I also suspect the "step of faith" in accepting a God of immeasurable power and authority creates other problems for certain individuals heavy on "left-brained" cognition. In such a case, maybe numbers and formulae serve as a useful cushion to the more convoluted matters of the heart.

But if ignorance can lead to stubbornness, then stubbornness can lead to rebellion. Let's face it, highly accomplished people like scientists and philosophers are not used to approaching a problem from a posture of "submission to" instead of "mastery over." If you refuse to cross over into the realm of faith, though, what will forever burden you is the inadequacy of science to ever deliver the bottom line.

For example, science cannot grasp Hebrews 11:3:

> By faith we understand that the worlds were prepared
> by the *word* of God, so that what is seen was not made out
> of things which are visible (NASB).

I used to think the "not visible" part referred to cells—or maybe atoms or even molecules—solid objects that are nonetheless invisible without sufficient magnification by a microscope. But that's not it. The passage means that right down to quarks, God fashioned all these things from an incomprehensible source completely beyond the reach of science. Furthermore, as was mentioned in chapter 14, all it takes is His spoken Word to either bring present realities, like light, into existence, or cause yet another animal or plant saltation in the fine tradition of punctuated equilibrium.

Now I realize that acquiescence to such a dominant form of "God" might be a tough accommodation. Yet for my part, I decided long ago to scale the one high but surmountable wall that has an Almighty God on the other side. Then all explanations, scientific or otherwise, come easier, and I'm relieved of having to continually scale one impossible evolutionary theory after another. No doubt about it. The only workable answer to the age of rocks is the Rock of Ages.

Chapter 25

A STELLAR DAY

*Examining the risks of
believing in Darwinism*

If you are having one—a stellar day, that is—it might be wise to skip this chapter. If you have just closed that big business deal, purchased that new vehicle you've wanted for so long, bested your arch-rival in that ultimate contest, got your work published, received a hefty promotion, or just met "Mr./Mrs. Right"…no need to be brought down. No need to reflect on the contents of this book—and the implications that you may owe reverence and thanks to something bigger than you. Savor the moment, because today the world is yours to command. You have risen above it all. You are creating your own meaning and destiny.

But if you realize being on top of the world inevitably has a downside, and if you feel at least some credit for your successes belongs elsewhere, you will find meaning in this quote by a man who has certainly been at the pinnacle more than once. "The more the universe seems comprehensible, the more it seems pointless." The words contain a touch of science because the source is eminent physicist Dr. Steven Weinberg, and the words are from his book *The First Three Minutes.* Dr. Weinberg and his writings have helped make the big bang theory a household term. He earned this notoriety by describing what might have taken place immediately after the birth of our universe an estimated

13.7 bya. And yet among all the science, other phrases in his book reflect his view that humanity is alone in an immense and impersonal universe, and all is doomed for oblivion. Weinberg's own summation indicated that pursuing science was his only sort of consolation in an otherwise meaningless world.

Why did Weinberg place such impassioned comments among the starkly cognitive terms of picoseconds, radioactive nuclei, millions of degrees Celsius, inertial expansion, gravitational attraction, and massive nebula? I suppose that in the face of immense time and space, even the most prominent among us could begin to feel insignificant as we contemplate our own worth. More than that, perhaps after someone explains away our existence as one big accident, that person must reflect as to implications of such a stance. In other words, perhaps all the random science that extracts the idea of God still packs a heavy religious punch, and church and state are not that easy to keep separated after all.

A Stark Choice

It takes great intestinal fortitude to live out the belief that God is "not," and I admire those who are at least consistent. As I said at the beginning of this book, agnostics often live lives very similar to atheists, they just don't have the strength of their convictions. Let's face it, you really have to stand up tall and beat your chest to say that when you die and they cover you up, you are no more than worm food.

It also follows that great courage is necessary to carry on while trapped in a reality where all is totally indifferent to one's existence. Philosopher Bertrand Russell was obviously a man of such "strength," for he was able to say, "There is something feeble and contemptible about a man who cannot face the perils of life without the help of a few comfortable myths." Well, there you have it. Russell was generally dealt the same hand we all receive—only an illusion of meaning sandwiched between vast reaches of cosmic meaninglessness—yet he left his mark. Though in Russell's own eyes his eventual passing could be no more biologically significant than the death of any simple life-form like a bacterium (save for the amount of compost resulting), all reports say that at death he did not falter and give in to some conjured deity.

Here is a personal story to show how skepticism is rampant in the world. In the heat of the day while building on a house together, I had a close friend ask me at point-blank range, "Why do you get up on a perfectly good Sunday morning when you could sleep in and get some needed rest, only to sit in church with a bunch of hypocrites and then throw your hard-earned money into

> Some days my plans for success get trashed, my car breaks down again...or love leaves me disappointed. On such days, the "crutch" of faith sure helps me to walk on.

a plate?" Good question! (I also had a former landlady put it this way: "If God wanted me in church, why did He make the Sunday paper so long?")

In one sense, my answer is multifaceted. Partly because I see more smiles on the faces of people with genuine faith, and I want to smile more than frown. Partly because too many of the people I meet without faith are too self-absorbed to be enjoyable. Partly because I believe people like me, my wife, and my children have lives not just defined by function, but by purpose and meaning. Partly because my faith challenges me to overcome my all too frequent negative attributes, which imparts an automatic benefit to those around me whether they have faith or not. And partly to avoid the punishment angle. (As a classroom teacher, I find the motivation perfectly acceptable when an unruly student still obeys the rules simply to avoid punishment.) For me, the above reasons are sufficient to pursue spirituality, and I actually do not need to rely on any of the crushingly convincing scientific and mathematical evidences contained herein to believe in a Designer.

However, I find a singular response to the "Why believe?" question if I adapt "Pascal's Wager" to the situation: "The evolutionist stands to gain nothing and lose everything, and the person of faith stands to gain everything and lose nothing." This means by adding the faith angle to my life I at least get to enjoy more smiles, find deeper meaning, have more of the preferred trait of selflessness, address my faults more regularly, and maybe avoid some nasty consequences. Then if I'm wrong, and all I gain is that hole in the ground like Russell and Weinberg, I believe I still come out ahead. Sure, some say you can have all the above and not have to "bow your knee," but for me it never quite worked that way.

There is one more reason. Some days my plans for success get trashed, my car breaks down again, I get beaten by my nemesis once more, people hate my writing, I get fired, or love leaves me disappointed. On such days, the "crutch" of faith sure helps me to walk on. Then I'm less embittered by the bad times, which in turn makes the good times more enjoyable. And someday when I'm faced with taking my last breath, I'll know with confidence that I've gained all I could on both sides of the veil.

———•———

On his deathbed, it is reported that Mr. Russell was asked what if he was wrong, and what would he say to God if he were to soon meet Him. Russell's alleged response was that he would ask God, "Would you mind answering me one wee little question? Why didn't you give us more evidence?"

Now I could be wrong, but at his impending passing Mr. Russell might have cashed in a bit of that impressive courage. He also seems to be positioning himself in case he needs to shift the blame of his disbelief to God for not being more convincing. (Hmmm. Did he never see a bright full moon setting in the cool, blue western sky while the sun rose circular and red through the eastern clouds? Did he never hold a newborn baby?) So if Russell is wrong, what will be his plea? As a learned and well-read man, which of the challenges in this book will he say he was never made aware of? Which of the challenges will he say he was acquainted with, but did not find reasonable or worthy of investigation? Or which of the challenges will he say rang true deep inside, but he faltered because God "blew it" by giving him free will and choice?

And what of Charles Darwin? Rumors of his deathbed conversion seem to be everywhere, but I have never found any evidence to that effect. (If he did, you would have to call it "re-conversion" I guess. After all, he was once a licensed preacher.) But history does say Darwin was deeply shaken at the premature loss of a young daughter, and his resulting prolonged sadness indicates he turned more to bitterness than to faith. Finally, what of all the other famous evolutionists named in this book? I wonder how they handled those deep chasms in life, chasms that people of faith more easily conquer when they, without hypocrisy, reach for their "crutch"?

The judge told the man before his bar, "Sir, you shall receive justice in my court." To this the man replied, "Your Honor, it's not your justice I desire, it's your mercy."

Justice or mercy. It will be one or the other, and we decide which.

Afterword

IT'S TIME

One of the most intriguing books on my bookshelf is titled *Shattering the Myths of Darwinism* by Richard Milton. In this book, Milton effectively challenges many of natural evolution's erroneous geologic assumptions, such as that the Earth's sediment layers were deposited at an average rate of 0.2 millimeters per year. (Milton shows that *uniform deposition,* like so many other Darwinistic beliefs, is plausible only in theory but never in reality.)

The intriguing part to me is, while Milton's book challenges nearly every other evolutionary concept, in his next-to-last chapter he declares,

> Let me make it unambiguously clear that I am not a creationist, nor do I have any religious beliefs of any kind... For anyone, anywhere, to say that I am a creationist, a secret creationist, a "creationist ally," or any other such weasel-word formulation, is an act of intellectual dishonesty by those who have no other answer to the scientific objections I have raised publicly.

Design is not only for people of faith, whether a specific or generic variety. In fact, only in a heavily biased mind—a mind programmed with a preconception—can Darwinism survive examination. Since Design is only about science, and its scientific teeth bite deep, perhaps fear over the pain causes Darwinists to avoid such honest examination.

But still, wouldn't it make sense for Darwinists to actually *invite* Design into science classrooms and laboratories? What better places to expose Design's fraud and then dismiss it for the quackery it's said to be? It is the perfect strategy—if Darwinists are right.

The trouble is, every time Design gets a fair hearing, too many respected scientists with impeccable credentials speak on its behalf, and everyday people with reasonable thinking skills are siding with them. In fact, people everywhere are wondering if evolutionists in their towers look less like wise oracles whom the confused consult for wisdom, and more like Rapunzel—stuck aloft without hair or assistance.

A Methodology

Having gone full circle, I would like to return to the book's title. I suppose the rationale for hostage-taking always remains the same. You have an issue about which you are absolutely adamant, but the majority does not share your view. However, you believe if you can generate significant publicity for your cause, you will draw sympathizers and create new converts. So you kidnap a prominent individual or hijack an important public icon, which brings automatic media attention, and then hope society will ultimately say your cause justified your methods.

I can think of no better analogy for what the extremists in natural evolution have done in commandeering science over the last century-and-a-half. And as I have noted before, you will find these extremists in all aspects of scientific research, publication, and education trying to prop up the crumbling edifice of Darwinism.

To hasten their departure through board decisions, court challenges, and revised legislation, we must not inadvertently aid the Darwinists. Those who insist on making their brand of religion part of the rhetoric force board members, judges, and legislators into umpiring religious squabbles instead of making rulings on scientific principles. That in turn allows the Darwinists to cry foul over the First Amendment—and the scientific validity of Design is no longer the issue at hand.

The most serious fallout here is that even faith-based people in the general population withdraw support as they begin to wonder whose form of creationism is calling the shots and how extreme the beliefs to which their children will be exposed are. So if you want the science of Design to get a fair hearing in boardrooms, courtrooms, and congressional halls—and take its rightful place in science classrooms—choose the right battlefields, as mentioned in chapter 14. The science of Design is powerful, and it's all you need.

Final Predictions

In my 58 years of living, I have found natural evolution being continually espoused from all the sources you would expect. I got my first true taste of the notion that God did not explain my presence in my ninth-grade biology class. Evolution was laid out pretty much as fact in my textbook—not even with a few qualifying words—and was presented as such. Since then the theory has been prevalent in my university science and philosophy classes, even promoted in college courses where the subject of human origins is not even germane to the content. Also, I have not been the least surprised to hear natural evolution expressed as fact in science-teacher symposiums, scientific and geographic magazines, sci-fi movies, museums, and media coverage of events, scientific and otherwise.

But beyond that, the assumption we are all products of mere chance has continually appeared in unanticipated places. I can recall an automotive magazine article on the history of an American sports car where the author stated the vehicle had "evolved over time, just like the dinosaurs, but in this case with expert help." Then there's a state wildlife department's video on the mountain cutthroat trout that carefully traces how its Pacific ancestor naturally evolved into several different species over millions of years, some of which miraculously crossed the Continental Divide to reach Colorado rivers.

And very close to home, I remember the unconscionable prediction to my daughter from her fourth-grade teacher that religion would be dead in 50 years. (Only 42 more to go.) It is incredible that an abjectly false assumption such as Darwinism could become so prevalent.

However, I predict that in no more than ten years, maybe as few as five, strict Darwinism will be a minority belief not only among people in society but also among science researchers and science educators. Within this time frame you will see a revolution where more and more politicians and board members vote to allow or encourage—in some cases even require—public-school science teachers to cover some form of alternatives to natural evolution in their classes.*

This increasing acceptance will then spread forward to the next wave of scientific research and literature, outward into related judicial decisions and media programming, and finally upward into university science education and teacher-certification programs to fuel the next generation. (I've been in the education business long enough to know that though colleges and universities should be leaders in public-school reform, they are usually the last to adjust to changes that are already underway.)

Is such a change truly possible? Consider this. Society tolerated smoking in public places for approximately the same number of years we have endured Darwinism. Though few seriously doubted that people's health was damaged by tobacco, we still inhaled secondhand smoke, dealt with messy ashtrays, and came home with stale-smelling clothes… as if we had no choice.

But rather abruptly, the population put its foot down. Then it took surprisingly few years to relegate smoking to confined places, where those who wanted to continue the habit despite the overwhelming evidence of its dangers could still exercise their rights. I see no reason why we can't do the same with the scourge of Darwinism.

If we can accomplish such an overhaul, also benefiting will be home-school and private religious school leaders. They will finally have at their disposal more scientific teaching materials now being developed by professionals from widespread fields. This will be quite a transformation, but surely holdouts will always remain. Yet how ironic if Darwinists eventually become the "Flat-Earth Society," one of their recently favored terms for those they feel have been blinded to the truth.

For the above to continue on its present course, all references to evolution as fact need to be strongly challenged wherever they are found. The proof is simply not there. It is time for natural evolution to wave the white flag of surrender. It is time for those attempting to cling to their unsubstantiated theories to release science from the stranglehold of Darwinism. And it is time for the rest of us to make sure it happens. *It is time.*

---

* And, as stated before, organizations like www.ISFED.org are committed to hasten the turnover.

Appendix

CLEANING SOME TARNISH OFF THE NAME OF CHARLES DARWIN

Why reading The Origin of Species *is a must*

"Sit down before fact as a little child, be prepared to give up every preconceived notion...or you shall learn nothing."

—Thomas Huxley, "Darwin's Bulldog" (1825–1895)

Why am I advocating reading *The Origin of Species?* After all, it is the one book by the one author that creationists believe let the evil genie of evolution out of the bottle—a genie that takes wonderment rather than gives it. I have three reasons.

First, *there can be no doubt that natural evolution is rife with scientific problems from within that are as damning as legitimate theological challenges from without.* In actuality, the better you understand Darwinism, and the book that spawned it, the more glaring its abject failures become. So study it thoroughly by all means available. It is only in *partial* understanding of the big bang, molecular evolution, genetic mutations, the fossil record, phylogenetic trees, prehistoric hominid skeletons, and so on, that you can hope to believe "self-made" is a viable theory. (Similarly, only in partial understanding of actual events in New Testament history can you believe in the "Judas Gospel" and the highly fictional portions of Dan Brown's *Da Vinci Code*.)

Second, *if creationists are going to effectively debate evolutionists, they must be conversant on all aspects of self-made theory.* There is weight in the statement that you do not understand another person's point of view until you can explain it to that person's satisfaction. Also, as a lifelong science teacher, academic honesty calls for me to cover in my classes the basic tenets of natural evolution fairly and firmly, and *Origins* is a proper inclusion. Apparently I do that effectively because I am certain I have helped some students along the road to atheism. On the other hand, when covering challenges to evolution, I am also certain I have given people of faith more reason to doubt self-made, and through "Design," the tools to stand strong in a challenge.

If I do my job, then, as is the custom of our people, each is free to decide. In my particular case, creationists will also be told they do not have to cower unscientifically behind a wall of six 24-hour days in an attempt to hold their ground. Students need to hear there are ways one can integrate what is valid in science (as opposed to what is not) with the veracity of Scripture, and maintain the integrity of both. And finally, my bottom line is that I want my own children to understand both Design and Darwinism for their edification and protection—Design for the facts and Darwinism for the fantasy. (Though the public school system is more than happy to oblige on the latter.)

Third, *Charles Darwin is not the "dark persona" some people of faith imagine him to be. Neither is he the consummate oracle of truth as most evolutionists see him.* The reason for both misconceptions is that the basics of *Origins,* and Darwin's own conclusions, have traveled far from the original. Just as the U.S. Constitution's First Amendment phrase "freedom of religion" has only by interpretation become "separation of church and state," so do many people believe they understand Darwin's work—though it has been altered since early on by the interpretation of others. Darwin's close associate, biologist Thomas Huxley, well deserved the moniker "Darwin's Bulldog." He, along with such as geologist Charles Lyell and, later, paleontologist George Gaylord Simpson, were aggressive both to make the theory of evolution public knowledge and to be sure it preempted the necessity of a supernatural being. However, if you read *The Origin of Species* with clear eyes, you will meet a Charles

Darwin much different than history purports, and you may agree his work went to places he never imagined or would have endorsed.

———•———

Before we get into the book, be forewarned that *The Origin of Species* is not an easy read. Darwin's boyhood English teachers must have gone on to careers as orators or attorneys because his long-winded phrases can be difficult to follow. Consider this single sentence on page 11, which to people acquainted with Darwin's literary style will be painfully familiar.

> Seedlings from the same fruit, and the young of the same litter, sometimes differ considerably from each other, though the young and the parents, as Muller has remarked, have apparently been exposed to the exact same conditions of life; and this shows how unimportant the direct effects of the conditions of life are in comparison to the laws of reproduction, and of growth, and of inheritance; for had the action of the conditions been direct, if any of the young had varied, all would probably have varied in the same manner.*

I'm not positive, but I think Darwin just said ancestry is much more a contributor to variations than environment. (Hmmm. Isn't that contrary to what evolutionists believe?) This tendency to ramble makes Darwin especially difficult to quote as to the essence of his thoughts. However, if you can navigate through the excess verbiage, be prepared for some excellent observations and intuitive thinking on his part.

Earlier Experiences

First, a bit of history on Charles Darwin may be useful. Born on February 12, 1809, the son of a prominent physician from a line of doctors, young Charles showed little enthusiasm for the family profession of medicine when he was sent to the University of Edinburg. His disappointed father withdrew Charles when he was 19, and sent him to

---

* All quotes come from *The Origin of Species* (New York: Bantam Books, 1999), a reprint of the original 1859 text by Charles Darwin.

the University of Cambridge to study, of all things, Divinity, according to another family tradition, the Anglican Church. At Cambridge he became constant companion to a botany professor named John Henslow who was also a traveling preacher of sorts. Henslow exposed Darwin to regular forays into the countryside to collect samples, and also to connections with the royal admiralty whose ocean voyages made available exotic specimens. Upon graduation at age 22, preacher-ready Darwin eschewed the allure of Henslow's role as traveling minister to pursue full time the avocation of specimen collector. Perhaps in response to his ever-disapproving father, he signed on in 1831 for a five-year circumnavigation voyage. As an unpaid naturalist aboard the HMS *Beagle,* Darwin experienced the excitement of exploring the entire world while it was still largely uncharted.

During these five years he took copious notes and brought back a wealth of specimens. (If you saw the movie *Master and Commander* starring Russell Crowe, the character of the naturalist reflected what Darwin's shipboard role was probably like.) Having bona fide scientific credentials upon his return, he was invited to be a member of the Geologic Society, and now had the time and connections to work on *Origins* while he bred pigeons on the side. It is easy to see the impact this journey had on Darwin's ideas. His book is filled cover to cover with references showing his excitement at visiting places like the Canary Islands, Tierra del Fuego at the southern tip of South America, and, of course, the Galápagos Islands. His exposure to so many ecosystems, and the resulting knowledge of the great variety of plant and animal forms, cannot be minimized, for his five-year job was to see and record the natural world as few of us get to do.

General Observations

Over 20 years passed between Darwin's circumnavigation and the writing of *Origins*. Obviously he had ample time to ruminate over his experiences, and you will find many clever and unbiased commentaries in his book. Some unique observations will, of course, favor the natural selection process. On page 11, for example, he wrote,

Not a single domesticated animal can be named which has not in some country drooping ears; and the view suggested by some authors, that the drooping is due to the disuse of the muscles of the ear, from the animals not being much alarmed by danger, seems probable.

Darwin's noteworthy observation was that domestic split-hoofed grazers in the mammalian order Artiodactyla, like the goat, tend to have floppy ears. He believed these were modified by disuse from their wild forebears who used to need erect ears to detect danger, but now in the safety of their pens could allow them to relax.

Darwin also built a reasonable case that the evolution of humans necessitated the evolution of domestic animals. He believed that as hominids began to build societies, they slowly incorporated wild animals in mutual protection, servitude, and companionship. Darwin even noted that the primitive and savage del Fuegans, who killed and devoured their old women, still had canines especially bred and trained to specific duties. To this he remarked on page 29, "For hardly anyone is so careless as to allow his worst animals to breed."

Use and Disuse

However, Darwin made several observations that he acknowledged were very difficult to explain with his developing theory, a theory he frequently called "descent by modification." He posed a very interesting problem about complexity in immature versus adult stages of certain arthropods. On page 360 Darwin stated,

No one probably will dispute that the butterfly is higher than the caterpillar. In some cases, however, the mature animal is generally considered as lower in the scale than the larva, as with certain parasitic crustaceans.

To explain, in ensuing sentences Darwin wondered why natural selection does not result in advancement over all metamorphic stages, and asks why a caterpillar, while appropriately inferior in locomotion to the adult butterfly, should have such an advantage in jaw structure and feeding ability. (It is true that voracious insect larvae from the order

Lepidoptera can quite literally strip plants of their leaves.) Darwin was also unsure about the effect of environmental influences on modification of body parts. On page 365 he remarked,

> Whatever influence long-continued exercise or use on the one hand, or disuse on the other, may have in modifying an organ, such influence will mainly affect the mature animal, which has come to its full powers of activity and has to gain its own living; and the effects thus produced will be inherited at a corresponding mature age.

As examples of this quote, other parts of the book refer to animals that live underground like salamanders and bats. Darwin wondered why some species overcame the darkness by developing very large eyes, while others lost their vision. At any rate, he obviously believed these adjustments in vision capacity were passed on to the offspring. In my opinion, Darwin's explanations of "use and disuse" are too Lamarckian—Lamarckian being that discarded theory that environmental influences can cause direct genetic changes, like giraffe necks getting longer as they stretch to eat tree leaves. (The example I use in my classroom is that the cutting off of adult mice tails, no matter over how many generations, will have no effect on the tail size of mice offspring. Sorry, Charlie, but environmental factors do not alter genes just by their proximity.) However, Darwin should not be faulted for not understanding inheritance, because the groundbreaking genetic work of Gregor Mendel had not yet become public, and the laws of heredity had not yet been formulated. Had Darwin understood even the basics of chromosomes, genes, and DNA, one can only guess how he would have modified his entire book.*

In retrospect, what is curious to me is that some of today's prominent biologists, with full knowledge of the laws of heredity, still believe use

---

* There is a postscript here worthy of Paul Harvey's "Rest of the Story." After Darwin's death, and the subsequent sorting of the many documents in his library, copies of Mendel's papers were found, unread—surely unread because pages not completely cut at the printers were still joined. In these unread pages, Mendel explained the true nature of inheritance and gene behavior, and also stated that laws governing breeding do not produce large-scale change in species but rather their stabilization. This fact was later beautifully verified in 1908 by the publishing of the Hardy-Weinberg law, which experimentally proved that the frequency of dominant and recessive genes in a population do not change but remain remarkably stable. Therefore, while the *theory* of natural evolution produces genetic change, the *actuality* of natural evolution produces genetic stability. One can only guess how history might have gone had Darwin actually read Mendel's book!

and disuse have creative genetic powers. You may get the same impression the next time you read a Darwinist's explanation of the role of mesonychids that were covered in chapter 18.

Quandaries and Questions

Evolutionary science credits these rat-like/dog-like predators of the early Cenozoic Era with becoming toothed whales by living and hunting close to shorelines. Though not directly stated, I always get the impression that the influence of water over time changed the animal's legs into flippers—like they fell in and had to paddle, or else. Check out your local biology book and see if that inference doesn't shine through.

Though Darwin's whole life was generally devoted to science, his most intriguing observations came directly from his five-year voyage. For example, in reviewing all his ports of call he observed on page 321,

> As yet I have not found a single instance, free from doubt,
> of a terrestrial mammal (excluding domesticated animals kept
> by the natives) inhabiting an island situated above 300 miles
> from a continent or great continental island; and many islands
> situated at a much less distance are equally barren.

Based on this data, Darwin wondered if evolution even takes place where climates are too uniform, or where the gene pool is too small for descent by modification to function to completion by generating mammals. Another quandary for Darwin was why regions so similar in climate and terrain, found frequently along the same latitude line, would nonetheless give rise to so many different types of organisms when being longitudinally a world apart. In his words on page 284, "Notwithstanding this parallelism in the conditions of the Old and New World, how widely different are their living productions!" (Exclamation point his.) Darwin felt if his theory were viable, identical environmental selection pressures should give rise to identical, or nearly identical, species, yet he admitted that was not the case. Conversely, Darwin had no explanation for the alternative instances where species could be so similar when they were remote climates, continents, and gene pools apart. He quoted another researcher on page 265 in saying,

If struck by this strange sequence, we turn our attention to North America and there discover a species of analogous phenomena, it will appear certain that all these modifications of species, their extinction, and the introduction of new ones, cannot be owing to mere changes in marine currents or other causes more or less local and temporary, but depend on general laws which govern the whole animal kingdom.

Agreed. But this acknowledgment of governing laws seems contradictory to another statement on page 258 where Darwin reinforces what has to be the blind and unpredictable direction of the evolutionary process by saying,

We can clearly understand why a species when once lost should never reappear, even if the very same conditions of life, organic and inorganic, should occur. For though the offspring of one species might be adapted (and no doubt this has occurred in innumerable instances) to fill the exact place of another species in the economy of nature, and thus supplant it; yet the two forms—the old and the new—would not be identically the same; for both would almost certainly inherit different characters from their distinct progenitors.

As is obvious, especially if you read the book, you will see that Darwin presented himself with at least as many questions as answers.

Fleshing Out Natural Selection

However, all of the above discussion could be termed "asides" because Darwin's main motivation in writing *The Origin of Species* was to set forth his theory of *natural selection*. This is the process where survival of the fittest would cull from an excess population those unable to compete, and drive the remaining species slowly forward in complexity. These following quotes capture the train of his thinking.

I have called this principle, by which each slight variation, if useful, is preserved, by the term Natural Selection, in order to mark its relation to man's power of selection. We have seen that man by selection can certainly produce great results, and can adapt organic beings to his own uses, through the accumulation of slight but useful variations given to him by the hand of Nature. But Natural Selection, as we shall hereafter see, is a power incessantly ready for action, and is as immeasurably superior to man's feeble efforts, as the works of Nature are to those of Art (page 53).

Every being, which during its natural lifetime produces several eggs or seeds, must suffer destruction during some period of its life, and during some season or occasional year; otherwise, on the principle of geometrical increase, its number would quickly become so inordinately great that no country could support the product. Hence, as more individuals are produced that can possibly survive, there must be in every case a struggle for existence, either one individual with another of the same species, or with the individuals of distinct species, or with the physical conditions of life (page 55).

Can it, then, be thought improbable, seeing that variations useful to man have undoubtedly occurred, that other variations useful in some way to each being in the great and complex battle of life, should sometimes occur in the course of thousands of generations? If such do occur, can we doubt (remembering that many more individuals are born than can possibly survive) that individuals having any advantage, however slight, over others, would have the best chance of surviving and procreating their kind? On the other hand, we may feel sure that any variation in the least degree injurious would be rigidly destroyed (page 69).

Slow though the process of selection may be, if feeble man can do so much by his powers of artificial selection, I can see no limit to the amount of change, to the beauty and infinite complexity of the coadaptations between all organic beings, one with another, and with their physical conditions of life, which may be effected in the long course of time by nature's power of selection (page 91).

I would call these pivotal comments by Darwin not only clear (despite the wordiness), but in many cases unassailable.

As Darwin fleshed out the mechanisms of natural selection, he occasionally made comments that are judged to be true even to this day, comments that have since put a crimp on his own theory. On page 353 he correctly observed,

> We may thus account even for the distinctness of whole classes from each other—for instance, of birds from all other vertebrate animals—by the belief that many ancient forms of life have been utterly lost, through which the early progenitors of birds were formerly connected with the early progenitors of other vertebrate classes.

Today's paleontologists verify Darwin's "utterly lost" statement when they estimate that as many as 99 percent of all species that have ever lived have gone extinct, so filled is the fossil record with forms that no longer live. And yet if so many transitional forms existed at one time to connect birds with earlier vertebrates such as reptiles, as Darwin thought, where were all the partial bird/partial lizard fossil samples? Paleontology offers barely a dozen fossilized bird-lizards, almost exclusively from one small county in Germany, and yet they must somehow account for today's tremendous bird diversity.

Darwin made another forceful comment on page 47 when he said,

> What natural selection cannot do, is modify the structure of one species, without giving it any advantage, for the good of another species; and though statements to this effect may be found in works of natural history, I cannot find one case that will bear investigation.

This seems wholly reasonable. How could changes in one species have any influence on the advancement of another? However, the five kingdoms on Earth are chock-full of special symbiotic relationships between plants, animals, monerans, protists, and fungi. In a "mutualistic" arrangement, where both species derive a benefit, the connections are incredibly complex, requiring many structures and instinctual behaviors on both sides to be present. But if changes appear piecemeal, as Darwin's gradualism requires, are useless organs and behaviors neutral at best, and more likely deleterious, until all is in place? (Once again, the common Design phrase here is "Nothing works until everything works.") The proper view would seem to be that such complex structures and behaviors arrived *simultaneously* on both organisms, which is straining the limits of credibility beyond the breaking point.

Consider the rather common example of a rain-forest flower with a blossom especially structured to allow only one species of hummingbird to feed from it. This bird must also cross-pollinate the flower as its only means of survival. The flower's constricted opening to the recessed stamens are especially fitted to the bird's long, sticky, and nimble tongue. But the flower's design would be useless without the bird's aerial acrobatics, and vice versa. As Darwin correctly observed about 150 years earlier, the "evolving" flower *cannot* influence the development of the bird, and again vice versa. Therefore, both would have to suddenly appear with two sets of absolutely interdependent parts and instincts from what would have to be independent sources. Would Darwin say natural selection has that much power and foresight? Would he say there is that much luck available, and not just for this example, but all the other mutualistic, parasitic, and commensalistic relationships that fill our planet? His own words seem to say no.

Theoretical Missteps

Conversely, Darwin made statements in his book that create scientific bomb craters. This quote from page 159 is a word-for-word rendition.

> The illustration of the swimbladder in fishes is a good one, because it shows us clearly the highly important fact that an organ originally constructed for one purpose, namely flotation, may be converted into one for a wholly different purpose, namely respiration...hence there seems to me no great difficulty in believing that natural selection has actually converted a swimbladder into a lung, or organ exclusively for respiration.

That has to make a natural evolutionist cringe. Where do you find supporting data, or even a theoretical imagination, for how to turn a fish's ballast bag into our lungs?

Besides, Darwin used the phrase "originally constructed for one purpose," and as I touched upon in the introduction, "purpose" is a word evolutionists should shun, for how can there be purpose without a "Purposer"?

"Function," I suppose, but in evolution nothing has purpose because purpose assumes intent, and intent assumes intelligence. Perhaps random forces could have produced a "job" or a "role" for a part of the body, but without a guiding intelligence how could intent even be mildly implied? So if you ever catch a Darwinist using the word "purpose," call them to task.

As rough as the swim bladder comment is to take, Darwin made an even bigger assertion based on another's observation on page 153.

> In North America the Black Bear was seen by Hearne swimming for hours with widely open mouth, thus catching, like a whale, insects in the water. Even in so extreme a case as this, if the supply of insects were constant, and if better adapted competitors did not already exist in the country, I can see no difficulty in a race of bears being rendered, by natural selection, more and more aquatic in their structure and habits, with larger and larger mouths, till a creature was produced as monstrous as a whale.

Obviously it is no understatement to say Darwin expressed great confidence in the power of natural selection. So where to start with this one? First, if the bear became a whale this way, we need to find evidence of insect-eating whales. Next we need to address the size differential, and flippers verses feet, and...Never mind. I'm going to move on.

Not Godless

If you have never read the book, and were to state the overall objective of Darwin in writing *The Origin of Species* beforehand, I'll wager you'll have a different impression after you finish. Most people I talk to say something like, "Darwin's purpose in the book was to show how life evolved from the simplest forms to the most complex by totally natural processes." Of course this is the belief mainstream science tends to promulgate, and the impression that it wishes to leave. However, it

> From comments throughout his book, only one interpretation of Darwin's central belief is possible—that animal groups like the equines were the work of God.

is a deception based on a grain of truth big enough to rival the Serpent when he told Eve in the Garden that if she touched the fruit, "she would not surely die." The overriding misconception evolutionists allowed to persist is that Darwin felt God did not have an active hand in the creation of life.

This is absolutely false. If *The Origin of Species* truly were about the accidental beginning of basic life-forms, *The Origin of Kingdoms* would be a much more appropriate title. Neither was the book about the natural origin of major body plans of life, *The Origin of Phyla,* or major divisions within those plans, *The Origin of Classes,* or major groups within those divisions, *The Origin of Orders,* or distinct relatives within those groups, *The Origin of Families.* It was not even about the beginnings of types within those families, *The Origin of Genera.* There can be no doubt to the crux of the dilemma that Darwin sought to solve. It was, "Which life forms did God make, and which species became variations on what was already created?"

If you believe this conclusion is speculation on my part, the ensuing analysis will remove any dissension. Let's return to the question of horse evolution mentioned in chapter 18. On pages 137 to 140 of his book, Darwin takes a detailed look at the genus *Equus,* which includes the zebras and quaggas of Africa, the wild asses of Asia, and, of course, the domestic horse. He correctly notes that many donkeys have transverse stripes on their legs, especially when they are young, and that the quagga has very plain bars not on the legs, but across the body. Then he recalls from his own experiences in the English countryside that many domestic horses, duns in particular, had at least faint stripes, sometimes on legs and sometimes on shoulders. He even remembers a Belgian carthorse that had stripes in several locations. For natural evolutionists, their explanation for these similarities is quite simple. They say all of these domesticated *Equus* species originated from a less complex common ancestor in the wild, like the fully striped zebra of course. (See the "horse sequence" on page 214.)

And the zebra originated from an earlier more inferior ancestor—and so on back to the first cell. But hear Darwin's summation on the matter. The following is a word-for-word rendition from page 140, except for the bracketed insert that identifies the "view" he explained earlier.

> To admit this view [the view that each of these Equus species was an independent act of creation] is, as it seems to me, to reject a real for an unreal, or at least an unknown, cause. It makes the works of God a mere mockery and a deception; I would almost as soon believe with the old and ignorant cosmogonists, that fossil shells had never lived, but had been created in stone so as to mock the shells now living on the sea-shore.

From this single quote, and from comments throughout his book, only one interpretation of Darwin's central belief is possible—that animal groups like the equines were the work of God. Not only that, also of Divine origin were the natural biological rules and processes that allowed the genus *Equus* to become the zebra, ass, and horse, *and* the artificial selection processes that allowed the horse to become the Belgian draft. And here is where evolutionists soil Darwin's name. They use his work to extend the obvious fact that man can alter *species* within a genera, and the distinct possibility that nature has done the same, into the impossibility that nature has produced not only new genera, but all the families, orders, classes, phyla, and even kingdoms of life.

Darwin Versus the Darwinists

Note the difference. Darwin said the general Equidae family of horses came from God, and then maybe or maybe not branched naturally. Evolutionists say the Equidae family came from the Procaviidae family, which includes the hyrax and the rock badger, that itself surely branched earlier from something else. Then evolutionists go on to imply Darwin would agree with the horse diagram they always use as proof. The "proof" you will find in any textbook dealing with horse evolution (refresh your memory from chapter 18 as needed) is a sequence of pictures beginning with the extinct hyracotherium. This four-toed creature said to be a relative of the hyrax looks to me more like a small dog than a badger. (First, the Darwinists often replace the name hyracotherium with "eohippus," which means "dawn horse." In my opinion, evolutionists prefer the name eohippus so the whole world knows that this hyrax, badger, dog, whatever, is on the way to becoming a horse and not a wolf, a bear, a cow, or some other mammal. Besides, the cow was too busy becoming a whale).

Once it hits the world running on its four toes, the hyracotherium/ eohippus of some 50 million years ago evolves forward into larger sizes (I've seen as few as four but as many as twelve steps) that look more and more horselike. With changes like hooves slowly becoming less toed and more solid, we eventually get the modern day horse. Done. And for decades, the evolution of the horse has been called something similar to "paleontology's *best*-documented example of a progression of species." However, if the word *best* is indeed accurate, Darwinists are in deeper trouble than they can imagine.

Darwinists know that horse evolution is under a tremendous cloud of doubt, even in their own camp. It takes very little research to see that there is absolutely no sequencing the rib count, toe count, tooth count, and lumbar vertebrae count in the alleged fossil examples, and specialists even admit to overlapping existence in different numbers of these body features. Also, there are unresolved continuity problems in geographic locations and body sizes. There are even admissions that specimens like the moropus and the incredible Hagerman, Idaho, horse have to be excluded as impossible to sequence. What's more, fossils of ancient hyracotheriums and modern horses have been found in the same strata. Sorry, but even if complete fossils could ever be constructed from today's disjointed fragments, they still wouldn't "stack." Consider this 1984 quote from a knowledgeable official working where such an exhibit exists:

> There have been an awful lot of stories, some more imaginative than others, about what the nature of that history [of life] really is. The most famous example, still on exhibit down-stairs, is the exhibit on horse evolution prepared perhaps fifty years ago. That has been presented as the literal truth in textbook after textbook. Now I think that that is lamentable, particularly when the people who propose those kinds of stories may themselves be aware of the speculative nature of some of that stuff (Colin Patterson, Senior Paleontologist, British Museum of Natural History).

Patterson's quote shows exactly how Charles Darwin is betrayed. The "Darwinian Trees" he included in *Origins* never suggest such leaps are possible, and the fossil record surely bears this out. These facts are now so obvious that even Darwinists are trying to remove horse evolution from public scrutiny because of the embarrassment it keeps causing. But beware—you might still find the horse sequence in recently replaced high school texts like *Discover Biology* published by Sinauer Associates, copyright year 2000. In *Discover Biology* you will find these horses in the section about "evidences and proofs for evolution," and the sequence is captioned with (no joke), "Evolution Is a Fact."

Unfortunately for Sinauer and its authors, horse evolution—paleontology's *best* example—has completely disappeared from most current texts. As I write this in 2005, my tenth grade daughter is using *Biology—Principles and Exploration* by Holt, Reinhart, and Winston, and the horses are nowhere to be seen. That fact alone should tell you all you need to know. The strange thing is that though horse evolution has "gone up in smoke," Darwinists continue to draw hypothetical trees for many other species, still trying to convince the public, and perhaps themselves, that rodents can diverge into the primates that can diverge into us, and so on. Darwin simply would not agree.

Darwin and Breeding Barriers

Let me also briefly reintroduce the myth of human evolution. Though this topic will be dissected in depth in a forthcoming book, suffice it to say that trying to sequence ancient hominids is more impossible than the horse dilemma. In *National Geographic*'s August 2002 issue, there is an article on prehistoric human remains found in Russia's Southern Georgia province in the town of Dmanisi. The presence of such bones in this location so defies present theories on African hominids that an exasperated researcher said, "They ought to put it back in the ground." (The person making the quote was never named, presumably wanting to remain anonymous.) But here's a better one from the files of "I wish I had said that." J.S. Jones and S. Rouhani, writing in the respected magazine *Nature*, made a 28-word statement that perfectly summarizes the entire content of part five on paleontology.

The human fossil record is no exception to the general
rule that the main lesson to be learned from paleontology
is that evolution always takes place somewhere else.

"Always takes place somewhere else." I get that.

Darwinian-style evolutionary trees are found in nearly every science
book that deals with the "origins" subject, but every one I have ever
seen violates Darwin's approach by including in the tree members who
cannot interbreed. The one drawing he included on pages 98 and 99
of *Origins* is suitable to explain how breeders could take the common
rock dove (wild pigeon) and in over 4000 years branch it into some
200 varieties like the carrier, homer, tumbler, and fantail breeds—all of
which can still interbreed. He would also use the "tree" to explain how
finches isolated on a chain of islands like the Galápagos could become
differing species as their gene pool adjusted back and forth by natural
means to changes in climate and availability of food.

But in reading *Origins* cover to cover, you will not find Darwin trying
to prove such things as horses evolved from badgers, doves evolved from,
say, sparrows, or finches evolved from—what—an archaeopteryx? On
the contrary, he acknowledged what is now commonly understood when
species mate. The only time it is possible to get more robust offspring is
in the crossbreeding of two of the *same species* from different ancestral
lines. Even grade school kids have heard that inbreeding between close
relatives should be forbidden because it brings negative results. This
protection against inbreeding is one of "nature's laws" that Darwin
validated with amazement when he wrote on page 83,

> How strange are these facts! How strange that the pollen
> and stigmatic surface of the same flower, though placed so
> close together, as if for the very purpose of self-fertilisation,
> should in so many cases be useless to each other!

As an example, the female stigma on the flowers of a Bing cherry
tree will *not* accept its own male pollen that is tantalizingly millimeters
away. Neither will it accept pollen from a Rainier cherry tree a few feet
away—same genus but different species—though it lands on the stigma.

But if pollen from two Bing cherry trees a few feet away are exchanged, you get on both trees those beautiful dark red fruits to enjoy.

And Darwin addressed the rest of the breeding barrier as well. He explained that crossbreeding just beyond species lines—at genera—is extremely rare, and if it does take place, the offspring will most likely exhibit sterility. When I dealt with fruit flies in chapter 19, I already identified sterility as a "slight" impediment to evolution. As proof, refresh yourself on the origin of the Tennessee mule, a sterile cross between horse and donkey— same genus but different species. Talk about a dead-end creature!

I personally find it strange that in theory, natural selection has become synonymous with the transmutability of species, when in practice, it is a stabilizing feature that establishes breeding "walls" between which only useful variations take place. And even though Darwin had great faith in the power of natural selection, his conclusion on page 374 stated that its functionality extended no farther than family, the fifth of the seven steps of classification.

> Finally, the several classes of facts which have been con-
> sidered in this chapter, seem to me to proclaim so plainly,
> that the innumerable species, genera and families of organic
> beings, with which this world is peopled, have descended,
> each within its own class or group, from common parents.

Later in his conclusion he reinforced the limits of natural selection with perhaps his most succinct statement in the entire book,

> Nature is prodigal in variety, and [stingy] in innovation.

How true, but considering all this diversity, what, or Who, is the Innovator?

Darwin's Doubt

If you doubt the conclusions attributed to Darwin, you are not alone. *Origins* is filled with his own self-doubt that his views were correct. In his introduction on page 4 he said,

> For I am well aware that scarcely a single point is dis-
> cussed in this volume on which facts cannot be adduced,

often apparently leading to conclusions directly opposite to those at which I have arrived.

Early in *Origins*, in chapter 1 on page 19, Darwin seems to have made his entire theory philosophic rather than scientific when he said,

> Certainly, a breed intermediate between two very distinct breeds could not be got without extreme care and long-continued selection; nor can I find a single case on record of a permanent race having been thus formed.

Later in the book comes chapter 6 titled "Difficulties on Theory." In this entire chapter, Darwin acknowledged challenges to descent by modification, and often admitted he was unsure how to respond to them. He even opened chapter 6 with the statement,

> Some of them are so grave that to this day I can never reflect on them without being staggered...

For example, in this chapter he clearly reinforced what he often repeated, that the fossil record will need to uncover a wealth of transitional species to validate his theory. Consider his words on page 150,

> Here, as on other occasions, I lie under a heavy disadvantage, for out of the many striking cases which I have collected, I can give only one or two instances of transitional habits and structures in closely allied species of the same genus; and of diversified habits, either constant or occasional, in the same species. And it seems to me that nothing less than a long list of such cases is sufficient to lessen the difficulty in any particular case like that of the bat.

Also, in the concluding chapter on page 379, he revealed enough knowledge of the fossil record to pen one of the book's most famous lines, a question that remains true today.

> Why does not every collection of fossil remains afford plain evidence of the gradation and mutation of the forms of life? We meet with no such evidence, and this is one of

the most obvious and forcible of the many objections which may be urged against my theory.

Even though paleontology was still in its infancy, there was enough common fossil knowledge for Darwin's staunch supporter Thomas Huxley to criticize him for subscribing to the questionable belief in gradualism. Though Huxley was destined to become perhaps the best known atheist of his day, he told Darwin to reject a common Latin phrase *Natura non facit saltum,* meaning "Nature does not make sudden leaps." (I guess Huxley was a "punk eek" man before it became an established theory.) Finally, in chapter 6 on "Difficulties" Darwin recorded perhaps *the* most famous line in the entire book that I already quoted. Though over 140 years of medical research has been applied to the miracle of vision, and even though nature in its "stupidity" installed our retinas backwards (remember that one in chapter 20?), this quote still stands the test of time.

> To suppose that the eye, with all its inimitable con-
> trivances for adjusting the focus to different distances, for
> admitting different amounts of light, and for the correction
> of spherical and chromatic aberration, could have been
> formed by natural selection, seems, I freely confess, absurd
> in the highest possible degree.

And the people said, "Amen."

God the Creator

The final quotes I want to offer from *Origins* are bound to be extremely distasteful to the evolutionists. These are the ones where Charles Darwin repeatedly acknowledges God as the Creator of life. Remember the quote from page 140 where Darwin in essence said it would be a mockery to believe God couldn't make some form of horse to start the process? Then how much more will these rankle the atheist?

> It is scarcely possible to avoid comparing the eye to a
> telescope. We know that this instrument has been perfected

by the long-continued efforts of the highest human intel-
lects; and we naturally infer that the eye has been formed
by a somewhat analogous process. But may not this inference be somewhat presumptuous? Have we any right to
assume the Creator works by intellectual powers like those
of man? (page 157).

To my mind, it accords better with what we know of
the laws impressed on matter by the Creator, that the production and extinction of the past and present inhabitants
of the world should have been due to secondary causes, like
those determining the birth and death of the individual
(page 399).

This last quote above, found in the second to the last paragraph of
the book, once again captures the mind of Darwin that is now so mis-
judged by interpretation. Here he reaffirms that the Creator made life,
and lots of it, and put them under the control of His natural laws. This
would put Darwin on roughly the same footing as Galileo, Newton,
Pasteur—exceptional men who worked to blend science with the faith
they possessed.

Of course many would say that Darwin, and the others, would have
become evolutionists had they understood the choices finally provided
by science in the twentieth century. And it is true that by the time
Darwin wrote *The Descent of Man* 15 years later, it appears he had suc-
cumbed to much more belief in the power of natural processes. But
strangely enough, "self-made" would never capture stellar twentieth-
century minds like von Braun's or Einstein's, and no twenty-first century
stalwarts seem to be picking up the fallen banner of naturalism.

Meanwhile Design is experiencing a rolling snowball effect. Still,
we must remember that at the time *The Origin of Species* was written,
Darwin's only objection to the present religious thinking of his day
was that each species was an independent act of creation, and once
made, was permanently fixed. He felt Earth's time was sufficiently long
to produce significant variations within the prescribed limits of God's
innovations, and that competition had even driven many species to
extinction. I would word the riddle Darwin worked to solve in this

way. "Where did God's sudden bursts of creativity end, where did the natural processes He instituted take over—natural laws within which man's artificial efforts are confined—and how do God's natural processes operate?" Read my previous statement over very carefully, because this is still the correct question for science to ask today.

The Scopes Trial

Every thorough investigation on Charles Darwin and his views needs to at least mention the Scopes Trial. In 1925, the sixty-fourth General Assembly of the State of Tennessee passed House Bill #125 that expressly forbid the teaching of evolution in any college or public school supported by state funding. Anyone in violation of the law was subject to arrest and a fine of a minimum of $100 upon conviction. That same year, a 24 year-old high school teacher named John Scopes was arrested and brought to trial under the new statute.

Both modernists and traditionalists saw this trial as a forum to advance their positions, and both enlisted high profile attorneys to present their cases. For the prosecution, the state hired William Jennings Bryan, three-time Democratic presidential candidate, who was now a nationally known crusader to deprive evolution of official status. The ACLU hired the most flamboyant defense attorney going, Clarence Darrow, whose agnostic views had already lead him to defend a variety of political and social outsiders.

> If you watch *Inherit the Wind,* try to remember that Hollywood's general bias against religion was already in play.

The location of the trial, Dayton, Tennessee, became a "circus" for that week (complete with live chimpanzees), as vocal and sign-carrying adherents from both sides sparred outside and inside the courtroom. Reporters from every news agency were present, and newspapers were kept supplied with front-page headlines. (If you are unfamiliar with the event, I suggest renting the 1960 United Artist release *Inherit the Wind.* The movie is a fictionalized account of the trial and has Spencer Tracy playing the role of Clarence Darrow, Fredric March as William Jennings Bryan, and Dick York as John Scopes. The success of Tracy's and March's acting careers might be open to debate, but York, of course, went on to more meaty roles like the original Darrin Stevens in TV's *Bewitched.*)

The general consensus is that Darrow got the best of Bryan when Bryan himself agreed to take the stand. Under Darrow's questioning, Bryan's defense of the Book of Genesis came across as less than scientific, and apparently his views had a touch of narrowness and even bigotry. With that psychological edge, Darrow said the defense had ended its case, and everyone waited to see if Bryan could make a comeback with his closing statements the following day. But he was outmaneuvered when Darrow suddenly changed his client's plea to guilty and paid the $100 fine. Then he walked away with his primary goals fulfilled, making the theory of evolution common knowledge and allowing people to actually believe monkeys could turn into men.

If you watch *Inherit the Wind,* try to remember that Hollywood's general bias against religion was already in play. As a three-time U.S. presidential candidate, Bryan was hardly the nincompoop Fredric March portrayed, and Darrow was not the compassionate and yet fatherly "cool cucumber" seen in Spencer Tracy. Also, the script that called for York to play a meek, sincere, and embattled science teacher never revealed that John Scopes was not even certified to teach science. Rather, he was a sympathetic shill directly employed by the ACLU to challenge the statute. Still, I suppose you could say the ACLU achieved a victory of sorts. And its never-ending attack on religion really reached a pinnacle 43 years later in 1968 when the U.S. Supreme Court in *Epperson v. Arkansas* declared laws forbidding the teaching of evolution to be unconstitutional.

Well, evolution is certainly common knowledge now, and in a complete reversal, references to creation in public school classrooms carry personal and legal risks—exactly the situation that must change. However, I must emphasize once again that it is *not* the evolution of Charles Darwin. Rather, it has become the extended views of Huxley and Simpson, and later Sagan and Dawkins, as well as countless others looking for a way to diminish or exclude God from their personal belief systems.

It makes me wonder how Darwin would feel if he knew the places his name has gone. I wonder how he would feel to know his name is now synonymous with atheism? I wonder how he would see all the doubts of his own theories in light of over 100 years of scientific advancement, and the work in "Design" in the last decade?

Then I wonder if he would feel like Martin Luther who nailed his 95 theses to the door of the church at Wittenberg in hopes of reforming the Catholic Church. (When the Reformation movement began to take hold, Luther pleaded with his followers not to call themselves after his name—Lutherans—but instead "become followers of the Lord Jesus only." Obviously that didn't work.)

And now, if Darwin's original theories are beginning to look superior to his contemporaries, we still shouldn't be "Darwinists" even if Pastor Charles Darwin, with his Bachelor of Arts Degree in Divinity from Cambridge University, should preach John 1:3:

> Through him all things were made; without him nothing was made that has been made.

An Invitation to Connect with the...

International Foundation for Science Education by Design

www.IFSED.org

Our Mission

IFSED is a nonprofit, board-supervised organization whose mission is to promote excellence in non-evolutionary science education.

Our Vision

IFSED has a vision to reclaim science from the fallacy of Darwinism and other concepts of "self-made" life. This vision will be achieved by supplying science education with cutting-edge academic and research information from a Design point of view, and promoting professional dialogue on the failings of natural evolution.

Services Available

1. Teacher and administrator hands-on training seminars on information such as Intelligent Design and irreducible complexity—to offer vital information and creative approaches on incorporating these into classroom instruction and district standards.
2. Presentations by engaging and humorous guest speakers on the Design movement for churches, parent groups, service organizations, and media outlets—to educate constituents on the problems with natural evolution.
3. Support and technical advice for school boardrooms, courtrooms, newsrooms, and legislatures where the issue is academic honesty—to give information on how alternatives to evolution can be offered, especially in public education from elementary school through college.
4. Retreats and field trips for students and adults to examine scientific sites firsthand—to prove Darwinism is contrary to the actual evidence.

Please contact IFSED for dates and times of the above-listed services.

Books and Materials

1. Bulk orders of *Reclaiming Science from Darwinism* at reduced cost.
2. A periodic newsletter called *Designated Science,* devoted to the current movement to reclaim science from Darwinism. This newsletter includes articles on current events, cutting-edge science developments, and legal issues, as well as editorials, humor, and other features.
3. A condensed, self-paced math tutorial that covers all the computational skills from basic number sense up through pre-algebra. This packet also includes math exercises on probabilities and exponential numbers with non-Darwinian implications.
4. A specific tutorial on basic teacher-effectiveness tactics regardless of the subject. This tutorial covers the best of professional educational practices and focuses on how to be a motivating and engaging teacher who maintains control while maximizing student learning.
5. Separate biology, chemistry, and physics self-paced tutorials that cover the basic principles, immediate applications, and current issues in these fields without the evolutionary implications. These tutorials, complete with a sampling of easy lab exercises, are suitable for either refresher or "crash" courses on these three subjects.
6. A selection of non-Darwinistic instructional activities, laboratory exercises, worksheets, and information articles for science education classes, philosophy classes, and discussion circles. *If you have such materials, please contact us about the possibility of getting them in print.*

Please contact IFSED for availability of the above-listed books and materials.

Welcome! IFSED is creating a partnership of people who endorse its mission and vision. If you have an interest in any of the above services or books and materials, you can contact us below. Please join us in promoting the scientific, social, and spiritual benefits of living in the truth of Design.

—Dr. Kenneth Poppe,
IFSED Executive Director

How to Contact Us

International Foundation for
Science Education by Design (IFSED)
PO Box 136
Masonville, CO 80541
Web site: www.ifsed.org
E-mail: admin@ifsed.org

"A marvelous, entertaining, physician's-eye view of the intricate functioning of the human body."
Dr. Michael Behe
bestselling author of Darwin's Black Box

What Darwin didn't know lies at the tips of your fingers... and everywhere else in your anatomy.

The founder of evolutionary theory didn't know that the function of every cell and every system in your body follows an intricate DNA blueprint. In fact, he didn't know much about the human body at all.

Drawing on the most recent research as well as years of clinical work, Geoffrey Simmons tells the real story about your amazing complexity:

- *The brain* resembles a continent swept by electrical hurricanes and chemical tidal waves that somehow makes sense out of reality
- *A fertilized egg* makes a journey as complex as the path of a golf ball that rolls 30 miles and lands precisely in the 18th hole of a course it's never seen
- *The immune system* contains multiple defenses that confine trillions of microorganisms to your skin, like passengers innocently sunning themselves on the deck of a cruise ship

What Darwin Didn't Know pictures the wonders of the human body in their true context—a marvelous system fashioned by an infinitely wise Designer.